STREET **SMART**

STREET **SMART**

THE RISE OF CITIES
AND THE FALL OF CARS

Samuel I. Schwartz
with William Rosen

PUBLIC AFFAIRS
NEW YORK

PublicAffairs books are available at special discounts for bulk purchases
in the U.S. by corporations, institutions, and other organizations. For more
information, please contact the Special Markets Department at the Perseus
Books Group, 2300 Chestnut Street, Suite 200, Philadelphia, PA 19103, call
(800) 810-4145, ext. 5000, or e-mail special.markets@perseusbooks.com.

Book Design by Linda Mark

Library of Congress Cataloging-in-Publication Data
Schwartz, Samuel I.
Street smart : the rise of cities and the fall of cars/ Samuel I. Schwartz with
William Rosen.—First edition.
pages cm
Includes bibliographical references and index.
ISBN 978-1-61039-564-9 (hardback)—ISBN 978-1-61039-565-6 (ebook) 1.
Local transit—United States. 2. Urban transportation—United States. 3. City
planning—United States. I. Title.
HE4451.S387 2015
388.40973—dc23

2015014716

First Edition

10 9 8 7 6 5 4 3 2 1

To my brilliant and beautiful wife Daria,
who has had to listen to me talk about transportation
ad infinitum and has stuck with me nonetheless.

Also, to my advisor and professor at Penn,
Dr. Vukan Vuchic, who made me see cities
through an entirely new lens.

CONTENTS

PROLOGUE

Bedford and Sullivan

I WAS BARELY OUT OF THE SECOND GRADE WHEN A TRANSPORTATION revolution changed my life.

It was 1954, and my best friend, Freddy Cohen, had announced that he was moving. And not moving a few streets from our block in the Bensonhurst section of Brooklyn—which would have been bad enough—but all the way to the other side of the country, to Los Angeles, California. No more buses and subways for the Cohen family. They were migrating to the most automobile-friendly city in the world.

It was a sign of things to come. The following year, my other best friend (you're allowed up to six when you're less than ten years old), Shelly Pepper, moved to Long Island. Barry Politik's family hung in for a few more years: *his* family didn't leave Brooklyn for Rockland County, a suburb north of New York City, until 1961. Then all three of my siblings moved to the 'burbs. By then, not only had Walter O'Malley torn the heart out of Brooklyn by moving the Dodgers to be closer to Freddy Cohen, but a team called the *Los Angeles* Dodgers had even won the World Series.

It was enough to make you hate O'Malley, along with Robert Moses, New York City's parks commissioner, whose stubbornness over building a replacement for Ebbets Field, the crumbling but beloved home of Brooklyn baseball, gave the Dodgers' owner exactly the excuse he needed to head west.* And he didn't go alone. Horace Stoneham, the owner of the New York Giants, followed O'Malley to California, leaving the even-more-decrepit-than-Ebbets-Field Polo Grounds for Candlestick Park, just south of San Francisco. Huge transformations in America's transportation infrastructure dominated all these decisions—not merely the lower cost of air travel, which made transcontinental road trips feasible, but the belief, shared by owners and fans alike, that driving a car to a ballpark was the best possible way to get there. In fact, that driving was the best possible way to get anywhere.

Although Dodger fans, more and more of whom had preceded the Peppers and Politiks to the suburbs of Long Island, could drive their cars to Ebbets Field, they couldn't park them anywhere near the place. Shoehorned into a city block at the corner of Bedford Avenue and Sullivan Place, it had no parking facilities at all. As early as 1952, O'Malley had hired the designer Norman Bel Geddes to design a replacement, one the *New York Times* called "grandiose" because of its—wait for it—"retractable roof, foam rubber seats, heated in cold weather . . . automatic hot dog vending machines, and a synthetic substance to replace grass on the entire field." But all that was window dressing. The key to O'Malley's vision was a parking garage adjoining the new ballpark big enough for seven thousand cars.

There was no way to put that kind of garage on the city block occupied by the old Ebbets Field. O'Malley proposed building the new

---

* This is not the last time Robert Moses will appear in this story; see Chapter 2.

stadium in a different part of Brooklyn. He was—so he said—willing to build the "grandiose" park himself, but he needed the land condemned. And that meant he needed the help of Robert Moses. Moses loved cars, but he had no time for sports. The feud between the two powerful and stubborn men played out over nearly three years, and people are still fighting over which one deserves more blame for the Dodgers' exodus. Or whether the blame resided instead on a set of impersonal demographic changes that were remaking America in the mid-1950s.

Of course, my ten-year-old brain didn't think in those terms, exactly. Mostly, I just hated Walter O'Malley. I was far from alone. The late *Village Voice* and *New York Daily News* columnist Jack Newfield tells a story of saying to fellow newsman and Brooklynite Pete Hamill, "you write on your napkin the names of the three worst human beings who ever lived, and I will write the three worst, and we'll compare." Each of them wrote the same three names, in the same order: Hitler, Stalin, and Walter O'Malley.

I was an adult before I realized we were both part of a revolutionary change in the way Americans lived, worked, and especially moved from place to place. Over the course of the next fifty years, the most important parts of the built environment—the streets on which we lived, played, and worked—were impoverished by the seemingly irresistible centrifugal forces of sprawl and suburbanization. My own block, 83rd Street between 19th and 20th Avenues, stopped hosting stickball games and the kid-run "83rd Street Olympics." It no longer featured a daily lineup of kids sitting on curbs as if they were benches.

The phenomenon occurred in nearly every city that had been built before the advent of the internal combustion engine. Bedford Avenue, in its various incarnations, was already at least two centuries old before the first Ebbets Field was built. If you had a time machine that let you position a camera at the corner of Bedford and Sullivan, and if you set that camera to take a photo every fifty years or so starting in 1600, you'd see Native Americans on foot give way to horses and ox carts—first Dutch, then English, and finally American—only to be supplanted by streetcars, buses, and automobiles. You'd see farms replaced by houses of commerce and houses of worship. During the last fifty years of your time-lapse movie, you'd see the original entrance to Ebbets Field, at the corner of Bedford and Sullivan, transformed into Public School 375, better known as Jackie Robinson School.

The lesson of all this wouldn't be just the obvious one: that change is constant. What that hypothetical stop-motion history of a Brooklyn intersection also shows is that while the modes of transportation change every few years (horse-drawn cabs give way to early internal combustion; streetcars are replaced by buses) and even the buildings themselves change every few decades, the intersection itself occupies the same space, the same latitude and longitude coordinates, as it did centuries ago.

Vehicles come and go. Buildings go up and come down. Roads last forever.

They even outlast revolutions. They were there through half a dozen revolutionary turning points during the fifty years before Walter O'Malley broke my heart. They were there for the epic of sprawling suburbanization that started after the Second World War, and pulled the Dodgers west. And most of them remain today, as another revolution is under way: the "Street Smart" revolution, which is the subject of this book.

〉〉〉

Before you read any further, though, you should know what this book is *not*. It's not a comprehensive look at all aspects of the business of moving from place to place. You won't find anything in here about freight transportation, except insofar as it is making it lots easier to have trucks deliver goods to your front door than for you to carry them home from a store. Nothing about air travel, or—except for the occasional ferry—ships and boats. As a corollary, you also won't find a lot about intercity travel, or rural life. *Street Smart* tells the story of a transformation in the common travel decisions made daily and weekly in the industrialized world generally, and the United States specifically. Its focus is a modest 9.72 miles—the distance of the average automobile trip, including work commutes and local shopping trips. Those kinds of journeys are what this book is about: about getting ourselves to work, to shopping, to social encounters, and to entertainment—how we've done so historically, and how we're going to be doing so in the future.

The first four chapters of *Street Smart* describe the huge implications for cities and suburbs in a world in which the private automobile is a less and less dominant component of a modern transportation network—though I may as well say it here clearly: the private automobile isn't going to disappear from the landscape of the industrialized world, and *Street Smart* isn't a recipe for doing away with it. It wouldn't be practical even if it were desirable, which it isn't. A car-free future is a myth: seductive but unreachable.

A dozen other myths, plausible but misleading, pervade the world of transportation. It's widely believed, for example, that building new roads parallel to congested ones will relieve congestion. Or that wider lanes are safer than narrower lanes. Planners and politicians regularly contend that the more lanes you add to an intersection, the more traffic it can handle; that moving a city's traffic faster will make that city function better; or that closing a congested street or knocking down a highway leads inevitably to gridlock.

One of the most enduring myths, and probably the most disheartening, is the belief that America's deteriorating transportation infrastructure needs trillions of dollars in investment. This one is especially troubling, because it has crept into the thinking of so many smart people at every point on the political spectrum. Replacing and "improving" deficient bridges, roads, and highways is hugely popular with some of the country's most progressive and most conservative voices because, we're told, it's good for the economy, good for the environment, and definitely good for the future prosperity of the country. As we'll see, though, the argument for a lot of those investments rests on foundations even shakier than the infrastructure itself.

If the first chapters of this book are descriptive, a history of the first decades of the automobile age and the mistakes that accompanied it, the next chapters are prescriptive; that is, they outline what forty years of practice as a working transportation engineer have taught me are the best solutions to our existing transportation challenges. This latter part of the book examines each of four key aspects of sustainable and useful urban transportation systems:

- Enough density and connectivity to make *active transportation*—mobility that comes from muscle power: walking and biking—a practical choice for significant numbers of people. (Chapter 5)
- Multiple methods of transportation (or what engineers call *multimodality*) and many points where they intersect (*multinodality*), such that transit networks don't depend on a single form of transportation or a dominant core to which all routes lead. (Chapter 6)
- Transportation plans that take full advantage of *intelligent systems:* everything from GPS-enabled buses to smartphone apps. (Chapter 7)
- Networks that are *accessible* everywhere, all the time, and by everybody. (Chapter 8)

》》》

If this combination of desired features in a transportation network sounds a little utopian, I can understand why. But, as you'll see in the chapters that follow, these traits of effective transportation systems are already being implemented all over the world in cities as big as New York and as small as Charleston, South Carolina, as far west as Los Angeles and as far east as North Korea.

North Korea?

In May of 2010 I met in Beijing with a contingent of North Korean officials who were part of a delegation accompanying Supreme Leader Kim Jong-il to China. I was there at the invitation of a former student of mine from South Korea, with whom I'd worked in 2005 on transportation options for a future reunified Korea. This meant, among other things, planning a route through the DMZ, the demilitarized zone between the two Koreas, which required a visit into the zone—a nerve-wracking visit, because it requires surrendering your passport.

The head of the delegation was a man my student called the "Viceroy for Infrastructure" (his actual title was chairperson of the Taepung International Investment Group—*Taepung* translates as "Great Wind" or, more directly, as "typhoon"). I spent a day or so in a conference room in which they first explained their ambitious transportation agenda: five new railroads, six airports, hundreds of miles of roads, several new ports, and an entire new city in the northeast part of North Korea, which is tucked just under Russia and hooks around the eastern edge of China. The new city sounded really cool. It was to be an international destination for trade and tourism and very environmentally sound. I was imagining a walker's paradise with narrow streets, beautiful boulevards, pedestrian plazas everywhere, bike lanes crisscrossing the city, and streetcars decorated with Asian motifs whisking people to and fro. Yes, there'd be some car parks but pretty much at the edges. I was dreaming of creating a real-life version of Disneyland. To say this got me excited is an understatement.

They then asked me about the planning and building process from project conception to completion. I felt I was back in a classroom as I explained the steps from establishing goals and objectives to problem identification to planning and then execution. My "students" dutifully took notes.

At the end of the meetings they indicated that they would like me to play a major role as the master planner, to become a kind of Robert Moses for North Korea. At that point a memorandum of understanding was drafted between me and the Democratic People's Republic. We then celebrated with a banquet in which we repeatedly toasted peace between the two countries. I felt I was on my way to a Nobel Peace Prize. Or possibly jail. Neither has materialized. There's been no follow-up since (Kim Jong-il died shortly thereafter) and I have no idea whether some of my ideas have been implemented. However, if there are skinny roads with wide, tree-lined sidewalks somewhere in Pyongyang, I'd be pleased.

But I wouldn't be totally surprised. All over the world, from Zurich, to Barcelona, to Bogotá, to Pyongyang, to Columbus, Ohio, mayors and city planners are building in a new way—or, more accurately, in an old, time-tested way. They are creating environments that are dense and connected, affordable and desirable, appealing both to smart employers and the employees they want to recruit. They're building roads and rails for a smart future. Or, rather, a Street Smart future.

At various places in this book, you may notice a casual inconsistency in the naming of a number of departments in the bureaucracy of New York City. Sometimes the "Department of Traffic" appears as the "Traffic Department," for example. This isn't carelessness, exactly, rather a recognition that the departments themselves, and the newspapers that cover them, are equally inconsistent. Nonetheless, please accept my apologies for any confusion.

MOTORDOM

ROADS ARE ONE OF THE DEFINING CHARACTERISTICS OF CIVILIZATION itself. The first roads date back more than ten thousand years, but the earliest ones were strictly for either two- or four-footed walking. The real history of *manufactured* roads begins with the invention of the wheel by some anonymous Sumerian engineer about seven thousand years ago. Since wheeled carts are a lot more useful on smooth roads than the alternative, stone-and-brick-paved roads followed elsewhere in ancient Mesopotamia and in India and Egypt. Roads paved with cut timber and logs are regularly unearthed in prehistoric England. The tree-ring patterns in the logs of such roads can be very precisely correlated with calendars, enabling scientists to demonstrate, for example, that the mile-and-a-quarter-long "Sweet Track" was built in Somerset in 3807 and/or 3806 BCE. The Roman Empire built flagstone roads that eventually covered more than fifty thousand miles and are still used in parts of Europe.

For obvious reasons, though, most of the world's manufactured roads appeared first, and lasted longest, within towns and cities. The streets of London and Paris were paved with cobblestones in the Middle Ages; Baghdad had boulevards made of a primitive kind of asphalt in the tenth century. New York got its first cobblestoned street in 1657, when it was still known as New Amsterdam.

Those urban roads were *built* for transportation, but they were *used* for recreation and commerce as well. Until the nineteenth century turned into the twentieth, horse-drawn carts trying to negotiate a road like Bedford Avenue would have had to dodge pedestrians who filled the street. Peddlers and other tradesmen were as entitled to the street as wagons. Children played in the middle of those roads, and adults met one another there. The one thing Bedford Avenue wouldn't have seen frequently was the automobile. Even during the first years of the twentieth century, cars were so rare that seeing one was still newsworthy.

All that changed in 1908, when the first Model T rolled out the doors of Henry Ford's Piquette Avenue Plant in Detroit.

The Model T didn't just change America's street culture. It's one of the few machines in history that actually deserves to be called world changing. Before the T, cars were a novelty item for the upper classes and, occasionally, a genuinely useful aid for farmers. Still, the revolution that Ford's "car for everyone" ignited wasn't immediate. From December of 1908 through the end of 1910, only twelve thousand Model T's were sold, at an average price of $850—relatively inexpensive, but still out of the reach of most Americans. In 1911, though, Ford moved manufacturing to a new state-of-the-art plant in Highland Park and turned out seventy thousand T's.

It was only the beginning. In 1912, Highland Park made 170,000 cars; in 1913, more than 200,000. In 1914, not only did the factory's laborers churn out 308,000 cars, but they did so at a salary that Ford had doubled, to the famous "five-dollar day." By 1915, when Highland Park produced more than half a million Model T's, the price had dropped under $300 each, which meant that Ford assembly-line workers needed to work only nine weeks or so to earn enough money to buy a brand-new car. And they did. As did millions of others. By 1924, more than half the country's seventeen million automobiles were Model T's.

All those Fords, along with Dodges, Packards, Buicks, and forgotten models like Brewsters, Biddles, and Westrofts, produced, for the first time, a conflict over the ownership of America's roads—what became known to historians as the "battle over right-of-way." Only a year after the introduction of the Model T, the pioneering city planner Daniel Burnham created a plan for the city of Chicago that was explicitly "providing roads for automobility." In 1922, the professional journal *Engineering News–Record* called for "a radical revision of our conception of what a city street is for." In 1923, the *Providence Sunday Journal* observed (in an article titled "The Jay Walker Problem") that "it is impossible for all classes of modern traffic to occupy the same right of way at the same time in safety."

They weren't kidding. Throughout the 1920s, motor vehicle crashes in the United States killed more than twenty thousand people a year—more than two-thirds of them pedestrians. Campaigns against reckless drivers appeared everywhere, accompanied by graphic stories of auto collisions, usually featuring children and young women. Editorial cartoons vilified drivers. Mobs attacked drivers who hit pedestrians. One Philadelphia paper urged (tongue-in-cheek—I think) that in order to be "in the height of fashion" when they were hurt or even annoyed by a car, "don't ask whether the victim was wholly or in part to blame. Suggest that the driver of the motor-car be lynched."

Against the protestors a coalition of new interests emerged: automobile manufacturers, rubber companies, the petroleum industry, car dealers, and the auto clubs found in every city and state (fifty of them had formed the American Automobile Association back in 1902). By the 1920s, the coalition had started to call itself—I'm not making this up—*motordom*. Motordom wanted streets converted from open spaces available for commercial and recreational uses to one thing and one thing only: arteries for motor vehicles.

In the middle of this battle were local merchants, who just wanted to buy and sell in peace, and who saw the reduction of traffic jams as a priority. In service of that goal, they hired engineers to come up with solutions, such as traffic signals and restrictions on curbside parking. This, to the automobile coalition, was heresy. The merchants and their engineers were attacked by motordom, which regarded *any* restriction as a violation of some newly hatched fundamental right. "There are already too many laws," wrote the engineering service manager of the Kelly-Springfield Tire Company in 1923. Alvan Macauley, the president of Packard Motor Company, called traffic control "a burdensome tangle of restrictive legislation."

You have to give those early automobile advocates credit. They saw, as their opponents did not, that only total victory would do. In 1926, they recognized an opportunity for a key victory in the battle over right-of-way, when President Herbert Hoover empaneled a hundred-member committee to draft a Model Municipal Traffic Ordinance—one that would, in the fullness of time, be the blueprint for traffic regulation all over the United States. The head of that committee was William Metzger, director of the Detroit Automobile Club. The Packard Motor Company's Alvan "Burdensome Tangle" Macauley served as well. So did nine delegates from other auto clubs, and eight from various automobile companies, tire and rubber companies, and auto insurers, along with four presidents of local Yellow Cab companies and the head of the National Automobile Dealers Association. On the other side were five representatives of the railway industry, and exactly one person who could properly be said to be an advocate for pedestrians: Howard S. Braucher, secretary of the Playground and Recreation Association of America. With the deck stacked so heavily,

it won't come as a surprise that the committee's final product cod-
ified the principle of "streets for cars." Pedestrians would, thereafter,
be confined to sidewalks and crosswalks. The Model Municipal Traffic
Ordinance of 1927 transformed city streets from a mixed-use public
space into thoroughfares for the exclusive use of cars (and, by the
way, underlined the deficiencies of streets like those around Ebbets
Field in a new, car-friendly, world).

The real target of the Model Ordinance, though, wasn't the pedestrian. It was the streetcar.

Horse cars—horse-drawn railways—in America date from 1832,
when the first one opened in New York, connecting Prince and 14th
Streets, but they really got going in 1852, when Alphonse Loubat developed the familiar grooved rail set flush with the pavement.

Loubat's cars were pulled by horses, but not for long. Hayburners
were a pretty unattractive power source in a world that had discovered
how to turn boiling water into mechanical energy. The first successful
use of steam power in interurban transport was in cable cars—vehicles
that were connected by a releasable grip to a constantly moving steel
cable that was operated by steam engines at the end of the cable line, a
technology that San Francisco wire-rope manufacturer Andrew Smith
Hallidie perfected in the 1870s. In the 1880s, Chicago had more than
1,500 grip-and-trailer cars operating on 86 miles of track. At their
peak, during the 1890s, America had 283 miles of urban cable track
carrying 373 million passengers annually.

In the end, however, cable cars proved too expensive, as laying
cable and track could cost up to $100,000 per mile. They were also
inefficient: most of the steam power generated to operate the system
was used just to move the cables themselves.

Luckily, another innovation appeared just in time: electric streetcars. In 1887, Frank Sprague, a one-time assistant to Thomas Edison,
started building the world's first electric transportation system, in
Richmond, Virginia, using flexible overhead cables. The small device

that rode atop the electrical cable was known as a "troller," soon enough corrupted to "trolley." Electric trolleys were faster than cable or horse cars, running at between ten and twenty miles per hour, and, since they weren't attached to a cable traveling at a constant speed, the trolleys were also able to accelerate. Maybe more important, they were also far cheaper than laying underground cables.

Electric trolley construction exploded in the years between 1890 and 1905, when American cities featured thirty thousand miles of electric street railway. Because one of the objectives of trolley lines was to bring shoppers into the commercial centers of American cities, they tended to be laid out like the spokes of a wagon wheel; all routes inevitably led downtown, which is one reason that central business districts grew so rapidly during the peak trolley years.

But electric streetcars deposited those shoppers on shelter islands in the middle of city streets—streets that automobile interests regarded as theirs by right. Motordom waged an unremitting campaign against electric streetcars from the 1920s on, arguing, for example, that streetcar passengers were punished by the need to walk across half a street's worth of traffic to reach their destinations. In this, they were aided by almost dizzyingly bad management by the streetcar companies, which were frequently both poorly capitalized and corrupt. Even those that were well run had severe handicaps in the battle against automobiles and buses: streetcar companies usually owned the six to eight feet of right-of-way required for their electric cars to operate and were therefore obliged to pay property taxes on them. They also had to pay for snow removal and even, in some cases, for streetlights along the trolley tracks. Meanwhile, public streets were, well, public. They were effectively a huge, though hidden, subsidy to cars and buses.

Worse still, streetcar companies depended on franchises granted by municipalities, and frequently got them by guaranteeing to hold

prices steady for an irresponsibly long time. In 1897, the Boston Elevated Company agreed to maintain a five-cent fare, including free
transfers, for twenty-five years, during which inflation cut revenues in
half and the company's expenses doubled.* As a result, the electric
streetcar industry peaked by the early 1920s, when probably nine city
trips in ten were still made on more than thirty thousand miles of
track on twelve hundred different urban transit systems and interurban railways. The number of electric streetcars actually topped out in
1917 at 72,911; annual ridership hit 15.7 billion in 1923 and started
to decline thereafter.

It's not too much to say that the streetcar industry was on life support by the 1930s, when the combination of a new federal law and an
illegal corporate conspiracy administered the coup de grâce.

The law came first. One reason for the streetcar industry's boom
was that America's streetcar companies were usually subsidiaries of
local electric-power generating companies. Power companies built
the early streetcar lines, then sold the electricity to operate them.
Everyone made out: the electric company had a reliable buyer of its
product, and the transit company could count on a dependable supplier. Or could until the Crash of 1929 and the Great Depression
that followed, which saw the collapse of fifty-three public-utility
holding companies. When a single group of them, headed by Samuel Insull, the president of Consolidated Edison, went bust, it took
with it the life savings of more than six hundred thousand investors.
Twenty-three other utilities defaulted on interest payments.

Washington's response was the passage of the Public Utility Holding Company Act of 1935, popularly known as the Rayburn-Wheeler
Act. Rayburn-Wheeler provided that public utilities would be confined to single states, that they could offer integrated service only to
a limited geographic area, and—especially—that regulated businesses

---

* A nickel in 1897 was worth only 2.4 cents in 1923.

(like power generation) would be prevented from subsidizing un-regulated ones (like transit). The practical result was that more than half the country's transit companies, carrying 70 percent of America's streetcar passengers, were sundered from their electric-power gener-ating parents. Utility holding companies declined from 216 in 1938 (when the Act went into effect) to 18 by 1950.

The objective of Rayburn-Wheeler wasn't to enrich the competi-tors of America's streetcar companies. It was to reduce the potential for abuse. And the potential was definitely there. Unregulated street-car companies that were owned by electric utilities were a classic moral hazard: whenever the parent company needed to improve its own bottom line, it could require its transit subsidiary to buy electric-ity at higher-than-market rates. If the streetcar company operated at a loss, no one cared. Even the automobile companies didn't care about the accounting tricks that utilities were able to play on the public, and there's no record that any of them lobbied for the provision in Ray-burn-Wheeler that forced utilities to sell their streetcar companies.

They were, however, prepared to buy them.

At the heart of the 1988 Disney movie *Who Framed Roger Rabbit?* is a nefarious plot to close down the Pacific Electric's "Red Car" mass transit system and to replace it with freeways. At the last minute, the story's villain, Judge Doom, the head of Cloverleaf Industries, is foiled in his plan to swindle the rightful owners of the property known as Toontown and evict its residents, lovable animated characters like Mickey Mouse, Bugs Bunny, and Betty Boop.

The animated characters were invented. The rest? Not so much.

For more than a decade beginning in 1936, two shell companies—National City Lines and Pacific City Lines, owned by General Motors, Firestone Tire, Standard Oil of California, Phillips Petroleum, and other huge companies with what you might call a strong bias in favor of gasoline-powered transportation—bought more than a hundred electric train and trolley systems in at least forty-five American cities, including Baltimore, St. Louis, Newark, and, of course, Roger Rabbit's hometown of Los Angeles.*

In 1946, a former streetcar engineer and retired naval officer named Edward J. Quinby exposed the owners of National City Lines, writing a thirty-six-page open letter to America's mayors and city councils. Quinby's letter began, "This is an urgent warning to each and every one of you that there is a carefully, deliberately planned campaign to swindle you out of your most important and valuable public utilities—your Electric Rail System." The letter worked—sort of. In 1947, National City Lines was indicted by the federal government for engaging in a conspiracy in restraint of trade.

>>>

That same year, the Schwartz family welcomed a new member. Me.

By then, my folks, emigrés from Poland, had been living in Brooklyn on and off for a little more than twenty years. The apartment where they were living when I was born, 170 Tapscott Street in the Brownsville neighborhood, was no roomier than the shtetl house they had left behind: two-and-a-half rooms—a kitchen and two bedrooms—for my parents, my two older brothers, one older sister, and me. Even after we moved to Bensonhurst when I was four years old, things were a little cramped. I shared a bedroom with my parents until I was eleven, which was when my oldest brother, Harold, got drafted into the army and my other brother, Brian, left for Brown University to get a PhD in physics.

---

* It wasn't the first time this particular tactic had been tried. In 1933, General Motors set up a subsidiary known as United Cities Motor Transport with the stated objective of buying transit companies in order to replace streetcars with GM-made buses. UCMT was shut down after the American Transit Association censured GM for using pressure tactics to get the city of Portland on board.

The nearest parks of any size were nearly a mile away. One of them, Dyker Beach Park, was mostly a golf course, anyway. And membership in the Jewish Community House on Bay Parkway, where Sandy Koufax had once played ball, cost money. So our little corner of Bensonhurst had no choice but to preserve the kind of city street that had predated the automobile. Eighty-third Street, between 19th and 20th Avenues, was our playground, ball field, and hangout. The street was where we played punchball, football, a local baseball-like game called triangle (it was hard to fit a rectangular diamond on a street that was thirty feet wide), Ring-o-leevio, Johnny on a pony, box ball, and hit the penny. Stickball is probably the best remembered of the street games, one in which a pitcher would throw a rubber ball—a spaldeen—to a batter who'd hit it for distance.* Home plate was a manhole cover, which we called a sewer, second base was the next sewer, first and third were usually the back tire of the Plymouth and the front tire of the Chevy parked on either side of the street, which was about the only time we needed cars for anything. My father's grocery store was only three blocks from our apartment.

We didn't realize it, but Bensonhurst was already more like a museum of a long-forgotten way of life—a kind of ethnic Colonial Williamsburg—than a picture of America's immediate future. Quinby had been too late. Four years later, when the conviction against National City was upheld on appeal, more than half of America's electric streetcar companies had been shut down, and most of the rest partially eliminated. GM, Firestone, Mack Truck, and National City Lines' other investors were fined $5,000; a few individuals were fined one dollar each. Fewer than eighteen thousand streetcars remained in service. Public transit traveled over and under city streets—New York's first subway line opened in 1904—but the streets themselves had been conquered by the internal combustion engine.

---

* A home run was two sewers on the fly. I'm told Willie Mays, when he played for the New York Giants, was a regular three-sewer hitter.

>>>

While cars and buses were taking over the streets of America's cities, another and equally important battle was going on for the roads outside them.

Country roads are very different from urban ones. For one thing, they appeared far later in history. Until the nineteenth century, in fact, roads outside cities were virtually certain to be made of packed earth: rough, flood-prone, and very unreliable.

The first method for improving them in a cost-effective way appeared around 1820, when a Scottish road-building obsessive named John Loudon McAdam figured out how to lay out a level road with proper drainage, using nothing but broken stone. His innovation—an eight-inch roadbed made up of stones "not to exceed 6 ounces in weight or to pass a two-inch ring," topped by two inches composed of stones with no dimension greater than three-quarters of an inch, the whole thing compacted with iron rollers into a sturdy aggregate—was simple, brilliant, and, most important, economical. "Macadamized" roads spread throughout the United Kingdom, Europe, and the United States, where the "National Road" that connected Cumberland, Maryland, with Vandalia, Illinois, was gushed over by an English visitor in this way:

> It is covered with a very thick layer of nicely broken stones, or stone, rather, laid on with great exactness both as to depth and width, and then rolled down with an iron roller, which reduces all to one solid mass. This is a road made for ever.

Macadamized roads may have been made "for ever" but they weren't made for cars. How could they be? Even in 1895, fewer than five hundred automobiles were operating regularly on US roads, mostly on those stone-paved city streets. Ten years later, in 1905, only about seventy-eight thousand had been registered in the entire country. The impetus for building those first macadamized roads did not come from cars, but bicycles.

The League of American Wheelmen was founded in 1880 in Newport, Rhode Island. By 1900, it was America's largest special-interest group. And the interest with which it was specially concerned was roads. Bad as dirt roads were for slow-moving horse carts, they were basically impassable for bicycles, which were then taking America by storm. In 1891, the League published a pamphlet, the *Gospel of Good Roads: A Letter to the American Farmer*, as the manifesto for the National League for Good Roads. A year later, they started publishing *Good Roads Magazine*. The campaign was explicitly intended to build a coalition of bicyclists, farmers, and railroad companies, each of which had an interest in road improvement: the cyclists for obvious reasons, and the farmers not just because they depended on those very undependable dirt roads to get perishable goods to market, but because a macadamized road allowed a two-horse team to pull the same amount of freight that had earlier required six horses. For their part, the railroads, which had laid more than two hundred thousand miles of track by the end of the nineteenth century, were aware that the value of their network could be multiplied many times by improving access to it. They even dispatched hundreds of "Good Roads" trains to rural stations, where they would build a few miles of macadamized roads using steamrollers, as a taste of what *real* road improvement could look like.

Those new-and-improved roads looked a lot different outside cities than inside. One reason was that the rise of automobile culture tracked, almost exactly, with the beginnings of the movement known as American Progressivism, and the first automobiles were embraced as a Progressive solution to the widely accepted notion that cities were basically incubators of immigration, crime, and tenements. To Progressives, cars provided an *escape* from cities, though the escape they provided was pretty rocky—before the twentieth century, there were virtually no paved roads between cities in the United States—and confusing, since no one had come up with a naming or numbering system for intercity roads. Rand McNally's first road atlases guided travelers by listing turns, landmarks, bridges, and forks in the road.

Those roads that did exist were built to handle—in descending order—bicycles, farm vehicles (horse drawn and gas powered), and the occasional recreational automobile. So important were bikes that by the end of the 1890s, the so-called sidepath movement had its own magazine, accurately though predictably titled *Sidepaths*, that advocated for protected bike lanes that "shall not be less than three feet or more than six feet wide . . . constructed within the outside lines and along and upon either side of . . . public roads and streets." No wagons, carts, or horses: bike paths.

But by the 1920s, America's cars had multiplied to the point that they were literally destroying simple macadamized roads. The rocks that composed the roads were relatively light, which meant that the millions of rubber tires kicked up a dangerous amount of dust and caused the roads to deteriorate rapidly. The immediate answer was found in the same long-gestating hydrocarbons that fueled all those new cars: mixing tar with macadamized stone, later to be replaced by the petroleum byproduct known as asphalt. By 1925, seventeen million cars rode on twenty thousand miles of concrete-paved roads—and more than two hundred thousand miles of "improved" macadamized roads.

However, while engineers learned how to improve intercity roads, they weren't much good at figuring out how to pay for such improvements. The railroads that had been the great transportation innovation of the nineteenth century had been built by privately owned corporations (though on public land, which was given to companies like the Union Pacific). Private capital for roads was available. The Long Island Motor Parkway, the first thoroughfare in the world restricted solely to cars and buses, was completed by William K. Vanderbilt at a cost of $2 million in 1908.* The Lincoln Highway, begun in 1913 as America's first transcontinental road, was the brainchild of the Indianapolis industrialist Carl Fisher, as was the Chicago-to-Miami Dixie Highway. But private dollars were limited. The logic that regarded urban trolley tracks as a private enterprise, but city streets as a public responsibility, was more and more appealing to advocates of an intercity/interstate road system.

Those advocates were compelled to fight against a long history of opposition to national road building. The original Articles of Confederation, hostile to anything that might result in tyranny by a national government, explicitly prohibited any such activity. It's a little easier to understand the suspicion that the eighteenth-century founders of the United States had for national road-building enterprises if you remember that highways—the word comes from the defining characteristic of such roads, which was that they were raised, usually a foot or two, from the surrounding land—were so expensive to build and maintain that they had historically been a royal asset. In fact, for centuries "highway robbery" was a capital crime because thievery that occurred on the king's roads was the next thing to treason.

The conventioneers who spent the summer of 1787 in Philadelphia changed all that. Article I, Section 8, of the Constitution that they wrote empowered the new federal government to establish "post offices and post roads," which provided a loophole through the ban on federal road building. Eventually. It took another 125 years or so before the Sixty-Fourth Congress managed to pass America's first federal roads bill, the Federal-Aid Road Act of 1916.

---

* Vanderbilt, a racing fanatic, built the parkway as a racetrack that could be used by the public on non-race days—for a toll of $2, or about $45 in current dollars. The parkway, which was built as a rich man's toy, was eventually acquired by New York for nonpayment of taxes, and only a few miles survive, as a portion of the Meadowbrook Parkway.

The 1916 Act provided $75 million in federal funds for rural "post roads" so long as they were free to the public. It was expanded and amended by the Federal-Aid Highway Act of 1921, which offered states matching funds—50 percent from the state, 50 percent from the federal government—for building roads deemed "militarily necessary." A fair number of roads still in use today were built using federal matching funds. The New Jersey Expressway, on which construction began in 1929, was an FAHA project. So was the very first freeway in Los Angeles, the Arroyo Seco Parkway, which opened in 1940. It seems likely that more and more intercity and interstate roads would have been constructed using the fifty-fifty formula of the FAHA had the Second World War not intervened. The final link in the chain of events that got the Dodgers to leave Ebbets Field was forged, not in Los Angeles, or even Brooklyn, but in Germany.

>>>

After Germany's surrender in May of 1945, the most powerful man in Western Europe was the supreme commander, Allied Forces in Europe: General Dwight David Eisenhower. He was, by all accounts, a fine soldier and a gifted administrator, but his true brilliance was logistics: matching resources to objectives. In 1919, Lieutenant Colonel Eisenhower had been part of the US Army's Cross-Country Motor Transport Train, an attempt to show the entire nation just how fast and impressively a modern mechanized army could move. It took sixty-two days to travel from Gettysburg, Pennsylvania, to San Francisco, California, on Carl Fisher's Lincoln Highway. It was predictable that he would be hugely impressed by the roads built by Adolf Hitler's inspector general of German Road Construction, Fritz Todt: the Autobahn.*

---

* The Autobahn's reputation considerably exceeded its real value, as either military asset or transportation system. Fewer than 2,200 miles of Autobahn had actually been built before the war began, and no more were built until well into the 1960s.

The story might have ended there, except that seven years later the general was elected president of the United States. He had written in his postwar autobiography, "Germany had made me see the wisdom of broader ribbons across the land," and he was now in a position to do something about it. The "something" was the National System of Interstate and Defense Highways, better known as the Interstate Highway System.

The Interstate Highway System was and is an extraordinary achievement, fully deserving of the superlatives that appear regularly in every account of its construction. The construction industry trade fair known as CONEXPO-CON/AGC named the IHS one of the "Top 10 Construction Achievements of the 20th Century." So did the American Society of Civil Engineers. In July 1999, *Engineering News-Record* celebrated its 125th anniversary with a list of the top projects for each year of the magazine's life. The entry for 1996 was the Interstate Highway System, on the occasion of its fortieth anniversary. It remains the largest and most expensive public works project in the country's history, one that changed literally every aspect of the way Americans live, work, and, especially, travel.

Like anything of such magnitude, it didn't appear out of nowhere. The 1921 Act—the one that funded "militarily necessary" roads—required the newly appointed head of the Bureau of Public Roads, an engineer named Thomas MacDonald, to create a map with more than seventy-eight thousand miles of roads "of prime importance in the event of war."* Eighteen years later, a 1939 report to the US Congress, titled "Toll Roads and Free Roads," called for a new highway system "designed to meet the requirements of the national defense in time of war and the needs of growing peacetime traffic of longer range." In 1947, MacDonald, still head of the BPR, produced yet another new map, this one containing "only" forty thousand miles of highway.

---

* What this meant, in practice, was a network that connected coalfields, foundries, and iron ports in order to maximize the nation's ability to build armaments.

What was missing in all earlier attempts was a method of paying for the new roads. The Federal-Aid Highway Act of 1956 fixed the problem by creating the Highway Trust Fund: a bucket of federal money with a designated source of revenue—a federal gas tax of three cents a gallon. Every penny collected in accord with the Act was required to be used for building the new highway system, with 90 percent of the costs coming from Washington and the remainder from the states that would, once completed, own the new roads. The Act budgeted a total of $25 billion, to be spent in roughly equal increments in each fiscal year from 1957 through 1969.*

The Act also specified just what sort of roads were to be built. Interstate highways were to have no crossings at grade; that is, any intersecting roads were to transect the new highway either by tunnel or bridge, with overpass clearances of at least fourteen feet (later increased to sixteen feet) to accommodate military vehicles. Each new highway was to have at least four lanes, each one twelve feet wide—some rural routes were allowed to be smaller—and to be designed for safety at speeds of not less than fifty miles per hour in mountains, sixty in rolling terrain, and seventy everywhere else. "Primary" Interstate highways would be designated with two digits, secondary roads that looped around them with three.

It's not as if no one had ever built such roads before. The Pennsylvania Turnpike had opened in 1940 and would form big chunks of two different primary Interstate highways: I-70 and I-76. The Holland and Lincoln Tunnels, which opened in 1927 and 1937, respectively, represented the state of the art in tunnel engineering. The George Washington Bridge (1931) and the Golden Gate Bridge (1937) were models for long-span bridges. The railroad engineers of

---

* Put as charitably as possible, the numbers were a little optimistic. The "National System of Interstate and Defense Highways" would end up costing more than $110 billion (more than $400 billion in current dollars) and the final leg wouldn't be completed until 1991.

the late nineteenth century had left behind a vast library of technical knowledge about soil, drainage, and grading, which is one reason that many of the highways that formed the IHS followed railroad rights-of-way. The challenge of the Interstate Highway System was one of magnitude, not technology: no one had ever built so *much* so *fast*, or to such inflexible specifications.

To maintain the schedule required by the 1956 Act, huge numbers of new engineers were urgently needed. And, since the Act essentially required that every one of the 42,500 miles originally specified (the number would eventually grow to 47,700) would look exactly like every other mile, those engineers needed a system of uniform training, and a method for sharing best practices. By 1956, the Servicemen's Readjustment Act of 1944, better known as the GI Bill of Rights, had put more than two million one-time soldiers through college, and thousands of them graduated from new but largely identical programs in traffic engineering at schools like UC Berkeley, Yale, and Northwestern.

Waiting for them were the American Association of State Highway Officials and the Highway Research Board, which served both as a clearinghouse for data collected elsewhere and a source of new research. A single example: in 1958, the AASHO built seven miles of two-lane road just outside Ottawa, Illinois, consisting of six loops and one long straightaway plus sixteen short-span bridges. Its pavement was made up of 836 test sections, each one a different sandwich of surface, base, and subbase, using different recipes of concrete and asphalt. Road tests at the Ottawa "lab" consisted of driving vehicles weighing anywhere from two thousand to thirty thousand pounds around the track and measuring road wear. AASHO engineers ran such tests continuously for two years before finally reporting the ideal balance of thickness and ingredients.

It was only one of the remarkable engineering achievements of the builders of the IHS, which invented new road-building techniques on virtually a monthly basis: huge finishing machines that could pave two lanes at once; steel rollers that vibrated while pounding pavement down; techniques for turning existing concrete roadways to rubble on site, as a base for a new highway (the formal terms are *rubblization* and *crack-and-seat*). Other machines made sections of concrete nine feet wide by six inches deep—slip-form pavers—that could be manufactured in factories and transported to building sites like enormous LEGO blocks. The IHS also featured safety innovations like reflective road markers, new guardrail designs, and reflectorized signs. The United States spent 2.6 billion person-hours to build the system. Most of those hours were well spent, indeed.

Most of them.

>>>

A clue to the great failing of the IHS is found in that 1939 report to Congress, which called for a "system of direct interregional highways, with all necessary connections *through and around cities*" (emphasis added). The IHS is a marvel for transporting people and goods between cities. But wherever it is routed "through . . . cities" it is almost always a disaster.

It wasn't intended to be. The system's original planners always imagined routes through metropolitan areas—though President Eisenhower was evidently so confused about his namesake project that the first time he realized it included urban highways was when he saw the construction on what would become the sixty-four-mile-long Capital Beltway. The engineers of the Bureau of Public Roads weren't evil. They actually believed that the Interstate system would reinvigorate America's cities, representing as they believed it did the "chance of a century to make our cities sparkle brightly among our Nation's brilliant collection of really wonderful cities . . . probably the greatest single tool" in solving the problems of urban blight.

They maintained their belief in the progressive character of re-inforced concrete, even in the face of opposition to building eight-lane-wide, limited-access roads that would slice through existing cities, leaving hundred-foot-wide scars at each interchange. In September 1957 (the same month that Walter O'Malley announced that the Dodgers would be leaving Brooklyn) the Connecticut General Life Insurance Company sponsored a symposium it called "The New Highways: Challenge to the Metropolitan Region." In attendance was Bertrand Tallamy, Thomas MacDonald's successor as head of the Bureau of Public Roads, now renamed the Federal Highway Administration. So was Lewis Mumford.

Mumford, a sociologist, historian, and the author of *The Culture of Cities* and *The City in History*, wasn't exactly full of admiration for the planners and builders of the Interstate Highway System. "If they had any notion of what they were doing, they would not appear as blithe and cocky over the way they were doing it." He blamed the "inclination to favor anything that seems to give added attraction to the second mistress that exists in every house right alongside the wife—the motor car."

Mumford was right in his criticism but not in his reasoning. It wasn't a love for cars that brought limited-access roads into American cities. It was love of money. To local politicians, the clinking sound of the Highway Trust Fund paying ninety cents out of every road-building dollar was sweeter music by far than the sound of any V8 engine roaring down the highway. A $100 million highway for $10 million? Or, sometimes, since state governments offered their own subsidies, only $4 or $5 million? With hundreds or even thousands of new construction jobs in your district?

No surprise that city planners and state transportation commissioners designed and redesigned their municipal road-building projects until they could qualify for Highway Trust Fund largesse.

The problem with all that "free" money wasn't just that limited-access roads *by definition* are the enemies of the street culture in neighborhoods where people actually live, like the Bensonhurst blocks where I grew up. If the only purpose of a road is to get from one place to another, the stuff that goes on in and around that road becomes not just unnecessary but dangerous: a distraction from safe, high-speed driving. Even worse, though, is that local city planners, who still had to pony up 5 to 10 percent of the cost of even HTF-funded roads, had a big incentive to do so where the cost of removing the residents was lowest. As a result, instead of arresting the decline of cities, the IHS paid billions of dollars to accelerate it, in precisely those neighborhoods with the least political clout and money. Families that might have been inclined to stay in a metropolitan area now had another, compelling reason to move to the suburbs that were sprouting like toadstools everywhere in America where a new Interstate could carry commuters from home to work and back again.

There were, of course, many reasons that suburbs looked attractive to America's post–World War II generation. Suburban living has had its appeal ever since some anonymous commuter took a stylus in hand to write four thousand years ago, "Our property seems to me the most beautiful in the world. It is so close to Babylon that we enjoy all the advantages of the city, and yet when we come home we are away from all the noise and dust."* Brooklyn itself was widely known as a "ferry suburb" in the early nineteenth century.

But there were special reasons for the 1950s explosion in suburban emigration that took the Cohen, Politik, and Pepper families out of Bensonhurst. The same GI Bill of Rights that educated the engineers who built the IHS also provided, through the new Federal Housing Authority, low-cost housing loans to veterans. But since the law was explicitly drafted to promote employment in the building trades, qualifying families could get thirty-year loans for purchasing new, single-family housing, but only five-year loans for repairing or

---

* This is an excerpt from a letter to the King of Persia, describing the "suburb" known as Ur.

renovating existing structures. Even worse, the manual used by the Federal Housing Authority to decide whether to underwrite home loans in the first place taught that "crowded neighborhoods lessen desirability" and that "older properties in a neighborhood have a tendency to accelerate the transition to lower class occupancy." By design, the law effectively made it cheaper to buy than to rent, and a *lot* easier to move to the suburbs. As taxpayers flowed outward from existing cities, money followed, first in a trickle, then in a flood. And since the places where the money stopped had streets, but neither streetcars nor buses and sometimes not even sidewalks (not that there was anything much worth walking to), a car was an absolute necessity. And once you could afford it, two cars, or more.

≫≫≫

Cars, and especially multiple cars, were not a necessity for everyone, of course. The Schwartz family had managed to get along very nicely without depending on cars for much of anything. From the time I was born until I left for graduate school, we had owned cars for fewer than ten years.

We never really needed one. My father walked to work from our apartment to his grocery store. While I was in high school, I walked too, saving my five-dollar-a-week salary plus tips. Like my brothers and sister, I walked or biked to school. Even after I entered Brooklyn Tech—Brooklyn Technical High School in Fort Greene, one of New York City's hyper-competitive scientific and technical high schools—in the fall of 1961, I got there by subway.

When I graduated high school, I applied only to the public colleges in what had just recently become the City University of New York—basically City College, Queens College, and Brooklyn College. Today, the city's system has seven four-year colleges, along with grad schools and community colleges, all of them charging tuition, but in

1965, they were all tuition-free. In my family, the idea of paying for college was a foreign concept. My brothers never paid for college: Brian even got a fellowship to Brown after getting his undergraduate degree for free at Cooper Union and City College. Why would I? I got into my first choice, Brooklyn College, and began commuting to classes in the fall of 1965.*

Ask anyone: 1965–1969 was a great time to be a college student. I was a member of a fraternity, partied, took part in student demonstrations, and dated. Though I still had to work part-time in my father's store, I did my best to make sure I worked there as little as possible. The best excuse for avoiding the grocery store was another job, so I took jobs anywhere I could find them. I was a mailman, movie projectionist, and—my favorite—cabbie. It's not that I had authority issues, exactly. But I loved being my own boss, and driving a cab was a pretty good simulation. As long as I brought back at least $60 at the end of each shift, I was allowed to keep 49 percent, plus tips. In a good week, I could clear $300—and since I was still living rent-free at home, by my senior year I was rich. Also stupid. I made the mistake of trading in my '60 Chevy for a very cool '64 Pontiac Grand Prix with white bucket seats. Turns out I wasn't the only one who thought it was cool. Within a year, it was stolen off the streets of Bensonhurst and I was reduced to riding a bike: in 1969, the opposite of cool. My stupidity, by the way, wasn't limited to making trade-in decisions. My embrace of driving—while I had a car to drive, that is—was contributing to the demise of something smart—walkable city streets—though I didn't realize it for years.

I did attend classes, too. In New York State high schools, students take standardized tests, known as Regents Exams, in a variety of

---

* My first semester I walked three long blocks (about a half mile) to Bay Parkway and caught the bus to Brooklyn College. By my second semester I had enough saved from the grocery store work that I could afford the $450 needed to buy a six-year-old 1960 Chevy Impala—the one with huge fins. After that, I always drove.

subjects, and at Brooklyn Tech I had scored the highest grade in the school on the physics exam. I wasn't particularly interested in physics, but I thought it was my calling, so when the time came to choose a major, physics was it. It was a good thing I did. I did well enough in my classes to get by but my grade point average tended to hover just below a B. It would have been a lot lower but for physics and math.

In the fall of 1968, after I entered my senior year, I started getting brochures from universities trying to lure me to apply to graduate programs in physics. It wasn't my grades that made me so attractive, but the fact that US colleges were producing so few physics graduates. I was flattered anyway. My plan was to put off life for another four to five years while I got a PhD in physics.

So I went to visit my brother Brian, who had graduated from City College with his own undergraduate degree in physics nine years before, had earned his PhD at Brown, and was then on the faculty at MIT. I wanted his advice about grad schools. Instead Brian told me, "You're twenty years old and you haven't been discovered yet. At best you will get admitted to a mediocre graduate school and spend the next seven years working on your PhD. Then you'll get a job at some obscure university and study the spin on the twenty-seventh electron of a copper atom."

I was deflated. Also scared. The Vietnam War was raging, and I had to go to grad school to stay out of the draft. (Little did I know that, because of the war, the Selective Service Administration was just about to reclassify grad students, even those studying physics, 1-A.) What was I going to do?

Over the weekend my brother peppered me with questions. "What do you like to do?" Party, I said. Girls. Music. He kept pressing. I disliked the suburbs, even the Boston suburb where Brian lived, which eventually reminded me that I liked cities. I told Brian. He mulled it over in his mind. "Well, you're good in math and science. Not *physics* good, but good compared to others." This is how Brian's brain works. He put math + science + cities in an equation, for which the solution was one word:

"Traffic."

It was a replay of the memorable scene in *The Graduate*, in which Dustin Hoffman's character, Benjamin Braddock, receives sage advice about the future from his father's friend in one word: "Plastics."

I was just as articulate as Benjamin. "Huh?" I replied. (I wasn't a very smooth talker.) Was that even a field? Brian told me MIT had been studying traffic and maybe that'd suit me. I did have an interest in traffic safety after my friend's brakes failed on his '55 Chevy and we crashed into a tollbooth. I had read Ralph Nader's *Unsafe at Any Speed*.

So I investigated graduate programs in the study of traffic and transportation and discovered them hidden away in the departments of civil engineering. I applied to a few schools and was accepted by MIT and the University of Pennsylvania. The choice wasn't especially difficult: Penn offered me a full fellowship, plus a stipend of $75 a week.

I promptly went out and bought a "new" 1970 Chevelle. Ten-plus years after the Dodgers left Brooklyn, I did the same, and headed south on Interstate 95. Destination: Philadelphia.

Fifty years after Henry Ford's Model T had transformed cars from luxury items to necessities, the victory of the automobile looked complete. It also looked, to a lot of people, inevitable: a historical tidal wave that could have taken no other form than the one it did.

But it wasn't really inevitable at all. The revolution that transformed America's roads, the one that really got under way in the 1950s, was the result of a sequence of decisions—to draft the Model Municipal Traffic Ordinance, to pass the Rayburn-Wheeler Act, to collude in the National City Lines conspiracy, to build the Interstate Highway System, and to fund the suburbanization of America through the GI Bill—that pushed an entire country in one automobile-rich direction.

By the time I started studying transportation, some people were already pushing back.

FOR EVERY ACTION...

I F BEDFORD AVENUE IS ONE OF THE GRANDDADDIES OF NEW YORK'S streets, the four-mile-long Grand Boulevard and Concourse, originally designed to connect the boroughs of Manhattan and the Bronx, is barely a teenager.

The clearest inspiration for the Concourse was Paris's Champs-Élysées, which is shorter but wider than the Grand Concourse; at its widest point, north of 161st Street, the Grand Concourse is "only" 180 feet from curb to curb. The Champs-Élysées has occupied the same Parisian acreage since the 1600s, but the Grand Concourse is very much a nineteenth-century creation. Like the Good Roads Movement, it was a child of the 1890s, one of America's purest examples of what came to be known as the "City Beautiful" movement, a reformist crusade marketed as a Progressive answer to the evils of late-nineteenth-century cities: tenements, slums, and corruption.

Which was, as it happens, also how Progressives saw the automobile itself.

Like other tributes to the reform-minded movement, such as the World's Columbian Exposition that dominated the Chicago skyline in 1893, Washington's Capitol Mall, and the Benjamin Franklin Parkway in Philadelphia, the Grand Concourse featured extremely wide roads, including a central thoroughfare fifty feet wide, two thirty-five-foot-wide access roads, eight-foot-wide medians, and twenty-foot-wide sidewalks, all of them heavily planted with gardens. It also shared with them a common history of replacing poor neighborhoods by the simple expedient of moving their occupants, well, anywhere else.

Whatever its built-in contradictions—the most beautiful cities, it turns out, aren't always the most livable, and roads wider than a football field aren't what you might call pedestrian friendly—the City Beautiful movement, like the Grand Concourse itself, was unashamedly urban. Construction on the Grand Concourse began in 1894 and finished fifteen years later, in 1909. By the 1930s, with a subway line running under the boulevard, the three-hundred-plus neo-Tudor, Art Deco, and Art Moderne apartment buildings that lined it had become an extremely attractive place for immigrant families that had graduated from entry-level neighborhoods like the Lower East Side or Bensonhurst. Half my father's family that emigrated from Poland between world wars ended up in the area.

Even the Great Depression couldn't destroy the Grand Concourse. The authors of the 1939 *WPA Guide to New York* commissioned by the New Deal's Works Progress Administration wrote, "The Grand Concourse is the Park Avenue of middle-class Bronx residents, and a lease to an apartment in one of its many large buildings is considered evidence of at least moderate business success. The thoroughfare . . . is the principal parade-street of the borough, as well as a *through motor route*" (emphasis added).

The "through motor route" description, and the date it was made, are both significant. In some ways, it has always seemed to me that the 1940s—the "Big Bad Forties"—marked a transportation revolution for New York, and the entire country, that was as big in its way as the introduction of the car itself. It was the architect who designed the Grand Concourse, an émigré railroad engineer named Louis Risse, who called for building "the most magnificent thoroughfare in the world," which

> will include not only a wide speedway, but a double boulevard for common pleasure driving, broad walks, promenades, cycle paths, all intersected by nine transverse roads, passing underneath the same, for the accommodation of railways and heavy traffic. . . . It will be a drive of extraordinary delightfulness and practical convenience, and will offer the peculiar attractiveness arising from the sense that one may drive for miles without encountering an interruption in the road or a change in its character.

The miles of uninterrupted driving Risse described were, in 1897, intended for horse-drawn carriages; that is, a bridle path. By the time the Concourse opened, in 1909, the automobile age was well begun. By the 1940s, America was embracing it like nowhere else on Earth. That's when another "through motor route" transformed the borough for which the Grand Concourse had been emblematic into a shorthand proxy for urban decay, and became an enduring symbol of the conflict over the ownership of America's roads. The intersection between the north-south Grand Concourse and the east-west Cross-Bronx Expressway* would come to represent not just one battle over the City Beautiful, but a rallying cry in a decades-long war.

---

* In New York, parkways (except for Olmsted's Brooklyn parkways and the Bronx's Pelham and Moshulu parkways) and expressways are both limited-access highways with few if any crossings at grade, but parkways ban commercial traffic and expressways don't. The first limited-access parkway—the Bronx River Parkway—was built in 1925; the first expressway—the Brooklyn-Queens Expressway—was proposed in 1936 but was delayed by the Depression until 1939.

>>>

The story of the Cross-Bronx began in 1945, six years after the publication of the *WPA Guide to New York City*. The Depression had ended; millions of American troops had gone to war and returned to a very different country. The differences they found in the New York metropolitan region were largely the work of a single man: Robert Moses (who had not yet started his epic battle with Walter O'Malley over Brooklyn baseball).

When Moses died, in 1981, virtually every obituary used the nickname he earned in life: the "Master Builder." If anything, it probably understates his accomplishments. Between 1924 and 1968, he built thirteen major bridges, including the Triborough and the Verrazano-Narrows, the longest suspension bridge in the world when finished. (Not a single Moses-built river crossing had tracks for either trains or streetcars, even though every major bridge built in New York City prior to 1910 was "tracked." On his last bridge, the Verrazano, he didn't even put a walkway or bike path.) Also the St. Lawrence power project and Lincoln Center. Also more than two million acres of parkland, 416 miles of parkways, 658 playgrounds, 10 gigantic public swimming pools, the Central Park Zoo, and the 1964 New York World's Fair. His vision of the model city of the future was dominated by towers, highways, and beaches, all of them designed to be accessible by automobile, even at the price of putting them out of the reach of pedestrians.

(His résumé doesn't just include an embarrassingly long list of projects, but an even more embarrassingly long list of titles. At one point, Moses occupied a dozen different positions simultaneously, including chairman of the Triborough Bridge and Tunnel Authority, New York State power commissioner, and chairman of the State Council of Parks, and he was both New York City construction coordinator and parks commissioner.)

Moses's plan for a six-lane expressway running east-west right through the middle of the Bronx was part of an even more grandiose proposal for one hundred new miles of highway construction in the New York metropolitan region. The plan had been gestating since 1941, when a "Bronx Crosstown Highway" was endorsed in writing by the New York City Planning Commission:

> an express crosstown facility across the middle Bronx is an essential part of a desirable highway pattern. Topographical conditions, high land values and heavily built-up areas make the construction of such a highway very difficult. However, its great importance would justify the expense involved. This highway would provide the only adequate means of east-west travel through the middle Bronx. It would connect New Jersey via the George Washington Bridge, connect with New England via Westchester County highways, and afford very essential relief for local cross-Bronx traffic. The Borough President of the Bronx has estimated that the cost of this improvement would be $17,000,000.

It took four years and the biggest war in human history to delay the plan, which had Moses's fingerprints all over it. He had built existing parkways on either side of the borough, and could see no better way to connect them than with a limited-access highway. By 1945, he had his chance.

For reasons of history and topography, the project was a brutally difficult engineering problem. As planned, the six 12-foot-wide lanes of the Cross-Bronx Expressway (plus another 10 feet on each side for shoulders) had to cross more than a hundred streets, half a dozen expressways and parkways, and six mass transit lines, five of them elevated trains and one a subway. It required bridging (or, in some cases, changing the flow of) three separate rivers and avoiding a thousand sewer, electrical, and water lines. If that weren't enough, Moses was determined to make the Expressway aesthetically pleasing as well, with parks, landscaping, and playgrounds along the right-of-way. I've met some of the men—yes, they're all men—who built the Cross-Bronx Expressway, and every one of them was hugely proud of the technical achievement it represents. They should have been. Not only did they lace a 100-foot-wide thread through a needle's eye that was only a 101 feet in diameter—a subway line runs *above* the Cross-Bronx and *below* the Grand Concourse—but they did it without touching the existing girders that held up six densely populated miles of apartment buildings and factories. Ernest Clark, the Expressway's designer, says they "took the stuff out with a teaspoon." He also calls it "one of the most challenging highway projects that had been constructed . . . one measured in inches and tenths of inches."

The biggest challenge in building the Cross-Bronx Expressway wasn't shifting dirt and rock, though. It was moving people.

In 1952, plans for the middle section of the Expressway produced the first substantial protests Robert Moses had encountered in nearly thirty years of building. The original route, which ran through the relatively poor East Tremont and Morris Heights neighborhoods, required demolishing nearly 160 apartment buildings and relocating 1,400 families, most of whom didn't want to be relocated. The political leaders of the Bronx proposed rerouting the Expressway three blocks to the south, through the northern portion of a park, which would have removed six buildings housing nineteen families. Moses refused, providing a laundry list of reasons, from unacceptably steep grading to the loss of the Third Avenue bus depot.

(As pointed out by Robert Caro in his biography of Moses, "It was out of character for Moses, who had no prior interest in helping mass transit, suddenly sticking up for the preservation of a bus station. Decades later . . . the truth came forward: Moses' friends owned vacant property or shares in the Third Avenue bus depot.")

As he had for four decades, Moses succeeded in steamrolling any opposition. In 1963, the final stretch of the Cross-Bronx Expressway was completed, ten years late and at a cost at least three times its original $40 million budget. As a reminder of how the federal government had become essential even to road building within cities, the last third of the Expressway couldn't have been built at all without a very healthy contribution from the Highway Trust Fund, for which it qualified after a few hundred yards were shoehorned into the plans for Interstate 95. It was, along with the Verrazano-Narrows Bridge, the Master Builder's last great success, and his swan song. By the time it opened, any notion that the Cross-Bronx Expressway would revive the Bronx specifically, and be a model for urban renewal generally, was the punch line to a joke. The Expressway hadn't just destroyed East Tremont. Despite all the care Moses and his engineers lavished on keeping the Grand Concourse as grand as ever—the Concourse, unsurprisingly, with its 180-foot-wide streets and monumental architecture, was very much in the Moses style—it was already sliding into a vicious cycle of poverty and crime.

Though there are many reasons for the decline of urban centers in the 1960s (city centers had trouble retaining their appeal even without limited-access highways crisscrossing them), the Cross-Bronx Expressway had made a dozen middle-class New York neighborhoods less and less desirable as places to live, and by the 1970s the Bronx had become a poster child for urban blight in America. The Grand Concourse's already narrow medians—eight feet wide, and barely able to support a single line of trees—were slashed by diagonal "sleeves" to permit easier movement from the access roads to the central roadway and back. If pedestrians needed another reason to avoid strolling along what had become of Risse's "broad walks, promenades, and cycle paths," the chance of being killed by a car moving at high speed from one portion of the Concourse to another definitely offered one.

>>>

To those of us in the business of transportation, the best thing to be said about the Cross-Bronx Expressway is that it is a really good cautionary tale. Even on its own terms—moving cars efficiently from one point to another—the Expressway remains a disaster. It is an overbudget, destructive, and ugly corridor that actually increases the congestion it was built to relieve. The portion that runs from Baychester Avenue to the Major Deegan Expressway has the distinction of being the most congested corridor in the entire country.

Looking back, though, it might be that the most enduring legacy of the Cross-Bronx Expressway was the template it created for organizing resistance to roads that are built for cars rather than for people. In 1953, the East Tremont Neighborhood Association, a tenant group formed to oppose eviction, had promised to block what they called the "Heartbreak Highway." They failed, of course, but it was their failed revolt, not the "successful" Expressway, that put its stamp on the future.

Ground zero for what exploded into a national and then an international highway protest movement was San Francisco, California. At the same time that Robert Moses was bulldozing the middle of the Bronx, the San Francisco Board of Supervisors was preparing to do roughly the same thing to their own city. The 1951 and 1955 San Francisco Trafficways Plans contain designs for half a dozen freeways that would have crisscrossed the City by the Bay. They had names like the "Crosstown Freeway," the "Mission Freeway," the "Golden Gate Freeway," the "Park Presidio Freeway," and the "Central Freeway." Only parts of the last two would ever be built. Even as most states and cities were frantically chasing money from the federal government's Highway Trust Fund, others were joining the same figurative barricades that had been built by the East Tremont Neighborhood Association.

The biggest (or, at least, the best remembered) was the so-called Embarcadero Freeway Revolt.

Construction on the Embarcadero Freeway, formally State Route 480, which would have connected the Golden Gate Bridge with the San Francisco–Oakland Bay Bridge via a route that ran along San Francisco's waterfront, began in 1958. Almost simultaneously, more than thirty thousand San Franciscans signed petitions protesting it. The *San Francisco Chronicle* called "freeways that barge along in an unyielding straight line, knocking down everything in their path, or that stride along as huge ugly elevateds, or that slash great gashes through residential business districts [are] a crime that cannot be prettied up."

Not subtle rhetoric, maybe, but effective. California law provided that no street or road could be closed until approved by local authorities, and this gave the San Francisco Board of Supervisors a de facto veto over any freeway construction within the city. They got the message their constituents were sending. On January 27, 1959, they passed Resolution 45, expressing opposition to the unconstructed portion of the Embarcadero/Golden Gate Freeway. And they didn't stop there. They formally opposed seven out of the ten freeways described in the 1955 Trafficways Plan they had approved four years earlier, calling for an end to "the demolition of homes, the destruction of residential areas, the forced uprooting and relocation of individuals, families, and business enterprises." In doing so, they planted the seed for what is today one of America's most vibrant and prosperous cities.

By then, Lewis Mumford wasn't the only voice raised against building transportation systems that gave priority to the automobile. After the Embarcadero Revolt, the movement against limited-access highways really started to get traction everywhere from Australia to the Netherlands. In April of 1960, an article entitled "New Roads and Urban Chaos," by a Harvard professor named Daniel Patrick Moynihan, argued that the Interstate Highway System was "bringing about changes for the worse in the efficiency of our transportation system and the character of our cities. . . . It is not true, as is sometimes alleged, that the sponsors of the interstate program ignored the consequences it would have in the cities. Nor did they simply acquiesce in them. They exulted in them."

Moynihan was on to something. Municipalities and neighborhoods protested highway construction in Connecticut, Colorado, Florida, Georgia, and Illinois. In New York, where it really began, Robert Moses found himself unable to overcome opposition to his proposed Lower Manhattan Expressway, which would have run through Chinatown, Little Italy, and Soho, or to his Mid-Manhattan Expressway, which would have bisected Manhattan at 30th Street. In fact, New York City is the only major city in America without an Interstate highway running through its central business district. I often say we have Robert Moses to thank for saving my hometown from at least some of the costs that a fifty-year-long mistake in transportation infrastructure imposed on the rest of the United States. He activated the Jane Jacobses and other anti-highway activists of New York City a decade before the Interstate system funding was in full swing.

The protests became associated with the civil rights movement, since the most at-risk neighborhoods tended to be the poorest and blackest; in Washington, DC, a black militant group handed out flyers demanding "no more white highways through black bedrooms." In April of 1962, President Kennedy sent a message to the Senate and House of Representatives on "The Transportation System" that called for a long-term program of federal aid to urban mass transit, whose riders were becoming increasingly poorer, blacker, and more Hispanic; in October he signed the Federal-Aid Highway Act of 1962.

Also in 1962, a marine biologist named Rachel Carson published a denunciation of the use of pesticides on the environment. As much as any book ever written, *Silent Spring* changed the world. But even before it inspired the modern environmental movement—the Environmental Defense Fund, which opened its doors in 1967, and the

Environmental Protection Agency, which was created in 1970, are direct consequences, as was my own embrace of the environmental movement—Carson's book changed transportation. Less than a year after the book was published, the Bureau of Public Roads announced that, starting in 1964, states would have to certify that any federally funded highway project had to take into consideration possible effects on fish and wildlife.

In 1965, in a telling bit of symbolism, the Embarcadero Freeway was removed from the Interstate Highway System.* Between 1968, when construction completely stopped, and 1973, when the first resolution was passed to tear down what remained, I completed my studies in the graduate program in engineering at the University of Pennsylvania.

⟩⟩⟩

After four years studying math and science at a very fast-track high school, and physics at Brooklyn College, grad school engineering was, well, different. My brother Brian, whose idea it was for me to study transportation engineering, says I was going from using perturbation theory to calculate the eigenvalue of an electron in a magnetic field to "We have two hundred feet in a parking garage; where do we paint the white lines to fit in ten cars?" He has a point. Anyone who studies physics knows that physicists never solve an equation with numbers; they do it all with letters. Numbers are beneath them. Problems that can be solved with numbers are jobs for the engineers. You know: the guys who weren't good enough for physics and had to settle for second place.

---

* What was left of the elevated highway on San Francisco's waterfront was finally demolished after it was severely damaged by the 1989 Loma Prieta earthquake. The waterfront—the Embarcadero—was redeveloped with parks, plazas, a tree-lined boulevard, and public transportation. It draws millions of visitors a year.

Guys like, for example, me.

I went from being a mediocre physicist to a star engineer. I won the Institute of Traffic Engineers Mid-Atlantic Student Paper Award for a treatise I did using calculus to explain how people parked inefficiently. I remember being handed the award by an old-timer who said he couldn't make hide nor hair of my complicated equations. I felt like patting him on the head. Thanks to Brian's advice, I was going to be part of a new generation of traffic engineers able and eager to use advanced math and science to solve the traffic problems of the future.

What I didn't realize, at first, was that advanced math and science—and, for that matter, engineering—weren't all that much help in *identifying* those problems. They're still not. Professor (later to be Senator) Moynihan sadly got it about right for engineers-past when he wrote, "Nothing in the training or education of most civil engineers prepares them to do anything more than build sound highways cheaply. In the course of doing this job, they frequently produce works of startling beauty—compare the design of public highways with that of public housing," and Moynihan showed no compunction about invoking the authority of engineers when I worked with him briefly, unsuccessfully, to ban tandem trucks from the Brooklyn-Queens Expressway. However, he continued, quoting John Howard from MIT, "It does not belittle them to say that, just as war is too important to be left to the generals, so highways are too important to leave to the highway engineers."

But if you can't trust the engineers, then who? The usual answer is "politicians." After all, most people figure that getting a four-way stop sign installed, or a bridge built, is essentially a who-you-know phenomenon. And God knows we've poured a lot of concrete over the years in places that made sense only after you found out which pols' well-connected pals were making money out of the deal. That said, corrupt though the political process can (sometimes) be, it's not the worst way to make investment decisions in transportation. The business of balancing different interest groups is messy and irrational, and often enough puts people in jail, but at least it doesn't delude anyone about objective fairness. For that, you need an economist.

Simple economics—simple common sense, really—suggests that we ought to invest in projects where the benefits outweigh the costs, and avoid those that don't. Transportation engineers can usually fill in the cost side of the equation with a lot of precision (though not always accuracy, as the history of cost overruns on everything from the Via Appia to the Cross-Bronx reminds us). This many man-hours, that much reinforced concrete, and presto: a budget.

Benefits are different. What is the value of widening a road? Installing raised pavement markers? From the time I entered grad school at the University of Pennsylvania to today, engineers have estimated benefits by calculating two things: increased speed and improved safety.*

Speed first. If a new bit of construction lowers estimated average travel time, it has positive value. Calculating how much value is a little more complicated. The term that engineers use is *appropriate travel time unit cost values* for each trip category. What that means in plain English is that benefits are larger for business trips than for social travel. Technically, there are more benefits in saving a corporate executive an hour on her commute than a teacher in his. Saving an hour on a once-a-week trip from Los Angeles to San Francisco is therefore worth more than saving ten minutes on a daily trip from the San Fernando Valley to Santa Monica. A passenger can do productive work while traveling, even at the risk of carsickness. Drivers can't, which makes the time a passenger spends on any given trip less costly, and generally worth less, than driver time.

If you add up the number of driver-hours that engineers estimate will be reduced by a new lane on the Interstate, and multiply that by their average hourly earnings, you get the speed benefit. Of course,

---

* In the mid-1960s, the curriculum for engineering students and the practice of working engineers added the measurement of both fuel efficiency and pollution control.

you have to trust that those estimates have some basis in reality, which is—I'm being nice here—a leap of faith. No one, up to and including Robert Moses himself, predicted that traveling the nine miles of the Cross-Bronx Expressway at rush hour would take forty minutes, at a peak average speed of fourteen miles per hour.

As with speed, so with safety. It's relatively simple (or at least practical) to build a model that will estimate how many collisions might be prevented by building a pedestrian bridge over a dangerous intersection, or eliminating a too-sharp curve in the road. But what's it *worth*? That is not a simple calculation at all. Fifty years ago, an economist named Thomas Schelling came up with the idea known as the "Value of a Statistical Life," or VSL,* which promised to measure the monetary value of saving one life. There are a couple of ways to do this. The "human capital" approach uses market productivity over the remainder of the saved person's life, in which saving the life of a cardiac surgeon is worth more than saving the life of a librarian, or saving a twenty-five-year-old is worth more than doing the same for a seventy-year-old. Or you can use a "comprehensive" or "willingness-to-pay" system: calculating the number of lives that would be saved by requiring side airbags in vehicles, for example, and dividing by the cost that such a requirement would add to an average vehicle's selling price. Then there's the "dead-anyway" effect, in which people with terminal illnesses value their lives a little, well, perversely: "I have a brain tumor; I think I'll cross against the light." Just to give you a sense of just how imprecise this system is, equally reliable estimates can set VSLs anywhere from $500,000 to $7 million each. The calculation, though, remains the same: estimate the number of VSLs saved by building that pedestrian overpass, and if it's greater than the cost, start breaking ground.

The problem with all of this isn't the obvious one. Once you get past the cold-blooded creepiness of it, you can see why we need to

---

* Schelling, a Rand Institute theoretician, also came up with the term *collateral damage*. The man was a phrasemaker.

put a value on incremental lives saved. Human life is priceless, but that doesn't mean that it has an infinite dollar value. If that were literally true there would be no reason to *ever* stop adding safety features to cars, streets, airplanes, and so on. Pretty soon, the cost would become ridiculous—cars armored like Abrams tanks, or airfares costing millions of dollars each. The real problem is that VSL calculates *only the benefits that can be easily measured.* Because it's hard (some might say impossible) to measure the value of a pleasant walk versus an unpleasant one, neither engineers nor economists are capable of giving it any value at all.

This problem—speed is quantifiable, livability isn't—infiltrates every aspect of transportation engineering. Consider the concept known as *level-of-service*, or LOS. Ever since 1965, two of the bibles of traffic engineering, the *Highway Capacity Manual* and *Geometric Design of Highways and Streets*, have given letter grades, from A to F, to roads according to level-of-service for a given hour (usually the most congested one of the day). A road with an LOS of "A," for example, allows all traffic to flow at or above speed limit, spaced twenty-seven or more car lengths apart.

The only place this kind of spacing happens in real life—that is, not at 5:00 a.m. on a Sunday morning—is in those television commercials where the one thing on the entire Pacific Coast Highway is you and your Audi.

From there, level-of-service grades are all downhill. "B" and "C" both have relatively free and stable traffic flow, and are the practical goals of road designers. By the time you get to a "D," cars are about eight lengths apart and flow is becoming unstable. An LOS of "E" is already unstable: like water at 32°F, about to solidify into ice. At this level of congestion, any disruption—a driver missing his cup holder and spilling coffee all over the front seat of his car—causes a shock wave that can catch hundreds of cars in a sudden traffic jam. Even that is still "better" than LOS "F" in which every car is unable to move until the car directly in front does so first. See "Expressway, Cross-Bronx; rush hour."

LOS was at the heart of the discipline when I first studied it, a heritage of the 1950s and 1960s, when the only concern about roads was congestion, and the only responsibility of transport engineers was relieving it via expansion. For a lot of engineers, it still is today, when—supposedly—the cost of being stuck in traffic is estimated to be $115 billion a year in the United States alone.

The idea behind LOS, like a lot of transportation engineering, seems sensible enough when you first encounter it. But it depends on the premise that the only function of a road is getting from point A to point B in the least amount of time. This turns out to be a pretty limited view of transportation. For one thing, it measures vehicles, not people; thirty people on a bus make just about the same contribution to LOS as a single driver. Because states and municipalities have hundreds of statutes on the books that require fees to be paid by any development that causes a drop in the average LOS, they also promote development in the least crowded neighborhoods, providing another unneeded impetus to suburbanization. An engineer and urban planner named John Fruin even went to the trouble of developing an LOS standard for pedestrians, in which a sidewalk with an "A" level-of-service is one where no one walks at all. "A" for absurd.

However, I shouldn't scold my fellow engineers. I might have ended up accepting a lot of this myself if I hadn't been lucky enough to have, as my academic adviser at the University of Pennsylvania, Vukan Vuchic.

Professor Vuchic was still in his mid-thirties when I met him for the first time (he had only been at Penn for a couple of years himself when I started). This was a good thing, since I was part of the generation that was raised on not trusting anyone over thirty. An émigré from Belgrade, Professor Vuchic had traveled all over the world and seemed to know what was going on just about everywhere. I can still recall him comparing transit in the United States with systems in European countries. He talked of the chandeliers in the subway stations of Moscow and the efficiency of its trains.

More than anyone I've ever met, Professor Vuchic opened my eyes as to how cities can be transformed, for better or worse, through transportation. The decline of the American city was front-page news in my college and grad school days. The murder rate climbed each year, population declined, buildings and even whole blocks were burned out (perhaps hardest hit of all was my birthplace, Brownsville). I pined for the good old days my older siblings talked about and which even I had tasted: Coney Island's Steeplechase Park before there was a Disneyland, Ebbets Field (for nearly sixty years I've carried in my wallet a very worn photo of me on the field with Brooklyn Dodger pitcher Sal Maglie in 1956), seeing the birth of rock-and-roll at the Paramount or Fox theaters on Flatbush Avenue, or the carefree days playing stickball on 83rd Street.

Sam "the Kid" Schwartz with Sal "the Barber" Maglie, August 12, 1956, at Ebbet's Field in Brooklyn. *Samuel I. Schwartz.*

Professor Vuchic explained how the decline of the American cities was inextricably linked to decisions the cities had made about transportation. We compared *modal share*—that is, the percentage of people traveling by car, transit, or on foot—in London, Paris, and New York. We then compared New York to other cities in the United States. Through his eyes we saw European city centers staying vibrant while many of our center cities were dying. We learned what a mistake it had been for US cities to get rid of most of their streetcars at the same time streetcars were going strong in Continental Europe. We saw the movement to create a sense of place in towns and urban centers through good design of streets. The crowds filling European plazas were testimonials to the value of such design. More than anyone else, Professor Vuchic transformed me from a student of *traffic* engineering (this is what it was still called) to a thinker about a much broader subject: *transportation*. I was already a lover of cities. Under Professor Vuchic's supervision, I became a lover of urban transit systems. I mourned the loss of streetcars as I learned what had become of them. I envied the European cities that still had them.

It was more than just an inspiring teacher, of course. By the time I arrived at Penn's campus in South Philadelphia, the environmental movement had become mainstream; the Environmental Protection Agency was established in my second year. Cars were bigger polluters per capita than buses, which were bigger polluters than trolleys or trains. They were less democratic, too. Transit wouldn't just clean America's air but cure what ailed America's cities and restore American democracy. When I graduated with a master of science in transportation engineering I was ready to return home, and get a job working for the New York City Transit Authority, the public agency responsible for running the world's biggest urban transit system.[*]

---

[*] OK. New York's system may not be the world's longest subway—depending on how the measurement is made, London's Underground has a claim—but it has, by far, the largest number of stations.

Unfortunately, they weren't ready for me.

Ever since 1953, when the Transit Authority had acquired New York's three separate subway systems, two bus networks, and what remained of the city's streetcars, almost all of its transit professionals had been former conductors, train engineers, and bus drivers. A graduate degree from an Ivy League school didn't even merit a response. So I floundered a bit. My first wife and I moved into a tenement on a rough street in a heavily black neighborhood in Brooklyn that was barely a stone's throw from the Ebbets Field Apartments and Prospect Park. No suburbs for us, not even after my wife got mugged on the Flatbush Avenue bus and her parents offered to pay us to move. I drove a cab to support us while sending out résumés, and after a few months I was offered a job at the Department of Traffic as a junior engineer. In March 1971, I showed up for work.

Unlike the Transit Authority, the Department of Traffic was used to college types. My colleagues were mostly graduates of the traffic engineering program at Yale, which had been turning GI Bill students into Interstate Highway System engineers for fifteen years. College was pretty much the only thing we had in common. The department's other engineers were car people, secure in the knowledge that their only job was moving cars faster. After two years studying the downside of the automobile, I felt like a traitor. I wasn't feeling a whole lot better about it when, twenty-one months after I started work, I got a lesson, though *not* the one I expected, in the practical consequences of overdependence on cars.

On Saturday morning, December 15, 1973, the forty-year-old West Side Highway, which runs along the Hudson River and connects the Brooklyn-Battery Tunnel with the Henry Hudson Parkway—both built by the unstoppable Robert Moses—collapsed under the weight of a truck carrying more than thirty tons of asphalt. It was as if someone had opened a concrete trapdoor, fifty feet long and thirty feet wide, dropping the dump truck and a passenger car to the street below, and flipping the truck on its back. Fortunately, no one died, but at first glance it looked as if we had just built a new exit ramp to the street below. A day later, the road was closed indefinitely (ultimately meaning "forever") "pending engineering studies." The long-term studies—What caused the collapse? How should the highway be repaired?—were given to others. The immediate problem—What to do with eighty thousand cars a day that would have to find an alternate route?—fell to me.

I would love to take credit for coming up with a brilliant solution that saved the city, but the truth is both more mundane and a lot more interesting. The predicted traffic disaster never appeared. Somehow, those eighty thousand cars went somewhere, but to this day we have no idea where. Or how, two years later, twenty-five thousand more people were getting into Manhattan's Central Business District.

What made this interesting is that it was a nearly perfect example of what the economist Anthony Downs named the Law of Peak-Hour Expressway Congestion and which another economist, Gilles Duranton, called *induced demand*. Boiled down to the basics, induced demand is what happens when the supply of a good increases and more of that supply then gets consumed: when a host puts out more cheese and crackers, her guests eat more cheese and crackers.

What this means in road (and bridge, and tunnel) building is not just obvious but as well documented as anything in transportation engineering: "If you build it, they will come." If you build more lanes on the expressway, more cars and trucks will use it. If you're lucky, congestion remains as bad as it was before you spent $50 million trying to relieve it; if you're not, it gets worse. It's like the Red Queen from the other side of the looking glass, who tells Alice, "Here, you see, it takes all the running you can do, to keep in the same place. If you want to get somewhere else, you must run at least twice as fast as that!"*

---

* Our old pal Pat Moynihan was on to this in 1960, when he wrote, "The number of automobiles increases to fill all the space provided."

The West Side Highway collapse was like that, but backwards: the counterintuitive phenomenon known as *disappearing traffic*. Nearly everyone, including most engineers, assumes that a constricted traffic artery behaves like a garden hose: reduce the diameter from one inch to one-half inch, and pressure increases. But drivers aren't water molecules. When a road's capacity is reduced, congestion doesn't necessarily increase. In fact, the biggest and best study of reduction in road capacity shows that lane closures not only cause traffic to decrease on the road's remaining lanes, *but only half the decrease reappears anywhere else*. This means that if two lanes are closed on a four-lane boulevard, it might carry only 60 percent of the cars it did before the closure; but if you look at every alternate route, you'll be able to account for only half of the "missing" drivers. In an urban setting, with alternate routes or public transit options—that is, one with at least some commitment to smart street design—20 percent of the boulevard's traffic will just disappear. "If you unbuild it, they will go away."

This wasn't obvious at the time, but unbuilding a replacement for the West Side Highway was a huge financial boon to the cash-strapped city, and not just because we avoided spending tens of millions of dollars in construction costs. The usual rule of thumb is that for every dollar spent on capital investments like bridges, roads, and highways, another 3 percent will be incurred on annual maintenance (or, at least, it should be). Moreover, well within their predicted lifespans, those bridges, roads, and highways need replacing; a highway deck lasts no more than forty years, twenty in regions with severe winter weather. Roads may last forever, but that also means that they consume resources forever, too.

>>>

It was gratifying to see the real world behave in a way that fit in with what I'd been studying for the past three years, which was that building more roads was the exact wrong way to improve transportation systems. And it was frustrating when the real world collided with the slightly unreal world of politics. When I began work at the Department of Traffic, John Lindsay had just finished his fifth year as New York City's mayor, and while he's remembered today mostly for a series of disastrous transit, teacher, and sanitation strikes, he also was environmentally conscious enough to recognize, earlier than most, that the last thing that the thirteen-mile-long island of Manhattan needed was easier access for cars. Even before the West Side Highway collapse, one of the first projects I worked on was a plan to ban cars from Midtown. We were just weeks away from implementing what became known as the "Red Zone" plan when the mayor got cold feet. To this day I still have one of the signs we made.[*]

An actual sign manufactured but never installed. In 1971 Mayor John Lindsay proposed banning cars from the heart of Midtown Manhattan bounded by Third Avenue on the east, Seventh Avenue on the west, 37th Street on the south, and 57th Street on the north from 11 a.m. to 4 p.m. weekdays. *Samuel I. Schwartz.*

---

[*] Mayor Lindsay also proposed, and I worked on, a plan to close Times Square to cars. Thirty-five years later, in 2009, the car-free zone known as Broadway Plaza was opened by then-mayor Michael Bloomberg and his transportation commissioner, Janette Sadik-Khan. More about this in Chapter 5.

In 1974, Mayor Lindsay, who was a true environmentalist, was succeeded by Abe Beame, who wasn't. One day, I was called to Deputy Commissioner Sam Hochstein's office along with a few other engineers. Were we there to discuss how to improve mobility for millions of New Yorkers? The best way to address the deteriorating bridges and tunnels on which the city depended? Whether to invest in new buses? In a pig's eye. We were there, Hochstein told us, because Mary Beame, the mayor's wife, had been stuck in a traffic jam on Fifth Avenue.

It's not that I was a complete naïf. I knew that policies weren't always, or even mostly, the result of rational debate about objective facts. Even so, this was pretty infuriating, not least because the reason for Mrs. Beame's distress wasn't a failure of the city's transportation network, but one of its successes. Early in the Lindsay administration, Central Park (along with Prospect Park) had been closed on weekends, and then, after a few successful years, from 11 a.m. to 4 p.m. every day from late spring to Labor Day. Mary Beame got caught in a summer closing.

New administration, new priorities. Sam Hochstein's engineers were given our marching orders. Or more accurately, our vehicular orders. We were charged with coming up with a justification for reopening Central Park to traffic twenty-four hours a day on weekdays. As director of traffic research at the time, it was my job to produce the report that would get the job done. I protested. I enjoyed playing hooky during the daily closings in another Olmsted masterpiece, Prospect Park, and had even met my wife Daria during one of them, as we both walked our dogs. Roy Cottam, a veteran Traffic Department engineer, tried to calm the assembled group, explaining this upstart kid by saying, "Sam's not like us, you see. He rides the subway."

He had no idea. I had gone to grad school with a predisposition in favor of walkable, traditional cities. By the time I left, I had replaced it with something even stronger: a first-rate education in the kind of transportation networks that made the cities I loved possible in the first place. I had learned the history of the "battle over right-of-way" and calculated the costs of building all those limited-access highways through America's urban neighborhoods. I didn't hate cars; still don't. But I wasn't very eager to make the city even more car friendly than it already was. This made writing the how-to-open-Central-Park report a sickening task. Sickening enough, in fact, that I went off the reservation. Instead of a justi-fication for reopening the park, I produced a report showing that for the most part the closings of the Central Park loop to cars had little impact on Fifth Avenue traffic. The only hour when I found a measurable impact was between three and four in the afternoon. I knew, however, I had to come up with something more or I'd be bypassed in the process. So I proposed that we should open the Sixth Avenue entrance to the park but only as far as 72nd Street. Essentially the park would remain car-free north of 72nd Street and on the entire West Drive. I produced a rigorous report and it worked. The park remained closed from 10 a.m. to 3 p.m. (we lost the 3–4 p.m. hour) and the Sixth Avenue entrance remained open (a vestige that remains today).

The Central Park incident was a reminder that New York had a less environmentally conscious executive running things. Though the Clean Air Act of 1970 required the city to reduce pollution, and the state and city, under Governor Nelson Rockefeller* and Mayor Lind-say, had agreed to a plan to limit automobile traffic by placing tolls on the bridges that led from Brooklyn, Queens, and the Bronx into Manhattan, Mayor Beame didn't believe in it. Though the plan had

---

* Malcolm Wilson, who became governor when Rockefeller was tapped by Gerald Ford to serve as Ford's vice president after Richard Nixon's resignation, was the sig-natory on the plan.

advocates everywhere from the federal government to the nonprofit environmental groups like the Sierra Club, they couldn't figure out how to get around the obstacles that the mayor (who was nothing if not a savvy bureaucrat) put in their way.

I showed them how.

To this day, Steve Jurow, who was then working as an engineer for the Natural Resources Defense Council, calls me his "Deep Throat." At a series of secret meetings in Brooklyn—some with Steve, some with a friend at the US Environmental Protection Agency, Gerard Soffian—I shared documents showing that the predicted massive traffic jams at the East River bridges were a fantasy. Others showed that overall traffic congestion wouldn't increase in Brooklyn (where the mayor had his strongest political base) but would actually improve.

My leaking worked—sort of. The now suspiciously well-informed Natural Resources Defense Council and other environmental activists were able to get a federal judge to order the city to put the tolls on the bridges. Only an act of Congress could stop it, but, unfortunately, that's just what happened. Two of our most progressive elected officials, Senator Daniel Patrick Moynihan and Congresswoman Elizabeth Holtzman, got a law passed that allowed the city to substitute the tolls with something else that would have the same beneficial environmental impact.

NRDC licked their wounds, and tried to figure out what the "something else" could be. That's when I surreptitiously developed a plan and delivered it to Soffian (things were getting hot then), who then passed it along to Jurow. A series of proposals set out in that plan were then submitted by NRDC to the US Environmental Protection Agency. They included, among other things, exclusive bus lanes on Madison Avenue and a ban on parking in Midtown and Downtown.

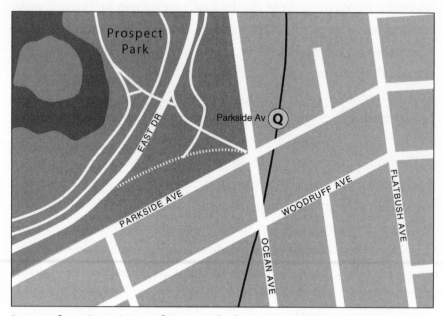

In one of my (many) acts of municipal sabotage, I erased an existing road that cut through a corner of Prospect Park. The statute of limitations has expired, I think. *David Smucker and Ranjani Sarode (Sam Schwartz Engineering) and Prospect Park Alliance.*

And it worked. The EPA approved it, which allowed a federal judge to order the city to implement the "NRDC" plan, which had been anonymously written by yours truly. I kept my mouth shut when I heard my colleagues at the Traffic Department complain about those damned feds in Washington who were dictating to us in New York what we should do on our streets.

What I thought, though, was (as they used to say in Brooklyn), "the noive."

Throughout the Beame years, I engaged in low-level sabotage of the Traffic Department's plans. I would widen a sidewalk to a decent size here. Eliminate a parking lane there. One time, a road that linked Brooklyn's Prospect Park to Parkside Avenue mysteriously disappeared from the city's plan. No one in government noticed as grass grew from asphalt.

Nothing lasts forever, though, and the Beame administration lasted less than most. In 1978 Ed Koch became mayor and appointed a new commissioner of transportation, a career engineer and Democratic clubhouse regular named Anthony Ameruso. Koch also named, as the deputy commissioner, David Gurin, the founder of an organization with the revealing name Transportation Alternatives. Gurin knew that his entire department was filled with the guys I'd met when I started in the Traffic Department seven years before—the ones whose dream was to pump as many cars into Manhattan as possible. He asked Steve Jurow, "Who can I trust?" Jurow told him: "Sam Schwartz."

In the spring of 1978, I was named assistant commissioner, Plans and Programs, for the Transportation Department. When I started at my new job, I took thirty top engineers from the old Traffic Department with me. I couldn't stop the car people from trying to bullshit me, but now the best of them were going to be working for me.

If my time at Penn had been an education in the theory of moving people from place to place, the next twelve years in the Department of Transportation were an education in the craft of the thing, and sometimes in getting them to move at all. In 1982, when I was appointed traffic commissioner, the city was issuing more than one hundred different kinds of special parking permits. Manhattan alone had more than two hundred different signs granting parking privileges to the, ahem, privileged. I managed to get many of the parking spaces back from the New York Police Department, the City Council, and even the mayor. My first meeting with Rudy Giuliani, then US Attorney for the Southern District of New York, was over my agents ticketing and towing his agents. The worst violators were the diplomats assigned to UN embassies and foreign consulates, whose unpaid tickets amounted to something like $50 million a year in free parking. Often enough, the diplomats chose to accumulate tickets rather than walk from their apartments on the East Side of Manhattan to their offices on the East Side of Manhattan, three or four blocks away.

When I announced that the only place they were going to get free parking in the future was in a game of Monopoly, I managed to anger not only the diplomats but their hosts in the US State Department. I was even asked to justify myself at the UN Secretariat, and I did, in front of scores of foreign dignitaries at the head of one of those horseshoe tables that are everywhere at the UN. I managed to unite all of them, for the first and last time, in a single cause: attacking me.

In 1982, parking in New York was an international outrage. Four years later it was a municipal disgrace, the biggest scandal to hit the city since the days of Tammany Hall. It began like the cold-open from some television cop show* when, in January 1986, the borough president of Queens, Donald Manes, slashed his wrists in what he claimed was a carjacking attempt, and later admitted was an attempted suicide. Over the next eight weeks, it came out that Manes had been financing his political empire through kickbacks from the city's Parking Violations Bureau. And he wasn't alone. The Bronx Borough President and the Democratic Party leaders of the Bronx and Brooklyn were sent packing off to jail. In March, Manes finally succeeded in killing himself, plunging a kitchen knife into his heart while on hold during a telephone call with his psychiatrist.

The headlines were all about Manes, of course, but nearly every major figure in the Department of Transportation was implicated, including the commissioner, Anthony Ameruso, and several deputies and assistant commissioners. I visited the traffic bureau's parking chief in the hospital; his face was a pulpy mess. He claimed he'd been hit by a car, but it looked a lot more like he had taken a vicious beating. George Aronwold, an administrative law judge in the Parking Violations Bureau, was murdered by the Colombo crime family.

The only part of the department untouched by scandal was the Traffic Bureau, my bureau. I was hastily appointed acting commis-

---

* A fictionalized version of the story is actually the plot of the pilot episode of *Law & Order*.

sioner, then first deputy commissioner of the entire DOT, as well as its chief engineer. Almost overnight, I was responsible for, and had authority over, New York City's highways, bridges, and parking violations. Ferries? Mine. General aviation? Ditto. And I was still head of the Traffic Bureau, which included two thousand uniformed traffic agents. If it ran over, or parked on, a New York City street, it was part of my job. The scandal—or, rather, the mayor's desire to clean up the scandal—had put me in a position to write the city's traffic laws, enforce them, and even adjudicate them.

Scandals will do that. But while it was a bribery scandal that got me a new office, there was a more costly one waiting for me when I got there, one that was a lot more revealing about transportation policy. The mayor, the public, and the Department of Transportation itself had been lied to about the condition of the city's bridges.

Since only one borough out of New York City's five is actually part of the mainland of the United States, nothing that affects the city's network of more than two thousand bridges is ever trivial. In June, my assistant commissioner, a veteran and highly respected engineer named Arthur Asserson, came to see me regarding an alarming report about the Manhattan Bridge. The Manhattan, which opened in 1909, is a pure suspension bridge; all the weight of the bridge's deck, including the traffic it carries, is supported by cables suspended from towers. And the deck of the Manhattan is big: seven motor vehicle lanes and four tracks for the subways, more than any other New York City bridge. In 1986, it carried about 350,000 people per day.

Despite my degree in civil engineering, I knew next to nothing about bridge engineering when Arthur and his team gave me the bad news. The cleaning crew sandblasting the bridge's anchorage—the attachment point for the bridge's cables—was, in the process, blowing it away. Half of what looked like steel was actually rust. Structural computations revealed that, at full capacity, with four subway trains on the bridge at once and motor vehicles filling the lanes—a normal rush hour—the Manhattan side of the bridge was mathematically in danger of collapse. That was enough for me. We immediately closed two of seven lanes carrying automobile traffic, and two of the bridge's four tracks, for what became four years.

It was then that I began asking questions about the city's other bridges. I learned that they were more complicated machines than I had realized, with loads of moving parts like bearing plates that allow the parts of the bridge to slide relative to one another, and rocker arms that let it respond to stress from different directions. And I learned my engineers believed the Williamsburg Bridge, which had been built in 1903, and now carried eight lanes of vehicles and two subway tracks, was in even worse condition than the Manhattan. The cables that supported its center span—each one nineteen inches in diameter, made up of 7,696 pencil-thin steel wires bound tightly to-gether—were fraying. Hundreds of broken wires were visible at the north anchorage. Calculations showed that the wires were breaking or losing strength at a frightening rate, and that the bridge would start to sag and be at risk by 1995. My engineers proposed recabling the bridge, which had two problems. First, it had never been done before. Second, it would cost about $250 million.

The city didn't have the money. Neither did the state. That left the federal government, which had agreed to pay for most of the cost.

Not everyone was happy about this. Some engineers, bridge en-thusiasts, said it would be nuts to spend a quarter of a billion dollars to recable the bridge only to end up with a bridge that had been the state of the art in 1903. For the same money, they said, you could build a new bridge, one that would meet "modern" standards.

Meeting standards, I soon learned, since the enthusiasts were kind enough to share drawings and plans, meant a bridge with wider lanes and longer approach roadways. In order to accomplish this, the new bridge would mean condemning a whole lot of property on both sides of the bridge. You might see this as a cost, but the bridge builders saw it as an opportunity, since the neighborhoods on the Manhattan and Brooklyn sides of the bridge, the Lower East Side and Williamsburg, respectively, were, in their minds, "blighted." Knocking blighted neighborhoods flat *and* getting a new-and-improved bridge? Everyone wins.

I had to figure out the best course of action, and that meant I needed to take a long hard look at the information I had been given. And not just the information itself, but the premises (I don't want to call them prejudices) that they were built on. I was determined not to authorize hundreds of millions of dollars based on a flawed analysis.

And it was flawed. The study that calculated that the bridge would sag by 1995 had used a computer model with a serious error. The cables had not ten years of useful life, but at least a hundred.[*]

But if the cables were better than expected, the structural steel was worse. Many of the twenty-foot floor beams that supported the deck were cracked and perforated. This type of corrosion was found to be the cause of the West Side Highway collapse. Similar cracks were found in just about every one of the steel columns that supported the trains and motor vehicles. During the afternoon rush hour on April 12, 1988, I got a call from my bridge inspectors to come out to the bridge immediately. With sirens and lights flashing I got there in 10 minutes. I hopped out and squeezed between a chicken shack (where chickens soon to become kosher dinners were housed) and a steel column. The column supported the subway to the north and the roadway to the south. It had split in the middle with a gaping gash the width of my hand. This was no crack; the steel column was now two beams, in effect, with no bracing, separating at a rate no one could calculate. But, eventually, maybe months, maybe days or hours, it would collapse,

---

[*] Credit for this realization goes to the legendary Blair Birdsall, well into his seventies at that time, who called the initial study "hogwash." He found a repetitive error in the very sophisticated computer model.

bringing the subways and roadway plummeting to the ground. It had to be closed immediately and completely, and that night I closed it down. It was the first time in history that one of New York's major bridges had ever been closed to all traffic. The bridge remained closed until repairs—Band-Aids, really—were completed in August.

Simultaneously, to figure out whether the feds and New York State would come to the party, I needed to compare costs and feasibility of a new bridge with rehabbing the old one. I proposed assembling a panel of world-class bridge engineers who would participate in the evaluation, and the feds agreed to support the decision of the panel. I held an international competition for firms to submit new designs as replacement for the Williamsburg.

The decision couldn't be made using traditional traffic engineering cost-benefit calculations. Though the original $250 million estimates for repairing or rebuilding were blown out of the water fairly quickly—they had nearly tripled, to more than $700 million—the "how much" wasn't as important as the "who pays." We needed federal money for either option. And the feds wouldn't pay for repairing a "substandard" bridge.

But what made the bridge substandard? Its lane widths. The "standard" lane—on Interstate highways, on the Cross-Bronx Expressway—was twelve feet wide, but the Williamsburg Bridge had lanes that barely exceeded nine feet; at the bridge's towers, the lanes were even narrower. The bridge had no shoulders or breakdown lanes, and had such low clearances that trucks couldn't use the inner roadways. This meant that it wasn't able to move the maximum number of cars into Manhattan as fast as possible.

But we didn't want to move the maximum number of cars into Manhattan. And we sure didn't want them going any faster when they got there. The bridge was still moving a quarter of a million people back and forth across the East River after eighty-five years, which seemed about right to me.

The Williamsburg Bridge debate revealed a fundamental truth about transportation, one that had never occurred to Robert Moses: the cost-benefit equations of traffic engineering, in which benefit number one was getting more drivers to their destinations more quickly, weren't based on impartial and unbiased math. They were a set of blinders that left only a very narrow set of options visible at all. Before the Brooklyn Bridge had been "modernized" in 1948–1949 by having its trolley tracks replaced with additional automobile lanes—the engineer responsible referred to the trolley tracks as a "horse-and-buggy remnant"—it transported four hundred thousand people a day to and from Brooklyn. Afterward? A hundred and seventy thousand. Even if you believed in increasing capacity, the argument for a new bridge wasn't especially persuasive.

It was the West Side Highway all over again. We could rebuild a bridge for $700 million, and leave the city with an ongoing maintenance bill of at least $20 million annually for the next thirty years *in order to put more cars on the streets of the country's most crowded city.* You could say the costs of the bridge outweighed the benefits, if there had actually been any benefits. This was another seemingly sensible infrastructure investment that wasn't sensible at all.

This is when the feds brought up benefit number two: safety. Wider lanes were, obviously, safer than narrower ones.

Only they're not. This time, the problem with the cost-benefit equation wasn't a faulty premise, but the data itself. In order to test the wider-lanes-are-safer-lanes hypothesis, I studied every crash that occurred on the bridge over a three-year period and marked each one on a map. If that notion had been true, I reasoned, more crashes would have occurred where the lanes were narrowest, that is, at the towers. Just the opposite turned out to be the case. The towers, it turned out, were the safest places on the entire bridge; my explanation is that when lanes get very narrow motorists drive more carefully. Even though every traffic engineer in the country had been taught the gospel of wider lanes, the opposite appeared to be true: "grossly substandard lanes seemed to be the safest of all." This was the traffic engineering equivalent of saying the Earth was round when the masses *knew* it was flat. Still, most engineers do not accept this fact.*

Even the feds couldn't argue with that. The Williamsburg Bridge, narrow lanes and all, was saved. And so were Williamsburg in Brooklyn, and Manhattan's Lower East Side, which are today two of the most vibrant and prosperous neighborhoods in the entire country, yet another instance of smart streets promoting thriving communities. The lessons of the Cross-Bronx Expressway had been expensive, but we were finally learning them.

One lesson: an awful lot of the transportation engineering consensus from forty years ago, from LOS to cost-benefit analysis, is what happens when you know more about *how* to do something than *why* you're doing it. But it isn't the only lesson. It took a while to realize it, but the decisions made about America's transportation infrastructure in the 1950s and 1960s came up short in other ways as well.

For another thing, for example, engineers and planners turn out to have been really, *really* bad at predicting the future, which is a big deal when you're building stuff that is expected to last decades if not centuries. They consistently extrapolated future needs from past trends, instead of saying, "This is what would happen *if past trends were to continue.*" No one asked what would happen if the trends didn't continue, much less whether they would have led to a desirable future.

Even worse, the big mistake about building stuff like the Interstate Highway System and the Cross-Bronx Expressway is that the engineers *used a period of rapid change as the baseline.* There's no era in

---

* Twenty years later, this was definitively proven in a study performed by the Transportation Research Board, which found that "there is no consistent, statistically significant relationship between lane width and safety . . . or increases in accident frequency" for automobiles traveling at intersections or in the middle of urban and suburban blocks.

American history when car ownership grew faster than it did during the 1950s. And there's no period when transit use declined so rapidly. Predicting the future transportation needs of the country using the 1950s and 1960s as a baseline was as helpful as projecting the future needs of the US Navy in 1945 based on a straight-line projection from the years 1941–1944.* This led to some incredibly jug-headed ideas: if the "demand" for parking in Philadelphia's Central Business District had followed projections, there would literally have been no room for anything other than parking lots in downtown Philly.

By the time I left my last public-sector job in 1990, the profession of transportation engineering had learned at least some of these lessons. A much more sophisticated perspective had finally taken hold about the future of mobility—it didn't hurt that so many of the 1950s-era engineers had retired—and a consensus had formed around the value of smart growth and multimodal transport systems (a fancy way of saying that the country needed a combination of heavy and light rail transportation, streetcars, buses, and cars). We engineers may have had tunnel vision, but we weren't completely blind.

What we finally saw was that America's transportation system was in crisis. We had spent the preceding forty years building thousands and thousands of limited-access highways to transport people from their homes to the places where they earned money and where they spent it. The average distance for both had been on an upward slope for decades. In 1960, when the United States had 64.6 million full-time workers, 9.4 million, or 14.5 percent of them, worked outside the county in which they lived; by 2000, 128.3 million were employed, and 34.3 million worked outside their home counties: 27 percent. Average commuting times inched up to more than fifty minutes a day. Because of induced demand, there was no engineering fix to this problem: no

---

* On December 7, 1941, the Navy had 790 ships; at the end of 1944, 6,084.

matter how many roads we built, or how well, people weren't getting from point A to point B any faster, partly because points A and B were getting further apart, partly because we had reached the limits of what could be done to improve automotive speed and safety even using the limited definitions of an earlier era of engineering doctrine. Transportation had fallen into a vicious cycle in which more and more resources were being spent to less and less effect.

And if that weren't enough, a transportation system that was almost entirely run on gasoline was clearly insupportable in the long run, given the obvious costs of a dependence on a commodity that was, more and more, found in some very dodgy parts of the world—and this was well before concerns about pumping billions of tons of CO_2 into the atmosphere.

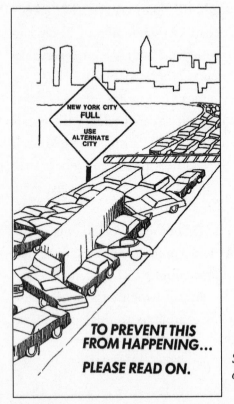

Samuel I. Schwartz (Department of Transportation).

It wasn't that the problems were unpredictable. A hundred different studies, by a thousand different engineers, planners, and urban studies professionals, had forecast not merely that the United States was strangling itself on its own tailpipes, but even how long it could continue doing so before the costs became insupportable. We predicted the need for draconian regulation, and for dramatically increased support for alternative forms of transportation. In the 1980s I crafted a brochure showing angry cars filling up every inch of a city by the year 2000. It was captioned, "New York City Full: Use Alternate City."

We predicted just about everything. Everything except the Millennials.

THE MILLENNIALS

T HE FIRST MEMBERS OF THE MILLENNIAL GENERATION WERE BORN
sometime between 1980 and 1982, but, like babies with *very*
indecisive parents, they weren't actually named until 1990. That's
when historian and demographer Neil Howe partnered with writer
William Straus on a book titled *Generations: The History of America's
Future, 1584–2069.*[*]

You might think that a book with that kind of subtitle was pretty
ambitious, and you'd be right. Howe and Straus had a theory that, ever
since America's earliest days, different generations had succeeded one
another in a predictable and regular pattern. Thus, what they called
the "GI Generation," born in the first two decades of the twentieth
century (this was before they got the moniker "The Greatest Generation") was succeeded by a "Silent Generation," which was followed

---

[*] The same generation actually goes by a few different names: Gen Y, the "echo
boomers," the Peter Pan Generation. Some European writers call it the "Precarious
Generation."

in turn by the Baby Boomers. America's seventy-five million Boomers are the parents of both Generation X (or Gen X)—whose birth years stretch from the early 1960s to the beginning of the 1980s—and a good-sized chunk of the Millennials, too, eighty million of whom arrived on the planet between the early 1980s and about 2004.

Each of Straus and Howe's generations had a distinctive flavor. The "Lost Generation," the cohort who became adults during the First World War, was notable for its sense of disorientation and confusion; members of the "Silent Generation," born during the Depression and World War II, were the first American generation smaller than the preceding one, which is one reason Silents experienced the largest increases in prosperity in recorded history. However, at the time they were first named, the oldest Millennials were still only adolescents, and a large fraction had yet to be born. This didn't stop Straus and Howe from making some predictions about their future traits. Most particularly, they and their followers argued that Millennials would be, like their Greatest Generation grandparents and great-grandparents, strong community builders, the "most civic-minded since the generation of the 1930s and 1940s." They would be charitable, politically engaged, non-materialistic, tolerant, and very concerned about protecting the environment. They would be the "We" generation.

They're definitely tolerant. About the rest, not so much.

There are lots of impressive-sounding academic papers about Millennial attitudes and how they compare to other American demographic cohorts. The most rigorous study is one that combined two huge representative samples collected over nearly fifty years—the Monitoring the Future study of high school seniors that has been ongoing since 1976, and the American Freshman survey of entering college students that has been conducted since 1966. The two studies, collectively encompassing more than 8.5 million surveys, are like a panoramic snapshot of the views of American eighteen-year-olds from the 1960s to today. Here's what they show:

- Eighteen-year-old Millennials are much more convinced that material success—getting rich—is important to happiness than either Boomers or Gen Xers. Specifically, 75 percent of Millennials say so, while only 45 percent of eighteen-year-old Boomers did (and only 70 percent of Gen Xers—the original "Me" Generation).
- Millennials are also a whole lot less concerned about keeping up with politics. Only 35 percent of Millennials thought this important, as compared to 50 percent of the Baby Boomers.
- When it came to saying that developing a "meaningful philosophy of life" was important, the score stands Boomers 73 percent, Millennials 45 percent.
- And, despite a widespread belief that Millennials are the most environmentally conscious generation of all time, they turn out to be, well, not. Only 21 percent of Millennials thought that taking care of the environment was critical, whereas 33 percent of Baby Boomers thought so. Three times as many Millennials as Boomers said they made no personal effort at all to help the environment. Even at the most mundane level, 78 percent of Boomers (and 71 percent of Gen Xers) said they made an effort to turn the heat down in winter; only 56 percent of Millennials did. Maybe even more relevant, when asked to identify the top five reasons for transportation choices or routines, Millennials placed "I care about the environment" dead last, behind saving money, simple convenience, or the opportunity to exercise.

With all that noise, it's probably unfair to hold prognosticators (especially engineering prognosticators) responsible for missing some fairly important stuff. What's way more interesting about the writers and researchers who wrote about the Millennials isn't what they got wrong. It's what they didn't get at all: Millennials have a *very* different perspective on cars and driving than their parents and grandparents. For fifty years, American families had been addicted to the automobile and had, as a result, built a car junkie's paradise for themselves. By the time the Millennials showed up, withdrawal was kicking in.

>>>

Let's take a look at the era that began in 2001, when the first Millennials graduated college, got jobs, and started families. Eight years later, in 2009, Millennials* drove 23 percent fewer miles on average than their same-age predecessors did in 2001. That is, their average mileage—VMT, or *vehicle miles traveled*—plummeted from 10,300 miles a year to 7,900, a difference of 2,400 miles a year, or 46 fewer miles a week.

It's not that they stopped traveling. While Millennials made 15 percent fewer trips by car, they took 16 percent more bike trips than their same-age predecessors did in 2001, and their public-transit passenger miles increased by a whopping 40 percent. That's 117 more miles annually biking, walking, or taking public transit than their same-age predecessors used in 2001.

When a cohort of the size of the Millennial generation changes behavior that radically, it's a little like what happens when a third of the people on board a ferry decide to move from starboard to port: the entire boat starts to list. Which is what is happening to the United States. In every five-year period from 1945 to 2004, Americans had driven more miles than they did the half-decade before. In 2004, the average American drove 85 percent more than in 1970. But by 2011, the average American was driving 6 percent *fewer* miles than in 2004.

---

* Actually, the research was done with a standard-variety census cohort: people aged sixteen to thirty-four. In 2009, this included those born between 1975 and 1993, a group with "only" a 90 percent overlap with the generally accepted description of the Millennial generation.

Baby Boomers and Gen Xers were a small part of the reason—they drove somewhat less in 2009 than in 2001—but the big cause was the Millennials. What makes this even more dramatic is that, by 2009, *only half the Millennial generation was even out of high school*. If all eighty million Millennials retain their current driving habits for the next twenty-five years, the US population will increase by 21 percent, but total VMT will be even less than it is today, and *per capita VMT*— the vehicle miles traveled per person—will fall off the table.

This is a huge development, made even larger by the fact that it came as a complete surprise, even to people who were supposed to be paying attention to the subject. Until about 2010, in presentation after presentation I referred to the driving public as a "stubborn lot." The only time there had ever been a substantial drop in VMT was during world wars, depressions, and fuel crises, and in each case, once the cause disappeared, a jump in VMT followed. Not this time. This drop was unprecedented. In January of 2004, Federal Highway Administrator, and, soon enough, Secretary of Transportation Mary Peters predicted that "VMT may double in the next twenty years." Even as late as 2008, when the "VMT Inflection Point"—that is, when vehicle miles traveled stopped growing—was already a four-year-old phenomenon, the federal projections were still assuming that the growth in driving would return to the same accelerating pace it had exhibited for decades. As the transportation consultant Jarrett Walker puts it, "This isn't prediction or projection. This is denial."

Some of the consequences of what happened when transportation officials weren't looking are unambiguously positive. Americans spent 421 million fewer hours stuck in traffic in 2011 than they did in 2005. For the first time, the number of cars being "retired" is actually greater than the number of new cars being sold.

Other results are more complicated. When the irresistible force of the Millennials hits the immovable object of America's car-centric transportation infrastructure, there are going to be a lot of very interesting side-effects. Gas consumption in 2014 was at a ten-year low, which is definitely a good thing for anyone who thinks that US foreign policy ought not to be driven by the need to secure sources of petroleum in dangerous parts of the world. But it's also the reason the Highway Trust Fund was on the brink of bankruptcy in 2014: less gas purchased means fewer gas tax dollars for roadways. In the same way, Millennial housing choices—about which more below— are revitalizing thousands of neighborhoods that were built before the convenience of automobile drivers became paramount, but are leaving a lot of suburban housing stock behind. In 2006—*before* the crash of 2008—urban planner Arthur C. Nelson wrote an article in the *Journal of the American Planning Association* that estimated that, by 2025, the United States will have 22 million unwanted large-lot suburban homes.

Housing values. Energy policy. Health costs. Taxes. The future of the car business. It's probably not possible to list all the implications of the Millennial turnaround on cars and driving. But there's one big question that can't be avoided: Why? Why, for the first time since the Model T, are Americans less interested in driving? There are dozens of answers to those questions in wide circulation among policy wonks, urban historians, and transportation engineers—some of them better than others.

One not-so-persuasive reason that I hear a lot is the economic one. In this version, the reason for the dramatic drop-off in driving among Millennials is the recession of 2008, which was not only the worst financial crisis since the Great Depression but hit the Millennials especially hard.

If you finished college in 2008 or 2009, you (1) were almost certainly a Millennial and (2) had a really hard time finding a decent job. Meanwhile, it was true that the price of a new or used car held pretty steady during the years after 2008, and, because interest rates declined even faster than per capita VMT, the real cost of buying a

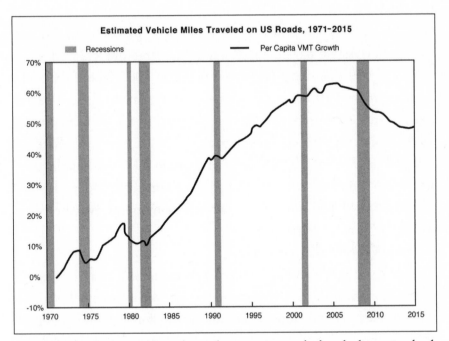

Estimated Vehicle Miles Traveled on US Roads, 1971–2015

For a century, Americans have been driving more each decade, bouncing back after brief declines for wars, or recessions. Until now. *David Smucker and Ranjani Sarode (Sam Schwartz Engineering) and Advisor Perspectives.*

car actually declined, at least for buyers who could get a car loan. However, the price of gasoline increased substantially. Between 2001 and 2010, in fact, the average American's bill for filling up the tank increased from $1,100 to $2,300 (in 2011 dollars). In this scenario, driving less was just a rational, and temporary, expedient.

It makes sense. Except that the decline in VMT among Millennials—and everyone, really—began in 2004. And it has continued through 2014, long after the worst effects of the Great Recession have passed. It's not that economic downturns don't affect driving behavior, it's that once the downturn is over, Americans have always returned to their cars. But not this time.

Moreover, if the Millennials were experiencing greater-than-average economic hardship as a result of the Great Recession, you'd think that the luckiest of them—those with jobs, and decent incomes—would be driving the same way their same-age predecessors did. But they're not. As we have seen, Millennials overall drove 2,400 fewer miles in 2009 than their predecessors did in 2001. Those with jobs do drive more—10,700 miles annually—but that's still 2,100 fewer miles than their employed same-age predecessors, who were putting 12,800 miles on their odometers back in 2001. Even more revealing: Millennials earning $70,000 a year or more in 2009 used public transit for twice as many miles as their affluent same-age predecessors did in 2001, they biked more than twice as many miles, and they even walked 37 percent more.

It's not the economy, stupid.

Nor can the Millennials' choices be explained away by college debt. Though recent college graduates are likely to have borrowed more money than previous generations to pay for their diplomas (and the amounts in question are larger than ever), there is no data showing a correlation between the amount of debt owed and the debtor's VMT: whether a particular Millennial is debt-free or owes tens of thousands of dollars tells you nothing about driving habits. Nor is environmentalism the cause. In a 2011 poll, only 16 percent of Millennials strongly agreed with the statement, "I want to protect the environment, so I drive less."

So if it isn't the recession, or debt, or environmentalism, then what has completely transformed the minds of a significant portion of a very large generation? A more plausible reason for the sea change in Millennial behavior is that they are the first generation that started driving in the age of Graduated Driver Licensing statutes. In 1996, the year the first Millennials were turning fifteen and sixteen, Florida enacted America's first comprehensive GDL program, which broke the process of getting a driver's license into stages. At the first stage, a learner's permit was granted upon passing a written driving exam, and the licensee was required to take a state-sanctioned driving

course, frequently one that cost $500 or more. The second stage of-
fered the new driver, after completion of a road test, an intermediate
license that restricted driving in substantial ways: no driving at night,
for example, or with other under-eighteen drivers. Only after completing the first two stages was a full license available. The GDL laws
decreased new drivers' mobility in order to increase their safety, and
they worked so well—fatal crashes involving sixteen-year-old drivers
dropped by a quarter between 1995 and 2005—that every state now
has its own version of a GDL program. And GDL programs don't just
delay driving; in many cases they reduce it permanently, since history shows that, if drivers haven't gotten licensed by the time they're
twenty, they're unlikely ever to do so. According to a study done at
the University of Michigan's Transportation Institute, "for all practical
purposes, for the cohorts born between 1939 and 1963 . . . all those
who wanted to get a driver's license did so by age 20." Anything that
slows down the process of licensing between the ages of sixteen and
twenty, or raises its costs, can have a very long tail of consequences.
This one sure does; a study from the AAA Foundation for Traffic
Safety revealed that only 44 percent of teenagers obtain a driver's
license within a year of becoming eligible for one. According to the
Federal Highway Administration, only 46.3 percent have a license by
the time they turn nineteen. In 1998, the number was 64.4 percent.

An even bigger reason for the decline in VMT among Millennials
isn't economic, or even statutory. It's digital.

The Internet, and the spectrum of technologies that have been
developed to exploit it commercially, have changed everything from
the way we buy groceries to the way we find romantic partners. It is
no big surprise, then, to find that it's changed the way we get from
place to place, too.

One way it's changed our mobility patterns—and by "our" I
mean anyone who has ever bought anything from Amazon, eBay, or
Walmart.com—is by changing the way we shop. By the time you read

these words, online shopping will account for at least 9 percent of all retail sales in the United States: more than $300 billion in 2014, up from "only" $134 billion in 2007. Not only are 190 million Americans hitting "buy" buttons on a regular basis, but they're spending more and more every year, for an average of more than $1,700 annually.

That huge diversion of consumer buying dollars from in-store to in-home has implications for the average American's VMT, but their magnitude is a little unclear. Back in 2001, shopping accounted for 14.4 percent of annual household VMT and 21.1 percent of the trips per household. But buying on the Internet doesn't substitute for bricks-and-mortar shopping trips on a one-for-one basis—some of the folks who study the phenomenon most closely find that online shopping adds to in-store purchasing as well. Some people try on a pair of shoes in a physical store, then order them online from Zappos; but others buy a new phone from Amazon and then hustle over to the nearest Best Buy to get a case for it. However, the overall effect is to reduce travel. One of the best studies estimates that every one hundred minutes spent shopping from home is associated with five fewer minutes in shopping travel time and a one-mile reduction in distance traveled. Every six hours spent shopping online substitutes for one entire shopping trip.

However, while the growth of online shopping is clearly reducing shopping travel overall, it's not so obvious that Millennials are more affected by the phenomenon than their Baby Boomer and Gen X parents. The real impact of the Internet on Millennial transportation choices is someplace else.

One of those "someplace else" possibilities is that the digital revolution affects travel for socializing as much as or more than it does travel for shopping. A 2011 survey by KRC Research asked different age groups whether they "sometimes choose to spend time with friends [via social media] instead of driving to see them." Only 18 percent of Baby Boomers answered "yes." Millennials? Fifty-four percent. The number one transportation trend identified by Millennials in a 2014 survey was "socializing while traveling."

So the big impact of the Internet might not be that it makes driving less essential, but that it makes other transportation options, particularly transit, more appealing. Millions of people of all ages have grown to rely on 24/7 access to the Internet, whether they're looking up a movie on IMDB while simultaneously watching it, or following a baseball game in real time on ESPN, or obsessively checking for Facebook updates, e-mails, and texts. But no one depends on that kind of access more than Millennials, or is more likely to feel unsettled when he or she can't have it. You can text on the bus or the train, but—hopefully—not while driving. Even better, you can do nearly everything on a hands-free transit option that you can do at home, including checking out the transit options themselves.

That's because the characteristic that really distinguishes public transit from the automobile is that transit delivers service according to regular schedules. Frequent users of transit, such as intercity commuters, spend enough time on the train or bus to learn those schedules, but the once-in-a-while user has been predictably intimidated by travel that requires knowing which track the 7:02 train arrives on, or whether you need a transfer to take the crosstown bus at Main Street. That was true twenty years ago, and even five. Not anymore. One thing the Internet does unambiguously well is to make information that used to be expensive and scarce now cheap and abundant. You don't have to spend ten years learning the commuting ropes to know whether the train or bus you're on is an express or a local, or even when it's going to show up. You just need a smartphone. Smartphones are also all that's needed to take advantage of other revolutionary new transportation options: ridesharing services like Via, car-sharing like Zipcar, and—especially—dispatchable taxi services like Uber and Lyft.*

---

* For more about the importance of information-rich transportation systems for Millennials and everyone, see Chapter 7.

However, these and other cool new businesses didn't *create* Millennial distaste for driving. They just exploited it. The question remains: why do Millennials find the automobile so much less desirable than their parents, grandparents, and great-grandparents did?

>>>

Woodbridge, Virginia, is a small suburb about twenty miles south of Washington, DC. Many of the fifty-five thousand residents commute to Washington each day and return home to the leafy suburbs replete with cul-de-sacs and single-family homes. The blocks are long, the roads are wide, and many of them lack sidewalks. In typical suburban fashion, buildings and strip malls are set back from the road with parking in front.

In 1996, at the end of a cul-de-sac called Standish Court, nine-year-old Morgan Whitcomb, inspired by her trips to Washington, DC, and the anonymous cities she saw on television, decided to design her own urban metropolis. Using sidewalk chalk, Morgan laid out a bicycle-sized street grid across the cul-de-sac. There were intersections, stop signs, one-way streets, and sidewalks. When she was done, the neighborhood kids would play "city," and ride their bikes or walk along the streets, following the traffic rules, hand signaling when they turned. One kid would stand in as a traffic cop to direct traffic at the intersection with a "signal." Eventually someone would become bored and the game would devolve into "cops and red-light-runner."

When it came time for college, Morgan chose Columbia University in New York City, which was, in terms of the built environment, about as distant from the DC suburbs as Mars. And she adored it. Today she is an engineer and planner working in my company's Los Angeles office in bike-lane design and bike-share planning for cities. She does so on a computer running very sophisticated programs rather than using a chunk of chalk on a strip of asphalt, but it's not hard to see the line connecting one with the other.

At Sam Schwartz Engineering, a relatively high proportion of employees are Millennials like Morgan. They're not completely typical, since so many of them live in big cities with good public transit systems—our home base is in New York, but we have offices in Chicago, Newark, Tampa, LA, and Washington, DC. In addition, most of them, like Morgan, are transportation professionals, many of whom returned to the kind of street smart urban neighborhoods that her grandparents left decades ago. When we began researching and writing this book, we asked them why so few of their generational compatriots were car owners and drivers. Their answers don't provide a statistically reliable snapshot, but they're intriguing, nonetheless.

In addition to financial reasons—not enough money, too much debt, a dubious economy—they had a lot to say about the psychic baggage that goes with car ownership. Almost every one of them saw car ownership as a burden rather than a benefit. While cars used to be symbols of freedom and maturity, they're now just another buying decision, and one that has to justify itself by increasing the buyer's convenience, not his or her status.

The most enlightening reason, though, might be this: Millennials are the first generation whose parents were more likely to complain about their cars than get excited about them.

I suspect this is because kids get their introduction to automobile travel from the car's backseat. There, they are captive audiences to high-volume parental annoyance about driving—"high-volume" referring to both decibels and frequency. Every generation has had the dubious privilege of learning an impressive number of curses while watching Mom and Dad drive, but Millennials were driven through more traffic jams, more often, longer, and farther, than any generation in history. They were the first generation to be chauffeured not just on family vacations or the occasional trip to the supermarket, but everywhere: To the mall. To soccer practice. To piano lessons. As a result, they observed more unpleasant driving than the Gen X, Boomer, and Silent generations added together. It's remarkable to me how many of my Millennial employees who grew up in suburbs subsequently opted out of a driving-dependent life. And, since they were the demographic cohort most likely to drive as adults—way more than city kids, anyway—their defection counted twice, the same way that a second-place team's victory over the team they're chasing adds a half game to the team behind and takes a half game away from the team ahead. By moving not to another suburb but to a walkable city, a suburban young adult electing not to drive isn't quite a "man bites dog" newsflash, but it is certainly a snap at what had been a routine rite of passage since the end of World War II. After fifty years of mistaken decisions about America's built environment, a lot of Millennials are looking for something different.

It's also not a coincidence that Millennials were far likelier to grow up with two parents commuting. This might have exposed them to more of the exhausted complaining—from both parents—that is too often the commuter's primary contribution to dinner table conversation. It seems plausible, too, that one reason that Millennials are less enthusiastic about suburban living is that they were exposed, from an early age, to the same sort of complaints about lawn mowing, roof repair, and mortgage payments. Moreover, while it's true that urbanite parents are probably just as likely to complain about household repairs and living costs within earshot of their children, when it comes to chauffeuring them, they have a lot less to complain about. Volunteer chauffeuring costs suburban families between $782 and $1,742 per driver each year. Urban parent chauffeurs? Only $218 annually.

On top of the pretty interesting and highly suggestive observations from the skewed sample of my younger staff are some objective engineering facts. We can see that the speed of automobile travel in moving from one place to another peaked around 1970. My driving id (or is it ego?) finds that depressing. Before that, cars were, as advertised, improving the daily trips to work, stores, and restaurants, at least for most people. Thereafter, although cars got more and more technologically sophisticated, and more and more roads and highways were constructed, America entered Red Queen territory. We were building as fast as we could, just to travel at exactly the same speed, and soon enough even that wasn't enough. Drivers found themselves spending more and more hours getting from place to place. From 1970 to 2004, they kept increasing the annual mileage on their odometers, but they weren't getting anywhere any faster.

Even worse, all that driving wasn't producing any more goods and services. Though otherwise smart people continue to equate more driving with a healthier economy, they're doing the math wrong. A new study from Michael Sivak, at the Transportation Research Institute at the University of Michigan, shows that, whether you look at mileage per dollar of GDP or fuel consumed per dollar, the relationship peaked in 1977. After that, it started a pretty steep decline, to the point that every mile we drive is actually producing no more economic output than it did in 1946.

And we're paying a *lot* more for that economic activity. When I started driving in 1966 I recall paying 25.9 cents per gallon of gasoline; anything more than 30 cents was a rip-off. This really, really cheap gas was too good to be true for long. In October of 1973, two years after I started working for the New York City Traffic Department, the Organization of Petroleum Exporting Countries instituted an embargo on oil shipments, which raised the price of a barrel of oil by 400 percent. The price of a gallon of gas at the pump rose from about 38 cents to more than 55 cents. Gas stations were asked by the federal government to stop selling on weekends, which made it impossible to buy gas on weekdays without planting your idling car in a line that seemed to stretch around the block.

Drivers were not happy about this. At the Traffic Department we had to institute traffic changes around gas stations to handle the long queues of idling cars.

Then, six years later, a second oil crisis, this one following on the heels of the Iranian Revolution, doubled the price of a barrel of oil yet again. Gas prices spiked from an average of about seventy cents a gallon to more than a dollar. More long lines at gas stations. More unhappy drivers. The gas crises were the only times I had seen traffic volumes go down significantly in my long career until 2005 or so. It wasn't the *cost* of gas that was keeping drivers out of their cars; it was the *difficulty of getting* gas. We made this observation after the supply crisis was over, when even though prices surged, VMT started rising again.

The purpose for reminding ourselves about the oil shocks and gas lines is not to make a purely economic argument. The price of filling a tank is, of course, higher today than it was before OPEC started flexing its muscles (and before China and India started putting millions of new cars on the road, thus increasing demand for a shrinking resource like petroleum). But it's not quite the whole story. Gas might have jumped to a price of $1.35 a gallon by 1981, but if you adjust for inflation, it was about the same as it was in the middle of 2014: $3.47 in current dollars. When the price of gas dropped below $2.00 in many parts of the United States at the beginning of 2015, it was still higher than the 1979 price in inflation-adjusted terms. In 1920, the height of the popularity of the Model T, gas cost 20 cents a gallon, which is equivalent to $3.87 in 2015.

Gas prices go up, and they go down. More important than the inflation-corrected price per gallon is how drivers *thought* about the cost of a fill-up. And repairs. And insurance. And traffic jams. From the second oil shock on, their daily commute and weekly fill-up gave them more and more reasons to be annoyed about tradeoffs demanded by the six- or eight-cylinder money pits taking up space in their suburban garages. By 2004, economists were calculating that what they called the *commuting effect* (an increase of about twenty minutes in commuting time daily) was about as costly, in emotional terms, as breaking up with a boyfriend or girlfriend. Being economists, they tried to put a dollar figure on these costs, and found that people who commute about forty-five minutes a day should demand nearly 20 percent higher salaries for doing exactly the same job.

It didn't stop there. I don't know what the discipline of economics finds so fascinating about commuting, but in 2006, two Princeton economists asked nine hundred women to rank the well-being produced by nineteen different activities. Having sex (the researchers call it "intimate relations," but they're not fooling anybody) came in first. Socializing after work came in second. The "morning commute" was dead last, just a little worse than "evening commute." And the effect of the commute on the ideal home in the suburbs, with or without the white picket fence, was damaging too. The comfortable suburban home that persuaded them to take on the commute in the first place might appreciate in value over time, but the enjoyment of it doesn't. People who move to larger houses adapt to the larger size almost immediately, at which point it offers essentially no increase in gratification. The stress of the commute itself, on the other hand, is cumulative: the more years it goes on, the worse its effects. The depressing and formal term for the syndrome experienced by long-term commuters is *learned helplessness*: the kind of pessimistic resignation that seems to happen to laboratory animals when exposed repeatedly to painful stimuli that they cannot avoid. The road-building and housing policies that had made millions of Americans completely hostage to their cars were, to put it in slightly less technical language, pissing them off.

So they complained. And, from 1980 on, the most impressionable listeners to their complaints were—you guessed it—the Millennials. The impression they got was very consequential: Cars made you happy the day you brought one home from the dealer. Afterwards, not so much.

>>>

When I mention, in speeches, conferences, meetings, and even at dinner parties, how Millennials' distaste for driving is changing America's transportation future, I can often count on someone reminding me that *her* nineteen-year-old drives everywhere. Or that the neighbors have bought cars for each of their teenage kids as they turned eighteen. I must be wrong, they say.

Part of this is my own fault. Like anyone trying to make a point, I tend toward hyperbole: "Millennials don't want to live in suburbs." "Millennials hate cars." Nuance gets a little lost. No one, least of all me, is suggesting that cars are going extinct anytime soon. Americans and Europeans and Asians will continue to buy cars and drive them. But a change in VMT occurring at the margins isn't unimportant. If only an additional 10 percent of the Millennial generation chooses to forgo a car-centric lifestyle, that means eight *million* Americans are deciding to buy cars less frequently (if at all) and to live in places where cars are less necessary. If you're in the business of selling cars for a living—if you're Ford or Toyota—learning that the number of cars purchased by people aged eighteen to thirty-four declined by nearly 30 percent from 2007 to 2011 is the opposite of good news.

And, if the Millennial attitude toward cars *isn't* marginal—if it represents a trend that will grow as they age and as the next generation appears—the change will be even more dramatic.

Carmakers haven't given up on Millennials. They hire specialized marketing firms that promise to unlock the puzzle of selling cars to this market segment despite a lack of interest in their product. They advertise on Comedy Central and Spike. They fund Internet campaigns. They change car colors—Chevrolet tried out "techno pink" and "denim." They know Millennials like physical activity, so they show SUVs with full bike racks headed to exciting off-road bike trails.*

Some of it will probably work. But most won't. Because a lot of those Millennials who still like driving are choosing to do so without the burden of car ownership. According to a 2014 study by the business consultants Alix Partners, car-sharing services like Zipcar or RelayRides are responsible for auto manufacturers selling half a million fewer cars from 2004 to 2014. If the trend continues (that is, unless it gets worse), another 1.2 million aren't going to leave dealers' car lots between now and 2020. It's not as if automobile manufacturers can make up for this shortfall by fleet sales to the car-sharing companies. Every new car they sell to a company like Zipcar equals thirty-two cars *not* purchased by civilians. Nearly one American household in ten is now a "zero-car" family.

Automobile manufacturers and oil companies, however, have some very attractive strategic options. Even as cars get progressively more difficult to sell to young Americans, they get easier and easier to sell to young Chinese, Indians, and Brazilians. The companies that make up the car industry, and especially the oil business, are international. They can continue to grow overseas even as they are barely holding their own in Europe and America.

Things are different for the other group at risk of a marginal but large change in American life choices. The suburbs themselves. If large numbers of young families decide they'd rather live in dense urban communities, the construction companies whose business is building suburban homes can't easily reinvest in Chinese homebuilding. More important, the people who are responsible for governing those suburbs depend on property taxes to pay for virtually all local services, from sewer repair to schools. They are in deep trouble if the

---

* There's something perverse about using bike riding to sell cars.

value of the properties being taxed declines. Which is why the biggest consequence of the changing attitudes of Millennials toward cars and driving is a powerful centripetal effect pulling Millennials toward urban life, replacing the centrifugal forces that spun their parents and grandparents into the suburbs.

In plain language, Millennials are moving to transit-friendly environments. According to a 2010 Brookings Institution survey, 77 percent of Millennials aged eighteen to thirty-five plan to live in urban centers—in "vibrant, compact, and walkable communities full of economic, social, and recreational activities." A 2011 survey by the National Association of Realtors found that 62 percent of people aged eighteen to twenty-nine—Millennials all—prefer living in an area with a mix of single-family houses, apartments, retail, libraries, schools, and access to public transit.* In a 2011 survey by the Urban Land Institute, 50 percent of eighteen- to thirty-two-year-olds said they preferred living in a walkable community, and an additional 14 percent said it was "essential." The 2014 TransitCenter *Who's on Board* report has similar and more recent statistics. Their survey reinforced the finding that the ideal neighborhood for under-thirties is predominantly transit-oriented: 16 percent said they preferred "urban, downtown, with a mix of offices, apartments, and shops;" another 16 percent chose "urban, residential neighborhood;" and 30 percent opted for a "suburban neighborhood with a mix of houses, shops, and businesses."

Maybe even more significant, almost half of Millennials who already own a car say they'd give it up if they could count on an alternative, and more than half would seriously consider moving to another city if it offered a wider choice of transportation options. Even Millennials living in cities that are relatively poor in such alter-

---

* Actually, everyone likes the sound of that kind of place. Though the percentages are highest among the young, more than half of forty- and fifty-year-olds reported a preference for living in mixed-use communities.

natives are eager to cut the cord that links them to a car: 64 percent of Millennials living in Nashville expect to live in a place where they don't need to own a car, even though only 6 percent of them currently do so.

Many cities are meeting the demand. After decades during which the number of residential building permits in suburbs and exurbs were three and four times greater than the number granted to urban areas, the relationship is being completely reversed. In New York City's metro area, the share of residential building permits in the central city was 15 percent in the early 1990s and nearly 50 percent by 2005. In Chicago, same story: 7 percent to 27 percent. Portland, Oregon: 9 percent in the 1990s, 26 percent in the 2000s. Boston, which started losing population to the suburbs in the 1950s, is now growing again, with a population larger than at any time since the 1970s.* In subsequent chapters, you'll meet a dozen different mayors, city managers, and transportation commissioners from cities large and small that are creating—sometimes re-creating—urban centers that are both lively and livable, where a car is a choice, not a necessity. They're building Millennial-friendly cities.

Whenever I meet with civic leaders in transit-poor cities and suburbs, I tell them, "If you don't want to lose your children, invest in transportation that doesn't depend on the automobile. Build walkable town centers." This has been my most effective line in getting hard-core drivers to sit up and *listen*.

---

* One consequence is that supply and demand are increasingly out of whack in desirable—that is, walkable—cities and neighborhoods. This leads inevitably to higher housing costs, and more and more stratification among Millennials: as prices get bid up, fewer and fewer low-earning families stay, which leads to a self-reinforcing cycle. Prices that go up tend to keep going up. One perverse result is that the highest-earning families end up with the lowest transportation costs. Households in drivable suburban neighborhoods spend, on average, 20 percent of their family incomes on transportation. Those in walkable neighborhoods, half that.

>>>

Jarrett Walker is fond of telling Millennials, "The foundation of orthodox transportation planning is our certainty that when you're the
same age as your parents, you'll behave exactly the way they do."
But maybe the real question isn't, "Why are Millennials so different
from their parents and grandparents?" but "Why were their parents
and grandparents so different from them?" The historical anomaly,
after all, wasn't the desire to live in densely populated, walkable
communities. That's how human beings have lived ever since they
started building permanent habitations, and then towns and cities, ten
thousand years ago. It's how most people still live outside the United
States today. What was different about the United States of America
(and a few other places) from the 1920s to the 2000s was the aspi-
ration of most people to live as far away from work and shopping as
they could afford.

For a long time, the bargain seemed a good one. Houses got bigger and more luxurious. By most standard-of-living measures like
per capita GDP, or wealth, or years of education, things consistently
improved. If the price was time (usually miserable time) spent commuting, it was an affordable one. And they got used to it. In 1995,
Daniel Pauly, a marine biologist who was studying the effects of
overfishing, developed a brilliant idea that seemed obvious in retro-
spect, mostly to people who lacked the smarts to see it themselves.
The concept, which Pauly called *shifting baselines*, is a cognitive hic-
cup that causes us to draw flawed conclusions about change by using
the wrong starting point for comparison. In fisheries, Pauly's special
concern, this led biologists to estimate human impact on fisheries by
comparing the number of available cod, haddock, or herring, not to
the population that existed before humans started pulling them out
of the sea by the millions, but to the population that existed when
the biologists started collecting the data. Every generation, Pauly

wrote, makes "a gradual accommodation" with the losses that occur during their lifetimes.

Some of the biggest losers, when we became a generation of drivers, were kids. As they were losing the kind of street smart childhood my own generation experienced, their parents, perversely enough, were gaining something else: anxiety. Though even suburban streets are demonstrably safer than they were fifty years ago, and cities *much* safer, parents have become so fearful about the strange experience of walking that they've forbidden their children to undertake it, at least not without some adults to provide security. This level of fear-driven parenting has gotten so pervasive that it has prompted a reaction. In 2008, a New York mother and journalist named Leonore Skenazy wrote a newspaper column about letting her nine-year-old son navigate his way home, all by himself. Predictably, attacks followed . . . but so did the "Free-Range Kids" movement, which Skenazy started shortly thereafter. Is it needed? The month this book was completed, two Maryland parents were investigated for criminal neglect when cops picked up their ten-year-old son and six-year-old daughter for walking one mile, with their parents' blessing (and with parent-supplied maps) from their local park to their house. A neighbor, forgetting how normal this used to be, had turned them in.

This sort of willful amnesia, when an entire population updates its own perception of just what, exactly, is "normal," is a good approximation of what occurred to American families from the 1950s through the 1970s. Their baseline expectations about the number of hours spent behind the wheel of a car every month kept shifting. The expectation was sustained by housing policies like the GI Bill that discriminated in favor of new housing, and by tax policies that discriminated against renters. It was enabled by transportation policies like the orgy of road building financed by the Highway Trust Fund. It was reinforced by white flight, by the almost deliberate destruction of inner city neighborhoods, and even by the well-intentioned but unhelpful Progressive disdain for city living. And it survived for decades.

Eventually, though, it turned out to be a losing game. For millions of people—not just Millennials, but also Baby Boomers in the process of downsizing their homes—the costs of suburban living started to outweigh the benefits. And furthermore, they also realized that there were even greater benefits to changing the scale and pace of living itself. And the realization that the best place to do so was on the kind of streets that were designed to do more than just allow cars to travel over them as quickly and safely as possible. On smart streets.

HEALTHIER, WEALTHIER, AND WISER

A joke:

> Two male traffic engineers were testing out a new bike path when one said to the other, "What happened to that old beat-up bike you used to ride?" The second engineer answered, "Well, I was sitting in the park yesterday, minding my own business, when this great-looking woman rode up, threw her bike down, stripped off all her clothes, and said to me, 'Take what you want.' So I took the bike." The first engineer nodded. "Of course you did. The clothes wouldn't have fit you anyway."

I know how that second guy felt. I like my own bike, too. Engineers, as a class, tend to like machinery in general, though most of them, in my experience, like four-wheeled machines powered by internal combustion engines a lot more than two-wheeled machines that run on muscle.* For a long time, I was no different. I loved cars. Most of the appeal came from the usual incentives: more freedom, higher status, better dating prospects. But I didn't just like *owning* that 1960 Chevy Impala with the big flat fins I bought with my grocery-store wages when I was a freshman at Brooklyn College, or even the 1964 Grand Prix I paid for with cab fares. I loved *driving*. I was good at it. And the more I drove, the better I got. By the time I was in my twenties, I knew a thousand different shortcuts and workarounds for every street in New York's five boroughs. I knew how to avoid double-parked trucks, how to time traffic lights, and how to find a parking space anywhere, anytime, and in the tiniest of spaces. In 1993, the travel publisher Fodor's even asked me to write a book they called *Shadow Traffic's New York Shortcuts and Traffic Tips*. I opened with "I hate traffic . . . I detest delays . . . from the day I got my driver's license I avoided driving with the hordes." Today I do my best to avoid driving altogether but I still must at times. When, in the mid-2000s, a car salesman tried to persuade me of the virtues of an onboard navigation system, I was a hard sell, indeed. When I finally got my first GPS-enabled car, the most fun I had using the thing was correcting the directions it offered, because I always knew a better way. (Those who drive with me regularly seem to think this is annoying; I can't see why.)

Even so, a part of me had been a closet cyclist ever since my Grand Prix was stolen in 1969 and I bought a secondhand bike to ride to Penn. That bike was stolen two years later in Prospect Park when I moved back to Brooklyn.

That secondhand bike was my first bike as an adult. I didn't know how to ride a bike until I was thirteen years old. I learned out of necessity on an old truck bike my father used for delivering groceries.

---

* Even so, a couple of engineering nerds—if this isn't a redundancy—have calculated that cycling is the most efficient form of transportation ever invented, with more than 98 percent of the energy produced by the rider actually transmitted to the wheels.

In those days a storekeeper was not allowed to own a delivery bike in Bensonhurst; he had to rent it from some characters with, as they say, "links to organized crime," for $8 a month, or $96 a year (about $780 today).*

With a tiny wheel in front and a heavy load of groceries in the basket, a truck bike wasn't easy to ride; every delivery boy flipped over headfirst on at least one of his first tries. But once I mastered the bike, I became a wild man. Traffic rules meant nothing. Stopping, other than at your destination, was a sign of weakness and meekness. I still remember one time under the "el" on 86th Street riding the wrong way in a tight spot between an oncoming car and a parked car. I squeezed through without stopping but I ended up with ten feet of chrome strip torn off the parked car in my basket. This being Bensonhurst, where damaging someone's car was akin to horse rustling in 1875 Texas, I got rid of the strip as fast as I could and kept on riding.

As a junior traffic engineer in the Traffic Department in the early 1970s I was probably the only man (there were no women then) who occasionally rode a bike. Bikes were for kids; real men drove Mustangs and aspired to drive a Caddy one day. I biked for recreation mostly through the 70s and then jogged through the 80s. I even completed the NYC Marathon in 1981. Even so, by the 1990s, I was living in Flatbush with my wife, a teenage son, a younger son and daughter, and three cars: one for each driver's license.

In 2000, though, we moved to Manhattan, and something changed. I discovered—or, rather, rediscovered—the pleasures of biking and walking, wherever possible.

We had moved from leafy Flatbush to Battery Park City, an exceptionally well-planned community at the southern tip of Manhattan. I had miles and miles of bike and walking paths outside the door

---

* I could go on and on about the mob in my neighborhood, but that's another book.

to my new apartment building. I could stroll or bike along the Hudson River. At times I'd walk the two miles home from work enjoying a different path each time. And I loved it. I felt I was living in this secret park with waterfront views right in Manhattan's Downtown; I was happy.

Until September 11, 2001.

Battery Park City is nestled between the World Trade Center and the Hudson River. It sits entirely on landfill made mostly from the excavation of the original twin towers. I walked by the World Trade Center that morning at about 8:30, fifteen minutes before the first plane struck. My wife was home in our apartment across the street from the site but luckily with only a river view—away from the direction of the World Trade Center. When she and my oldest son, David, who lived a few blocks away, made it around the wreckage to get to my office, they were covered with ashen debris. It was the last I saw of either office or home for weeks. Since Manhattan south of 14th Street was closed off, I worked on transportation engineering for the Battery Park City Authority while living with relatives in Connecticut and Brooklyn.

We returned home in late September but it was never the same. The fires burned till December. Every day moving vans took our neighbors away. After six months, my wife had had enough. Where to move to next?

This time I decided to follow my father's footsteps. In 1951, he had moved us from Brownsville to Bensonhurst to be within walking distance of his grocery store. In 2002, I did the same, moving to an apartment in Greenwich Village, eight blocks from my office on Houston Street. There were seven different ways to walk from my home to the office, one for each day of the week. Every day I'd pick a different side street and always find something new. Depending on the wait for the elevator, the entire trip took between ten and eleven minutes, and I wasn't anxious or rushed for a single one of them. As a boy, I had been a bit discomfited by the fact that my father walked to work, while most of the other fathers drove. Now I knew my father was the wisest of them all. He picked his home to minimize travel.

Despite all this, I didn't entirely trust that I'd discovered anything useful about the future of transportation. I knew I *felt* good about walking and biking. But I also knew that I was *supposed to feel good*. Much of what I read now professionally is pro-cycling and pro-walking, sometimes embarrassingly so. Some of the most frequently published writers on the subject of smart transportation are practically messianic, and heresy, such as suggesting that privately owned automobiles might have any place at all in some ideal future transportation infrastructure, is severely punished. Support for cyclists and pedestrians was in tune with my political sympathies, my social contacts, and even my bank account, since my company is frequently hired by clients interested in transforming the world into a less automobile-centric place. In 2012 we even self-published a book with the advocacy organization America Walks, *Steps to a Walkable Community*. If your work is advising municipalities how to build walkable communities, you probably should like walking.

There were other questions: Were alternatives to driving getting better, or was driving itself just becoming more miserable? Had the alternatives been better all along? Does adding a few miles of cycling and walking to your daily routine improve your mood, or does driving degrade it? Both?

The fact that crankiness is a frequent result of commuting by car more than about twenty-five minutes each way isn't really in dispute. As the last chapter pointed out, people regard long commutes of any sort as the equivalent of cleaning out a clogged drain. Five days a week. With your bare hands. And they're right. Longer commutes are associated with higher blood pressure and more frequent headaches. But they're far worse for commuters who choose to drive than for those who take an alternative, generally mass transit by rail. The constant road vibrations experienced by drivers, and the inability to stretch or move while experiencing them, puts pressure on the discs of the lower back, with the predictable result: more lower back pain. The physical toll isn't even the worst of it. The psychological stresses of long-distance commuting by car can be even higher. Part of the reason is that it's much more difficult to adapt to driving for forty-five minutes each morning than, for example, taking a train. Even the most unpleasant train commute departs at about the same time daily, occupies the same amount of time, and requires so little attention that it's even possible to sleep while shuttling back and forth. Car trips, on the other hand, are far more variable, more subject to delays due to road construction, traffic, and weather. For the same reason that it's easier to adapt to a noise, even an annoying one, when it occurs at the same rhythm and frequency, than to one that is constantly changing pitch and volume, it's less stressful to commute long distance by train than by car.

Driving does offer some compensating advantages over mass transit, of course, including a greater sense of autonomy and control.* But one of the seeming conveniences of driving—that getting from home to work doesn't force you to walk any farther than from your kitchen to your garage at one end, and from your employer's parking lot to your desk at the other—isn't a benefit. It's a liability.

The big-time health benefits of walking are not a secret. More than a century ago the English historian George Macauley Trevelyan began a book titled, simply, *Walking*, with the line: "I have two doctors: My left leg and my right. When my body and mind are out of gear . . . I know that I shall have only to call in my two doctors to be well again." He knew what he was talking about. Walking thirty minutes a day—as little as a mile at each end of a daily commute, for example—lowers the risk of heart disease by up to 40 percent,

---

* Or maybe not so much. See Chapter 7.

reduces the risk of Type 2 diabetes by as much as 60 percent, and can cut the risk of stroke by a third. Osteoarthritis? Walk thirty minutes a day, and reduce your risk by 18 percent. In the 1990s, Japan's Osaka Company began surveying its employees in order to get a handle on the impact of lengthening the distance they walked to work, and their risk of higher blood pressure. Every additional ten minutes spent walking to and from work was associated with a 12 percent reduction in hypertension.

Then there's the not dying part. The Cooper Center Longitudinal Study, whose database now contains more than a quarter million records from more than a hundred thousand people, representing 1.8 million person-years, found that low fitness was the strongest predictor of death in any given year—more than obesity or even smoking. The Harvard Alumni Health Study, which followed more than seventeen thousand subjects for nearly twenty-four years, found that walking thirty minutes a day cut mortality by nearly a quarter. It doesn't do your waistline any harm, either.

However, the reasons to choose walking or cycling, or even mass transit, over driving aren't just the negative ones, nor is it just that walking and cycling improve your cardiovascular health (though they do). My subjective reactions to incorporating walking and cycling into my daily routine were objectively true. They make everyone feel a whole lot better. Any kind of exercise, but especially regular, moderate exercise like walking and cycling, increases levels of serotonin, norepinephrine, and dopamine: the neurotransmitters whose lack is a prime cause of depression. A study at Duke University compared a brisk thirty-minute walk three times a week to taking the antidepressant Zoloft. Walking worked *at least* as well. It's not like this was a single outlier study, either. A group of health economists in England studied eighteen years of data on more than eighteen thousand commuters who had been surveyed about their own mental health: whether they felt worthwhile or worthless, slept well or poorly, how well they coped with life problems. The more time they spent walking—or on public transportation—the higher their scores. As one of the researchers put it,

> You might think that things like disruption to services or crowds of commuters might have been a cause of considerable stress. But as buses or trains also give people time to relax, read, socialise, and there is usually an associated walk to the bus stop or railway station, it appears to cheer people up. . . . Our study shows that the longer people spend commuting in cars, the worse their psychological wellbeing. And correspondingly, people feel better when they have a longer walk to work.

For me, though, the biggest advantage of getting around using my feet for something other than operating a car's accelerator might be that it makes me smarter. Or, at least, less stupid. The reason is a little seahorse-shaped section of my brain—yours, too—called the hippocampus, two of which are located just under the center of the temporal lobe. The two hippocampi are critical in storing and creating memories. They're the part of the brain first damaged by Alzheimer's, and the one where amnesia due to oxygen deprivation occurs. Even if we avoid amnesia or dementia, though, memory gets a lot less useful the older we get, largely because the hippocampus naturally shrinks as we age.

It doesn't have to. Though a lot of otherwise well-educated people still seem to think that a brain cell, once lost, is gone forever, this isn't true at all. So long as you continue to produce a protein known as brain-derived neurotrophic factor, or BDNF, your brain will build new neurons and strengthen the capacity of existing ones. How to increase BDNF production? Exercise, of course. Study after study shows that more exercise improves memory and cognition, in every animal from humans to rodents. Yes, rodents. Wire an exercising mouse up to an MRI and what you'll see is more neurogenesis—more production of nerve cells—in our old friend, the hippocampus. Which allows me to say, with a straight face, that when it comes to the hippocampus, size matters.

〉〉〉

Getting to work by foot or on my bike would make me a lot healthier, a good deal happier (or less depressed), and a little bit smarter (or less forgetful) even if I were the only one in New York doing so. There are even researchers who believe that walking, in particular, was so critical for human evolution that intelligence itself was a side-effect of bipedalism. But there's another benefit, one that has implications not just for individual commuting decisions but for a whole spectrum of transportation policies, from the way we design intersections to the speed limits we set. Choosing to drive less improves society's mental health, too.

This isn't exactly a new idea. In 1950, Disney produced a cartoon entitled *Motor Mania* that starred Goofy as a Jekyll-and-Hyde character who transforms from placid and gentle Mr. Walker into a psychotic bucket of rage—Mr. Wheeler—once he steps into the driver's seat of his convertible. Goofy's "windshield perspective"[*] is even more powerful today. A 2013 study found that neighborhoods, streets, and even people look very different to drivers than they do to pedestrians, cyclists, or even bus riders. People driving cars, for example, are a lot more likely to be suspicious of unfamiliar streets and hostile to less affluent neighborhoods. When subjects were shown four different ambiguous videos—a girl texting from a park bench,

---

[*] The phrase was originally coined in the 1990s to describe the belief, widely held among transportation officials from engineers to traffic cops, that everyone (even in New York) gets from place to place by car. It's now mostly used to express literally what it says: the way the world looks from behind a car's windshield.

for example—the ones who saw the incident as it would have appeared from the front windshield of a car rated the actors as more threatening, less considerate, even less educated than subjects who saw the video from the viewpoint of a pedestrian, a cyclist, or a bus rider.

This is because *what* we see is largely determined by *how* we see. Driving demands tunnel vision—literally. A 2010 simulation produced by the National Association of City Transportation Officials shows that a driver's "cone of vision" automatically excludes peripheral information, and that the faster a car travels, the more that cone narrows: moving at thirty miles per hour gives drivers less than 25 percent of the amount of visual information that they receive at fifteen miles per hour. The lack of visual context makes for snap judgments; and because drivers have to be more alert to rapidly developing dangers in a way that pedestrians aren't, those snap judgments tend to be negative ones.

The good news is that, although driving makes us more suspicious, walking makes us more hopeful. I know this sounds a little odd coming from someone who lives and walks in New York, where, as the joke goes, a tourist asks for directions by saying, "Can you tell me how to get to Central Park, or should I just go f&%k myself?" But it's true. Our sense of psychological well-being is a function of the number of positive contacts we have daily with others—not just friends and family, but strangers and neighbors. And those positive contacts are a lot more frequent outside a car. Cars do their very best—with their micro-controlled climates, audios, and even scents—to seal the driver away from the rest of humanity (and from the impact they themselves have on the environment: noise, fumes, and particulates) inside an aluminum box. It's actually a very weird development: cars offer a wholly artificial micro world. Maybe it's to parlay the car as a mobile suburb.

Once again, I'm not going to ask you to take my word for it. A neuro-economist (an academic specialty that you don't come across every day) named Paul Zak has written an entire book on how the hormone oxytocin—the "trust" hormone, associated with both childbirth and breastfeeding—is produced whenever we have a trust-building interaction. It's suppressed when we have a stressful interaction. "Oxytocin surges when people are shown a sign of trust."

It's not just that oxytocin makes individual people more likely to trust others; it promotes more trust, empathy, and compassion in an entire community. Things that cause a surge in oxytocin make us more empathetic and compassionate. And research shows that, wherever people can walk without fear of being run over by a car—and, even more important, without worrying about their children—they produce more oxytocin. Walt Disney didn't know anything about the neurochemistry of oxytocin when he built the original Main Street at Disneyland, a thoroughfare that is so pedestrian friendly that parents let their kids walk right down the middle of the street, side by side with trolley cars, but his intuition was correct: reduce threats, increase happiness.

Social cohesion and trust are improved just by *living* in a place with less traffic. Though the social costs of a physical environment dominated by the automobile have been debated ever since the Model T, the best (and still the most cited) study of the subject dates to the late 1960s, when Donald Appleyard, then professor of urban design at the University of California, Berkeley, performed a rigorous survey of three residential streets in San Francisco. On the surface, the streets seemed close to identical: same topography, similar demographics, and, of course, the same weather (in San Francisco, a pretty changeable thing). They differed in only one significant respect: the number of vehicles that traveled along the street on a typical weekday. On average, fewer than two thousand cars traveled down one street daily; on another, the number was eight thousand. On Appleyard's "Heavy Street," sixteen thousand vehicles a day. The residents of each street were then asked to complete detailed questionnaires about their respective networks of friends and acquaintances.

The results weren't unexpected, but the degree of difference was still startling: residents on the street with the lightest traffic had, on average, three close friends living on the same block; those on the heaviest, less than one. The people living on "Light Street" had more than twice as many acquaintances on their streets as the people living on "Heavy Street." Asked to draw pictures of their blocks, they included more, and more accurate, details. When Appleyard performed follow-up interviews on his subjects, they explained why: on a heavily trafficked street, "home" meant that part of the world that was inside the doors of their houses or apartments. On the lightly trafficked ones, the concept had a very different meaning—people living there consistently referred to the entire block as "home."

One reason that Appleyard's results continue to be cited is that they've been replicated in places as far afield as Bristol, England, and as close to the original study as Contra Costa County in California. That's where Appleyard's son, Bruce, performed a similar study in 2005, this time with kids. He surveyed and interviewed children living on lightly and heavily trafficked streets to see how the number of cars passing in front of their homes changed the way they saw their neighborhoods.

Again, more traffic equaled less community. Like his father, Bruce Appleyard asked his subjects, groups of children, aged nine to ten—to draw maps of their neighborhoods: where their schools were located, their friends' houses, places they liked or hated. Children who lived in heavy traffic neighborhoods could barely include any detail about their own blocks, much less their neighborhood. The main road in front of the school attended by both groups of kids is lined with trees; the kids who lived on heavily trafficked blocks, whose parents were—sensibly—fearful about letting their kids even walk across their own streets, drew no trees at all; the ones on lightly trafficked streets did. Kids who lived on less walkable, more heavily trafficked streets drew maps made up of random paths, disconnected from one another, and certainly unconnected to any larger community. Kids who lived on streets that permitted them to travel on foot drew accurate maps of their routes to and from school and playgrounds. And they included a lot more playgrounds; those who lived on walkable streets found 40 percent more places to play than those who didn't. Depressingly but unsurprisingly, the more traffic that kids were exposed to, the more likely they were to show streets and intersections as dangerous. Appleyard's conclusion? "As exposure to auto traffic volumes and speed decreases, a child's sense of threat goes down, and . . . ability to establish a richer connection and appreciation for the community rises." Or, as one of Appleyard's ten-year-old subjects who was lucky enough to live on a walkable block put it, "I like my naborhod [sic] because I have lots of friends, and because I can play there when ever I want."

I have yet to find a study that shows how walking increases romantic opportunities but it certainly worked for me when in 1971, after graduating from Penn, I moved back to Brooklyn to the Prospect-Lefferts Garden area. For the most part the neighborhood is made up of great stone or brick houses on tree-lined streets named Maple and Midwood. I, however, lived on Beekman Place, which, despite the ritzy-sounding name, consisted of six-story buildings and no trees on a rundown, dead-end street abutting busy Flatbush Avenue on one end and the open cut of the Brighton subway line on the other. My walking, needless to say, was on the prettier blocks or in nearby Prospect Park, where I met Daria, the woman I would eventually marry (and, more important, stay married to).

I did have a secret weapon: my dog, Pepita. Once, in my bachelor days, I yelled at Pepita for stalling in the middle of Flatbush Avenue (she was never on a leash) only to hear a throaty voice, attached to a leggy brunette, asking, "Is that the way you treat all your women?" A brief fling followed. It's a treasured memory—one I wouldn't have acquired had I crossed Flatbush in a car.

>>>

Although the discovery of all the hard data and sophisticated research that reinforced my prejudices in favor of less car dependence was satisfying, it was puzzling too: if living in dense, walkable towns and cities made people healthier and happier, how in hell did we ever get in this mess in the first place? What was it that made moving to the suburbs so damned appealing?

The answers are, like the subject, complicated. Some people did—and still do—dream of a house with a fence in front and a garden (or swimming pool!) out back. Others sought out suburbs as an escape from cities that seemed, and often were, dirty, crowded, and dangerous. A lot of families continue to shop for a suburban school district in search of what I call the Lake Wobegon Effect: a place where all the children are above average and therefore get an above-average education (though their math must be a little below average if they believe this to be true). But the best explanation for why Americans overwhelmingly chose suburban living for more than fifty years, and so many continue to do so today, is money. They voted with their wallets, for suburban houses whose cost per square foot was so much lower than that of the available housing stock in densely populated urban centers.

But that just pushes the question one step further back. Why did suburbs enjoy such a cost advantage? One reason is that it actually was more efficient to build in places that didn't have much existing construction in place, even when the new houses needed new sewer, telephone, and electric lines. For the same reason, building a new road is often cheaper than widening an old one, where half the cost can be *de*struction, rather than *con*struction, and a quarter goes to maintaining the existing traffic on the road under construction.

But there's a big difference between the kind of efficiency that can be quantified by a physicist and the sort studied by economists. The velocity-time graphs used by physics students to study acceleration might look a little like the supply and demand curves that economics students use to study prices. They're not. Demand curves can be manipulated. If we—and by "we" I mean all of us, acting through our local, state, and federal governments—decide to do so, we can alter the supply of most things, and thereby change their prices. If a rent-control law keeps prices below what people are willing to pay for housing, the housing supply contracts; if a new zoning law favors construction in a previously vacant area, the supply expands.

Which is exactly what happened with the GI Bill's requirement that government-guaranteed home loans go only to *new* construction, or the Eisenhower administration's decision to build forty thousand miles of heavily subsidized highways. The relative advantage of car-dependent suburban living didn't come from the impersonal forces of the market in action, but from a sequence of decisions made by fallible human beings, decisions that could very easily have gone in an entirely different direction. In some other countries, including many in Europe, they *did* take a different direction. Europe still has some nineteenth-century streetcars that have run uninterrupted to this day, including the Blackpool Tramway in England and Budapest's electric tram. Fifty years of sprawl in America then does, in fact, look a lot like a fifty-year mistake—one that didn't have to happen.

Which made me wonder whether we could, as a thought experiment, rewind that bit of history, and ask whether a society that depended on hundreds of millions of driving trips daily was actually more cost-effective in the long run. What if an environment that made driving less appealing was actually more economically efficient?

There are a lot of reasons to think it would be. It's not just that traveling to work by car is expensive in monetary terms, though it is. The total average cost of driving, including depreciation, maintenance, and insurance, runs about 61 cents a mile, and since the average automobile used for commuting to work contains only 1.1 people, every commute costs a little more than 55 cents per passenger mile. This means that, if you're an automobile commuter traveling twenty-five miles each way to work, you're spending around $30 a day for the privilege, not including the cost, if there is one, to park. You're also spending an hour every day for which, unless you're a cabbie or bus driver yourself, you're *not* getting paid, and during which you're not doing anything productive at all. For the average American, that's another $24. In transportation, time really *is* money.

During the fifty years we've been running this very expensive experiment in voting-with-your-wallet transportation policy, has it been worth it? Are we more prosperous, on average, than we would have been without spending hundreds of billions of dollars subsidizing automobile commuting? The subsidies definitely changed behavior; the United States still leads the world by a lot in vehicle miles traveled, even after the current decline. More than 85 percent of us depend on cars for almost all our transportation needs. But it's getting harder and harder to argue that this has produced an optimal amount of prosperity. One reason is that, paradoxically, all that driving seems to be correlated with lower economic productivity. Put another way, the more "inefficient" roads are, the more economically efficient are the areas they serve.

Here's the root of the paradox: within the developed world, the measure that seems to indicate the most mobility—VMT—is negatively correlated with productivity measures like gross domestic product. Moreover, region-by-region, the more mobility is constrained by tolls or congestion, the higher the GDP. Even though congestion costs Americans $121 billion in wasted fuel and unproductive time annually, a study from Texas A&M's Transportation Institute found a powerful correlation between per capita traffic *delay* and per capita GDP; and the correlation wasn't negative, but the opposite. For every 10 percent increase in traffic delay, the study found a 3.4 percent increase in per capita GDP. It's not that congestion itself increases economic productivity, but that places with a lot of congestion are economically vibrant; those without, not so much.

In fact, in a paper published just as I was completing this book, a group of anthropologists and systems scientists found that density has been powerfully associated with prosperity as much in the ancient cities of pre-Columbian Mexico as in twenty-first-century Manhattan (though the prosperity of the four thousand archaeological sites they found was measured in monument building and house size rather than GDP). The reasons seem to be the same, though: density promotes more, and more frequent, social interactions—and social interactions are essential for all forms of human productivity, from harvesting crops to selling razor blades to performing music to building factories. This isn't a function of simple size. It isn't just that larger cities just make more stuff than smaller ones; in both ancient and modern communities, the more interactions there are between people, the more output there is, even when population is held constant. As an economist would put it, density results in increasing returns to scale—and congestion seems a small price to pay for that.

The opposite is also true: policies intended to reduce congestion, usually by building more and wider roads, lead to lower productivity, and therefore less money in the average family's bank account. There are two big reasons why. The first is that, despite all the faith that we put in markets to allocate resources in the most efficient way, when it comes to roads, we are apostates. We assume that all those drivers—like all those suburban home buyers—are making free-market decisions to drive on all those new roads. But then we do an absolutely terrible job of creating a free market for driving. We don't put a price on all that use. We make some roads free, and some subject to tolls. Some are paid for by gas taxes, some not. It's as if we had opened a fruit market where apples were a buck apiece, and pears were free; even if shoppers preferred apples, you'd still be unable to keep pears in stock. The existing road system, all too often, works the same way, with drivers making decisions about the routes they take based on completely artificial—usually political—decisions about whether and how much they're going to be charged for using a finite amount of concrete and asphalt. This is the opposite of efficient.

Professionals have a technique for figuring out the optimal solution to congestion problems, one that minimizes both time and cost. It's called a *Wardrop Equilibrium* for the English transportation analyst John Glen Wardrop, who formulated it in 1952. He assumed that travelers would, over time, choose the shortest route under prevailing traffic conditions, the route that can't be improved by picking another one. After a bunch of travelers successively adjust their routes, a situation with stable routes and flows appears: an equilibrium. Wardrop formalized this with two principles: first, that a point exists where "no driver can reduce his journey time by a new route" and second, as a consequence, "average journey time is at a minimum."

In order for this to happen, though, drivers need to pay a higher price for traveling on a desirable route, or at a popular time. Otherwise, you can't get to equilibrium, because average journey time can't ever reach the most efficient state. So long as they have no price signals that tell them how, and how much, they would benefit by commuting at different times, drivers will inevitably commute inefficiently. The airlines have figured this out; that's why they charge wildly different prices for seats depending on when they are reserved. This is what congestion pricing is all about.

I first heard the term *congestion pricing* at one of the monthly Midtown Circulation meetings I held in the late 1970s, when I was an assistant commissioner at the New York City Department of Transportation. To be fair, they weren't my favorite way to spend time. In fact, they were about as productive as herding cats through a fish cannery, mostly because the attendees were intrinsically at cross-purposes—they included community members and representatives of business groups, pro-driver associations like AAA, and pro-bike organizations like Transportation Alternatives. We would discuss how a new computerized signal system would make speeds go up or how changing parking regulations and targeted enforcement could reduce congestion. But, in my heart of hearts I knew the answer was far simpler: fewer vehicles. I just couldn't figure out how to get there.

And then, one day, I learned. The guy who taught me was a prototypical absent-minded professor wearing a worn tweed sports coat with elbow patches and trousers from another era. His name was William S. Vickrey and he was a professor of economics at Columbia University. He quietly pointed out the futility of trying to improve travel for cars in such a dense area. He talked about how hotels and airlines raised prices at Christmastime when demand soared. He talked about how a car, especially a driver-only car, was the least efficient way of using space, which was the most precious resource in Manhattan. And that we should treat it the same as any other precious resource: put a high price on it. He called it congestion pricing.*

In 1980 I had a chance to do something about it. I wrote a traffic regulation that would prohibit driver-only cars, Vickrey's least-efficient vehicles, from entering Manhattan for free from 6 a.m. to 10 a.m. Effective September 1980, they would have to use a tolled bridge or tunnel to enter.

It didn't exactly work out as I hoped. We were sued by some of the same people that used to make those Midtown Circulation meetings such a breeze, including AAA and the Metropolitan Parking Association (a trade association—this is actually a euphemism for "lobbyist"—representing New York's garage operators). Injunctions. Delays. And then, the verdict: I—or, rather, the City of New York—

---

* I kept in touch with Professor Vickrey on and off during the years and was elated one day in October 1996 when I heard on the radio that he had won the Nobel Prize for Economics. I planned to call him to congratulate him and suggest we celebrate. Sadly I never connected with him again, though. He died three days after the announcement. The Nobel Prize can only be awarded to a living recipient. I'm at least glad he lived long enough, eighty-two years, to learn he had won.

did not have the authority to discriminate between driver-only and carpool cars. That power rested with the state, whose governor, Hugh Carey, no great friend of Ed Koch's (not that there are many real friends in politics), had no interest in provoking AAA.

I am nothing if not stubborn. In 1987, I introduced a similar plan as part of a series of traffic relief strategies. More than a thousand businesspeople marched on City Hall to protest the "draconian plans" of Schwartz and Ross Sandler, the city's new transportation commissioner, who had replaced Anthony Ameruso, then fighting a perjury indictment connected to the scandal at the Parking Violations Bureau. Full-page ads were taken out in all the dailies saying, "Commissioner Schwartz: Stop Fouling Up Midtown Traffic." (I was told later by Mel Kauffman, the real-estate tycoon who placed the ads, that the original version was "Stop F%&king up Midtown Traffic." He later became a client.). Once again, I learned that mayors and governors find it difficult to get people to pay for something valuable that they think they've been getting for free, and the plan went nowhere.

If insanity is, as they tell us, repeating the same behavior and expecting a different result, I probably should plead guilty. In 2001, I was called to a meeting to discuss a platform paper on transportation that I had written for the team representing a dark-horse candidate for mayor of New York City. (Full disclosure: I had written dozens of similar papers for candidates and elected officials, but this was the first time I had been paid for it!) A major element was congestion pricing.

I entered the candidate's office on Lexington Avenue and was led to a desk in the middle of a very busy floor where I first met Michael Bloomberg. I liked him instantly. He was no-nonsense and a numbers person—my kinda guy. He had read it and peppered me about congestion pricing. He didn't like it, or so it seemed. It was unfair, unworkable, and likely would hurt business. I countered and parried and thought I gained some ground but it was hard to tell. His first term came and went with nary a mention of congestion pricing.

In 2003, however, things changed. Mayor Ken Livingstone turned London into the first Western city to implement congestion charging, as they called it.* I was jealous, of course. Congestion pricing was invented in New York decades before by a professor at Columbia but London beat us to it.

Competition is a powerful thing, especially to a man like Mike Bloomberg. After London beat New York in the competition for hosting the 2012 Olympics, the mayor got, shall we say, motivated. In 2007 he took up the cause. He got about as far as anyone, which is to say, not very far. While the New York City Council held a largely ceremonial vote in favor, the state legislature, which needed to pass legislation enabling the city to set tolls, never even held a vote.

Congestion pricing, however, is about as hard to kill as Rasputin. As of this writing, I am advocating for another congestion pricing plan, this one known as Move NY, and it may even be on the way to being implemented as you read this. Or not—I'm used to disappointment on this subject. The reason is that when you give something valuable away for free, demand is essentially infinite. As a result, urban traffic congestion just keeps getting worse. I may be a little unhinged on the subject of congestion pricing, but the really insane idea, the one we keep trying over and over again with exactly the same crappy results, is fixing congestion by building more roads.

There's another reason for the congestion paradox. Why is increasing congestion, generally thought of as a bad thing, associated with greater economic prosperity, a good thing? It's because most of the measures of transportation efficiency tend to focus on mobility. But mobility isn't what's really important, for either happiness or prosperity. What matters is *access*. And it's just as easy, and a lot more efficient, to improve access—to stores, or entertainment, or employment—by decreasing the distance between, for example,

---

* Singapore had actually done so in 1975.

home and supermarket than it is by increasing the speed by which to get from one to the other.

That's how the paradox is resolved, about why people without cars in more densely populated neighborhoods get where they need to be more efficiently than drivers in sparsely populated suburbs. The Walker family (remember Goofy) lives in a neighborhood where they can walk half a mile at a not very brisk pace from their front door to a drugstore. Takes them ten minutes. The Wheelers, on the other hand, live in a place where the nearest drugstore is five miles away, and even when the roads are clear of traffic and they make all the lights, it takes them fifteen minutes to drive there and park. The Wheelers have superior mobility. The Walkers have superior access, though, because, when it comes to access, proximity is ten times more important than speed. And access, not mobility, is what drives prosperity. We're not just happier, healthier, and smarter in denser communities. We're richer, too.

This is true even in places that are thought of—correctly—as expensive. Some of the American cities with the highest housing costs, places like New York, Washington, DC, San Francisco, and Seattle, are also among the top ten metropolitan areas in total affordability, precisely because they are the *least* expensive to get around in. San Antonio, for example, looks like a bargain when housing is the only measure, cheaper even than Detroit or Indianapolis. But transportation costs in San Antonio are nearly $3,500 more a year than they are in San Francisco (and nearly *$5,000* more than in New York). Not a bargain at all.

The conclusion seems inescapable, at least to me. Though most Americans, and a very significant number of people around the world, will continue to depend on the automobile for commuting and shopping well into the foreseeable future, for a larger and larger number of people, the benefits of living in dense communities outweigh those of lightly populated suburbs. And now *they're* the ones voting

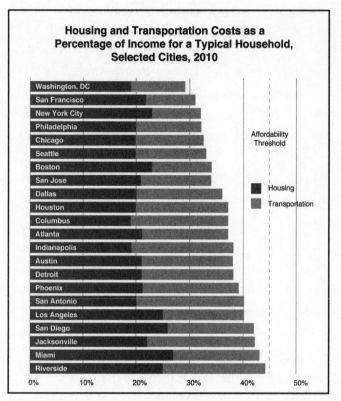

Housing and Transportation Costs as a Percentage of Income for a Typical Household, Selected Cities, 2010

When you add transportation costs to your budget, New York doesn't seem quite so expensive. *David Smucker (Sam Schwartz Engineering) and CityLab.*

with their wallets, moving to places that offer proximity and access instead of mobility. In fact, that's one reason the rents are higher in places with enough density to provide good mass transit: they're the most desirable places to live for an awful lot of affluent and well-educated people of all ages, but especially Millennials. The ones who are old enough to have completed college and are therefore most able to afford living in the most densely populated neighborhoods in the country are choosing to do so in record numbers. The percentage of twenty-five- to thirty-four-year-olds with a college degree living in close-in neighborhoods—those within three miles of a city's central business district—was 43 percent in 2000. By 2010, it was 55 percent. Meanwhile, college degrees were found in only about 35 percent of households outside the urban cores. It's not just that driving has become more unpleasant than it used to be—though it has—but that other alternatives are becoming *more* pleasant. Seen in this light, it looks a lot like the universal love affair with the automobile and everything that went with it was the historical anomaly: an accident of history.

After the Second World War, the United States occupied a historically unprecedented place in the world. While the entire planet had suffered through a decade and a half of depression and war, in 1945, America was the only place that was richer than when the whole mess started: more prosperous in absolute terms, and enormously wealthier than any other nation in Europe, Asia, or Africa. It also occupied a very sparsely populated continent, compared to anywhere in Europe and Asia. The temporary wealth advantage and the permanent geographical one combined to build the highways and the suburbs that defined America from the 1950s through the 1970s.

They continue to define the country today. The car isn't going away. One reason is that, as above, roads are—mostly—forever. All those suburban housing developments and sprawling municipalities were made possible by the automobile, and no one is going to walk away—pun intended—from a trillion-dollar investment. There's another reason, too, which is that people like cars. Or, more accurately, they like the *idea* of cars, the version of automobile travel that is a staple of thousands of hours of television commercials every year: families in their four-wheel-drive SUVs visiting and—a pet peeve of mine—driving on spots of unspoiled natural beauty. Testosterone-heavy drivers racing down uncongested and beautiful country roads, or performing controlled skids through urban traffic: "Professional driver on closed course. Do not attempt." Even though the reality rarely lives up to the dream, dreams matter. Though ideal car travel is, by definition, available only when everybody doesn't pursue it, that isn't going to change everybody's behavior.

The good news is that it doesn't have to. As we saw in Chapter 3, even the Millennials haven't stopped driving. They've just slowed down. No reasonable prediction suggests anything but a change at the margins: instead of 85 to 90 percent of all travel by automobile, perhaps "only" 75 percent or so.

But that 10 percent difference is hugely significant. It will determine how much of our national income should be invested in highways, and how much in subways; how much in sprawl, and how much in density. Entirely because of this marginal change, the future looks a lot more like the pre-automobile past. Only better. Easier to navigate, more accessible, and definitely safer, for pedestrians, transit users, *and* drivers. You know: smarter.

The consequences are gigantic, especially for the cities and towns that want to be part of that future. In the chapters that follow, we'll visit dozens of them that are remaking themselves as attractive choices for the growing number of people who have joined the street smart revolution.

CHAPTER 5

WALK ON BY

ANCESTRAL HUMANS DISCOVERED THE JOYS OF BIPEDAL WALKING something like four million years ago. The earliest known maps are about fourteen thousand years old. We started counting around twelve thousand years back, and writing things down maybe seven thousand years later. Which means that it only took about five millennia to come up with the term, "walk scores."

Actually, I should have written Walk Scores™. The Seattle-based Internet entrepreneurs Matt Lerner, Jesse Kocher, and Mike Mathieu founded Walk Score, Inc., in 2007, convinced that the ease of walking in a particular neighborhood could be quantified as a single number. Walk Score's scale ranges from 0 (Oro Grande, California, in the middle of the Mojave Desert, for example, is categorized by Walk Score as "car dependent," which may understate the case) to 100 (322 Eighth Avenue, in New York, the main office of Sam Schwartz Engineering, is rated a Walk Score "Walker's Paradise," not that I'm bragging). Walk Scores are now a feature on the real-estate website

Zillow as well as the websites of thousands of realtors. Millions of people access the service daily, using its mapping algorithm to discover how close a particular house or office is to amenities like parks, entertainment, and shopping.

The algorithm is a long way from perfect. Houses a block away from one another can have Walk Scores that are fifteen or twenty points apart. Though it's constantly improving, Walk Score's route calculations have sometimes assumed that pedestrians can literally walk on water to get to the nearest drugstore, and have a particularly hard time quantifying the difference between walking a quarter mile in flat-as-a-pancake Kansas City and along San Francisco's Filbert Street, which climbs thirty feet in every hundred.

The larger point about Walk Score, though, isn't its accuracy or even its methodology, but its success. Walk Score has demonstrated, if anyone needed further convincing, that walkability matters not just to urban planners and apostate traffic engineers, but to people looking for places to live and raise their families. Those people do so not just because a house or apartment in a walkable community makes for a pleasing lifestyle but because, since they're so sought after, they're also extremely good investments. Supply, meet demand.

And Walk Score is just the tip of the walkability-quantifying iceberg. The web-driven mapping company Maponics offers a tool called "Context Walkability" that provides walkability scores using data on everything from the complexity of intersections to crime, weather, and population density. Walkonomics and RateMyStreet are smartphone apps that quantify the walkability of hundreds of thousands of streets in the United States and United Kingdom based on user reviews. Walkability is also evaluated qualitatively using "walking audits" like PERS (for Pedestrian Environment Review System), which was developed by the UK's Transport Research Laboratory as a way of collecting and analyzing all the elements of the streets on which people—Londoners, at first, but PERS is now used worldwide—record crossings, routes, intersections, the width of sidewalks, and even feelings of safety while walking. Walkability is hot. As the song says, "Something's happening here."*

What it is, though, ain't exactly clear. About the only thing I know for sure about walking—other than that I like it myself—is that people want more of it. Survey after survey shows people want to live and work in walkable communities. They also want to shop there, which is why the people who sell them stuff are on board, too. A study of Toronto retailing showed that, in urban settings—that is, excluding covered malls and other retailing venues where virtually everyone arrives by car—the people who spend the most, and shop most frequently, arrive at their favorite stores on foot (and, occasionally, by bicycle). Another study demonstrated that, all other things being equal, walkable shopping areas in Los Angeles produced up to four times the sales of those in strip malls. There's a reason that retailers pay a premium for corner locations, and it isn't that drivers slow their cars down while turning: more pedestrians converging on your store equals more sales. Every way you slice the data confirms that what all the polls say is true: people want more walkability. Why, then, is there so little of it? Why is there such a mismatch between the supply of, and the demand for, walkable neighborhoods? Is it because, as one observer wrote, "Americans would like to live in places that don't really exist"?

Not really. They want to live in places that do exist, but there are far too few of them. This is one of the reasons that housing in San Francisco or New York or Washington, DC, is so expensive, and it's definitely the reason that living in the coolest—I mean the most walkable—parts of any city or town is the most expensive of all.

---

* For readers too young to have more than a vague familiarity with the phrase "something's happening here," it comes from the Buffalo Springfield song "For What It's Worth," which commemorates the 1966 curfew riots on one of the most walkable, and famous, streets in all of Los Angeles: the Sunset Strip.

Every point added to a Walk Score address correlates to an increase in property value of between $700 and $3,000, which can mean a bump of more than $30,000 even between those parts of town that are merely "very walkable" and those that qualify as "pedestrian paradises."

Which is a problem, but also an opportunity. By definition, only a few neighborhoods can be the *coolest* places to live. But that doesn't mean that we can't make everywhere *cooler.* All we have to do is change the way we think about streets.

>>>

Portland, Oregon, is the poster child for what has become known as *active transportation* in America—not just walking but bicycle commuting or even rollerblading, any kind of mobility that depends on human muscle power. This can make Portland's residents a little smug about the Rose City, but they've earned the right. Vehicle miles traveled have fallen 20 percent further in Portland than the US average, and the typical Portlander drives four miles less and eleven minutes less than the average American daily. Exhibit A (there will be more) is the Portland Bureau of Transportation's "Skinny Streets" program.

Skinny streets are just what they sound like: a reduction in the dimensions of roadways by modifying municipal standards. There are dozens of benefits for putting streets on this sort of diet, including increased safety, lower resurfacing costs, and even a reduction in heat re-radiation, which is one of the causes of what are known as "urban heat islands": metropolitan areas that are warmer than the areas surrounding them because of surfacing materials. Since the stuff used to pave roads and parking lots stores short-wave radiation from the sun, and then returns it with interest as heat, cities get hotter than they would otherwise be, which is not something we really need more of in an era of underlying global warming. But the best thing about skinny streets is that they promote active transportation, both by slowing down cars and by permitting the widening of sidewalks.

The campaign to put America's streets on a diet dates back to 1999, when a pedestrian advocate named Dan Burden published a fifty-two-page document titled *Street Guidelines for Healthy Neighborhoods* and set out, with illustrations and maps, recommendations for reducing the width of residential streets from the typical thirty-six feet (or more) recommended by the American Association of Highway and Transportation Officials to no more than twenty-eight feet, with parking on both sides.

A year later, in November 2000, the state of Oregon published their own version, *Neighborhood Street Design Guidelines: An Oregon Guide for Reducing Street Width*, complementing their adoption in 1991 of a Transportation Planning Rule that obliged governments to minimize street width wherever possible. And they did. A twenty-eight-foot-wide street with parking on both sides has room for only one traffic lane, which sounds crazy, but not in Portland, which has literally hundreds of miles of two-way streets on which drivers have to wait their turn to pass. These aren't farm roads; the Portland ordinance allows skinny streets in residential areas with densities of nearly nine homes per acre.

Road diets are not just a Portland obsession. San Francisco has completed the most road diet programs in the country—more than forty as of this writing. That includes Valencia Street, which was a four-lane road until 1999, when the traffic authorities got out their paint buckets and restriped the street with two traffic lanes, a center median that permitted left turns but no through traffic, and, for the first time, bike lanes.* In 2012, San Jose started implementing its own version of a road diet, part of a new plan for pedestrian

---

* The naysayers predicted an increase in bike collisions. They actually declined, despite a 144 percent increase in bicycle riding on the street.

safety, that turned half a dozen streets from one-way to two-way. The reason? For any given street width, traffic will be slower if it travels in two directions rather than one, and anything that slows traffic enhances walkability. As a bonus, two-way streets improve connectivity as well.

Well, of course, you might say. Portland and San Francisco are just the kind of places where you'd expect an irrational zeal for walk-and bike-ability. But that doesn't really explain Batesville, Arkansas, population a little more than 10,000. That's where Mayor Rick Elumbaugh, a one-time phys ed teacher in the Batesville Public Schools, is transforming the small town's Main Street by narrowing it to one lane with angled parking, and replacing traffic signals with curb extensions—building out the sidewalk at intersections, both to reduce pedestrian crossing distance and, because extensions prohibit parking, improve driver visibility—all on the advice of Dan Burden's Walkable and Livable Communities Institute.

Then there's Barcelona.

In June 2014, I got to cross Barcelona off my bucket list, when business brought me to the Catalonian city—yes, I know it's in Spain, but no one I met there seemed to identify themselves as Spanish—on the northeast corner of the Iberian peninsula. Like most Americans, I first saw Barcelona up close and personal on television, during the 1992 Olympics. It's probably a good thing for Catalonian tourism that most of us waited until then; everyone I met reminded me that it was a lot less attractive twenty-five years ago. The small beach was ugly, poorly maintained, and not used very much. Now? It's four times bigger, and the pride of the city.

The transformation of the city began with the slogan "Barcelona Posa't Guapa" (BPG) which translates as "Barcelona Be Pretty." Most slogans don't do much more than sell T-shirts, but this one was different. The Catalans had determined to beautify not only their capital city's physical appearance but their collective state of mind. Before the campaign, as one Barcelonés said to me, citizens would show their tempers as they drove: honking horns, yelling at each other, as if to reinforce every negative stereotype of Latin behavior. BPG enjoined them to calm down, to treat each other with civility. It may have succeeded, though you couldn't prove it by my experience; at least one driver did get out of his car and berate my cabbie for who knows what.

The infrastructure, though, was transformed.

While I was in Barcelona I met with Adria Civit, the city's equivalent of a transportation commissioner. In Barcelona, as everywhere, names matter, so when, a dozen years ago, they renamed the "Traffic" department as the department of "Mobility," it was a sign of a larger change. In Barcelona, walking (which is rarely considered a mode of transport anywhere) is considered "mobility," and it's monitored, measured, and reported in a Sustainable Mobility Plan that is issued every two years. In 2012, about half of trips in Barcelona longer than ten minutes were on foot or by bike, and only 26 percent of all travel was by car or motorbike. By 2018, Mr. Civit told me, they want to reduce that to 21 percent by increasing walking, biking, and transit, while simultaneously making car travel less attractive.

When I asked him how he intended to make cars less appealing, he answered with a three-part plan. First, lower speed limits. All one-way streets in Barcelona (and most of the others) have a speed limit of thirty kilometers per hour (not quite nineteen mph). Second, limit where cars can drive. The Portal de l'Àngel, in the Ciutat Vella shopping district, was converted into a pedestrian street thirty years ago. The initial reaction was less than enthusiastic, with residents and retailers panicking about lost business, but the neighborhood is now so popular that it has the highest rents in the entire country. "Then," he said, "threatening letters were sent to planners; now, if cars should come again, they'd shoot you."

For strategy number three, aimed at making the streets safer and more attractive to pedestrians, Adria leaned in and barely above a whisper said, "One of the secrets is this: narrow lane widths make people drive slower. I make the lanes very, very narrow."

Barcelona likes narrow lanes—and when I say narrow, I mean *narrow*: typically less than nine feet wide, and sometimes, when they really want to slow things down, less than eight. In the United States engineers typically press for traffic lanes that are twelve feet wide even in urban areas, though a few brave ones might get away with the occasional eleven- or even ten-foot width. *Bus lanes* in Barcelona are less than ten feet wide. Parking lanes are even narrower: six feet, seven inches. It made me feel vindicated for making the case back in 1986 for narrow nine-foot lanes on Williamsburg Bridge.

As always, programs intended to improve pedestrian and cyclist safety resulted in increasing active transportation. Those narrow lanes don't just make the sidewalks wider, they make the streets safer for everyone. But it isn't just about the lanes in Barcelona; crosswalks are set back ten to twenty feet from intersections so that turning vehicles can get a better look at pedestrians, and a flashing yellow light is angled so that drivers see it as they turn, reminding them the pedestrians have the right-of-way. In 2013, 168 pedestrians died in traffic collisions in New York City, population 8.4 million. In the same year, in the city of Barcelona, with a population of 1.6 million, the number was 10.

There are obviously a lot of important reasons to want to reduce collisions between pedestrians and cars, including saving hundreds of lives, and thousands of trips to emergency rooms. But one of them is improving walkability. Any initiative intended to promote walking or biking is a non-starter so long as pedestrians and cyclists don't feel safe. As a result, measures to slow cars down are a necessary part of any active transportation program. It's almost a law: the more you slow down cars, the more you increase walking. There is such a strong connection that when I talk about designing roads to slow down cars, I frequently get asked why we don't just lower the speed limit. That's when I get to explain the "85th percentile rule."

In traffic engineering, the 85th percentile rule holds that posted speed limits should be set to a speed that 85 percent of the drivers are at or below, based on clocking actual traffic movement. Or, put another way, if traffic engineers monitor a particular street that carries a hundred cars an hour, and eighty-five of them are traveling at or below thirty-five miles an hour, then that should be the posted speed limit. This also means, of course, that fifteen cars could be racing down the street at fifty mph. The 85th percentile rule (which has been around at least since 1964) is not just another way of ignoring the needs of everyone except motorized traffic; it's a way of letting drivers themselves decide what the posted speed limit ought to be, by their own behavior.

As you've already figured out, the 85th percentile rule virtually guarantees that one car in seven will be exceeding the speed limit at any time. And it strongly argues that just crossing out a sign's speed limit and replacing it with another won't get the job done. If 85 percent of the cars were traveling at or below thirty-five miles per hour before you changed the speed limit, they won't start traveling at twenty-five miles per hour just because the signs changed.

Nonetheless, there are proven ways to slow traffic down, using a suite of techniques known as *traffic calming*.* Drivers just naturally drive more slowly on a narrow street than on a wide one, similarly on narrow lanes versus wide lanes, and they slow down when they approach a roundabout or *chicane* (an unnecessary curve in the road) or when a speed hump is placed in their way, or when the curb is extended into traffic lanes at pedestrian crossings. That's why traffic-calming measures don't just reduce crashes—though they do, as much as 70 percent—but are associated with a 20 percent increase in walking. Traffic calming is a way of making the 85th percentile rule work

---

* It's actually a literal translation of the German word *Verkehrsberuhigung*, which is evidence for the European origins of both the term and most traffic-calming measures themselves.

on behalf of more than just lead-footed drivers. By changing driver behavior, it can change the speed limit, as well.

Calming traffic isn't the only tactic used to reduce the anxiety of pedestrians and so get them to walk more. Refuge islands, which are protected areas in the middle of multilane, two-way streets that allow pedestrians to cross one direction of traffic at a time, do the same thing, as do raised medians and even countdown timers at crosswalks, though they're usually insufficient. The most dangerous metropolitan areas in America for pedestrians—in order, Orlando, Tampa–St. Petersburg, Jacksonville, Miami–Fort Lauderdale, and Memphis—have some refuge islands and raised medians (to be fair, not very many) but there's only so much you can do to make a road carrying six to eight lanes of traffic traveling at more than forty miles per hour safe to cross, and these cities have a *lot* of them.

In any case, while making walking safer (both actually safer and *perceptibly* safer) is a necessary requirement for maximizing active transportation, it isn't really the entire story. It's like sidewalks themselves: people who live in neighborhoods with sidewalks are 47 percent more likely to meet the recommended exercise guideline of thirty minutes a day than those who don't. But to really put the activity back into transportation, the sidewalks need to be both *purposeful* and *pleasurable.* The best kind of active transportation promotes walking to places with some practical significance—shops, for example—and is designed so that people enjoy themselves getting there.

Practicality first. Walking and cycling are prevalent in cities with the highest Walk Scores—places like San Francisco or New York—less because of safety than utility. It's not just that these cities were built out before the automobile became the country's dominant form of transportation, which meant that their streets were built to a different scale than those of newer cities and suburbs. It's that they have constantly refreshed the number and quality of useful destinations within walking distance of where people live and work. The destinations change over the years—diners become wine bars, for example; peep shows on Broadway turn into Crate & Barrel outlets—but they usually don't disappear.

When they do disappear, however, or where they were never there in the first place, opportunities to improve walkability don't vanish. A lower starting point means greater potential for improvement. Pasadena, California, was once so car-centric that in 1915 it had the highest rate of automobile ownership in the world. But the city just northwest of Los Angeles is now planning to narrow portions of Colorado Boulevard—the route of the Tournament of Roses Parade, and where the Beach Boys' "little old lady from Pasadena" terrorized both pedestrians and other drivers. The plan is to shrink the boulevard, which carries up to twenty thousand cars daily, to as little as two lanes, with the space created used to widen sidewalks and build mini parks. Next door, in Eagle Rock, two lanes of Colorado Boulevard have already been converted into three miles of bicycle lanes and landscaped meridians. Results? The kind of development that attracts people to live in denser communities—theaters, restaurants, and shopping—is increasing so fast that three thousand new residential units have been built within two blocks of Colorado Boulevard in the last decade alone.

And Pasadena isn't the only place in Southern California with encouraging news about walkability.

>>>

More than fifty years after Walter O'Malley and the Dodgers moved west, I finally accepted that Los Angeles wasn't the enemy of all that was good and virtuous in the world. Or, more accurately, I realized why it wasn't, as I had originally thought, a bloodsucking vampire luring its victims with the promise of a carefree, sunny, and auto-centric culture. LA wasn't the vampire. It was the victim.

Eventually, even I figure things out.

My "aha!" moment came on a visit to the Los Angeles Department of Transportation in 2010 to meet with General Manager Rita Robertson. Hanging on the wall of the GM's office was a photograph of Broadway and 7th Street in downtown Los Angeles. The caption read: "The busiest intersection in the world." And I always thought it was another Broadway—the one in Times Square.

Broadway and 7th was once widely, and accurately, known as the crossroads of the entire western United States. Los Angeles's version of Broadway, then and now, was the only direct route into downtown Los Angeles from the north, and 7th Street the city's only direct east-west route. As a result, images of the intersection over the decades are an especially useful visual record of the modern history of traffic and transportation. A photo taken around 1910 shows sidewalks full of pedestrians, two streetcars, a horse-drawn cab, a steam-powered truck, and a single car, probably (it's hard to make out) a Model T Ford, which had been introduced only two years before. Another picture, from fourteen years later, is full to bursting with streetcars, dozens of cars, and even more pedestrians—not a surprise, since in 1924, when that photo in the general manager's office was taken, Broadway and 7th had 504,000 people crossing it every day. (For comparison's sake: 5th Avenue and 42nd Street in New York City then had about 400,000 crossings daily and Paris's Place de l'Opera, 384,000.) By 1930, the daily number in the LA intersection was more than 750,000.

It never hit that level again. Photos taken in 1938 and 1958 show a marked decrease in the number of pedestrians, and even cars. By the time someone took a picture in 1974, the overhead wires for LA's streetcars had vanished, as indeed had the street's foot traffic. The intersection that had once housed the city's landmark theaters and retailers was the next thing to a ghost town: made, and unmade by the automobile.

A century later, though, it just might find itself competing again for the title of the busiest pedestrian intersection in the world. With more than 3.8 million people spread over nearly five hundred square miles, and another 15 million in the Long Beach/Anaheim/Los Angeles County metropolitan area, LA is now the second most populous city in the country—and it has rediscovered walking. With a vengeance.

Eric Garcetti, the city's forty-second mayor, is certain of it.

The evolution of Los Angeles, from the archetype of a car-loving metropolis without walkable communities or even a real downtown to what might be the most forward-thinking transportation municipality in the United States, had been under way for some time before Mayor Garcetti took the oath of office in July of 2013. The largest public transit supplier in the metropolitan area, the Los Angeles County Metropolitan Transportation Agency and its Metro Rail subsidiary—the third largest such agency in the country, providing 1.6 million trips daily—runs seventy-three miles of light and heavy rail through eighty stations in three aboveground and two belowground lines, and has been doing so since 1990.* It is now the sixth busiest urban rail system in the country, measured by passengers per route mile.

LACMTA is a county agency, though. The Los Angeles Department of Transportation, the one with the 1924 photograph of the intersection of Broadway and 7th, reports to the mayor of the city of Los Angeles. And while the new mayor took office with a very long to-do list, including negotiating contracts with the city's municipal employees and fixing a huge number of budget problems, he also had transportation on the brain. Which was why I returned to Los Angeles

---

* Everything that goes around, comes around. Most of those lines follow routes once taken by the Pacific Electric Red Car and LA Railway Yellow Car streetcars, which were purchased and closed down in the Los Angeles version of the National City Lines conspiracy.

in 2014. He had hired my firm to help write a strategic transportation plan, one that would remake the streets of the City of the Angels.

It was a massive challenge. Los Angeles has more car-friendly asphalt than any city in the world: 7,500 miles of roads, nearly 15 percent of the city's 486 square miles (and that's without counting the city's nearly twenty freeways, eight of them part of the Interstate Highway System). Mayor Garcetti wanted those streets to be smarter, so he decided to make them walkable.

The demand was there. Where Angelenos *could* walk, they walked a lot. Santa Monica's Third Street Promenade had been closed to automobile traffic since the 1960s. Farmer's Market in LA's Fairfax district, since the 1930s. Both were packed with people shopping, strolling, and hanging out seven days a week. The heart of Los Angeles's downtown—yes, Broadway and 7th—is a Walk Score "walker's paradise." So is the West Hollywood area around Melrose Boulevard. Pasadena's Colorado Boulevard and Los Angeles's Echo Park neighborhood aren't far behind. Garcetti wanted to provide the same level of walkability found in Los Angeles's most pedestrian-friendly locales in as many other neighborhoods as he could.

As we've seen, walkability can't happen until streets are safe—and LA's weren't. The project we began working on in 2013, and which became the mayor's signature transportation program, started by recognizing that nearly half of Los Angeles's traffic fatalities were pedestrians and cyclists. Even worse, the number of children and the elderly who were killed by cars while walking was double the national average.

The answer? Vision Zero, a commitment to reducing pedestrian traffic fatalities by 100 percent—to making them vanish. We redesigned a Safe Routes to School program, proposed a system of re-timed signals, and introduced Los Angeles to "continental (or 'zebra') crosswalks": prominent two-foot-wide stripes parallel to the traffic flow, alerting drivers that they are approaching a pedestrian crossing.

All of the proven traffic-calming measures, from extended sidewalks to skinny streets, are now being implemented in different LA neighborhoods. At a few locations, the city is even reintroducing diagonal crossings: "scrambles" that allow pedestrians at all corners of an intersection to cross simultaneously and in any direction, including diagonally across the center of the intersection. Because diagonal crossings stop traffic from all directions, they can reduce crashes by as much as 50 percent.

We also proposed a number of ways of making bicycles more useful for Los Angeles's millions of bus riders, not just by extending the city's longest existing bike path along the Los Angeles River but by adding bike racks to the buses operated by the LA Department of Transportation, including the DASH (fifty cents a ride, twenty-five cents for seniors), Commuter Express, and CityRide systems, responsible for twenty-five million trips a year. Our plan also called for bike racks at transit hubs.*

But the big deal, to the mayor, the media, and to us, was the Great Streets Initiative. Part of it was literally that: identifying fifteen different LA streets that weren't—yet—Pasadena's Colorado Boulevard or Santa Monica's Third Street Promenade, and adding the kind of traffic-calming architecture and zoning improvements that will make them appealing as places to work and play, not merely drive through. Garcetti understands that street-level improvements don't just improve the streets themselves but revitalize the entire surrounding neighborhood. By investing in a one-mile stretch of Lankershim Boulevard in LA's San Fernando Valley, the city can expand the existing—and successful—NoHo Arts District. "Great Streeting"

---

* Our work on the strategic plan wasn't exclusively devoted to walkability. The plan also proposed improving the city's use of Transportation Demand Management computer systems; transformation in the city's systems for truck freight management, including designated routes and parking for trucks; and an advanced modeling simulation system for special events. However, *all* of them were intended to improve the safety and appeal of the city's streets.

Crenshaw Boulevard pushes the vitality of the Hyde Park neighborhood farther south. The program that targets Central Avenue in the heart of Los Angeles's South Central district is intended to revive the city's historic Jazz Corridor, and the Dunbar Hotel, where Chico Hamilton and Charlie Mingus used to play.

Another component of Great Streets, the mayor's "People St" initiative, may turn out to be the most successful of all. Residents can now, by simple application, ask the city to build three different sorts of public spaces on existing streets. *Plazas*, for example, convert underused street space into public areas furnished with tables and seating. *Parklets* are smaller versions of the same idea: liberating two or three street parking spaces, and transforming them into twenty-foot-long (or longer) spaces, each the width of a parking space, complete with benches, planters, tables, and even shade trees or umbrellas. *Bike corrals* use the same footprint as parklets for bike racks, which encourage cycling, and preserve sidewalks for walking. All of the People St initiatives remake LA's streets and punctuate the city's sidewalks with potentially hundreds, or eventually even thousands, of spaces for people-friendly seating.

A number of commentators have noted the resemblance between Mayor Garcetti's Great Streets (or, at least, his vision for them) and the traditions of street life in Latin America. *Latino Urbanism* (a phrase coined by James Rojas, a city planner from East Los Angeles) is a catchall term for the ways in which public and private space get blurred in Mexican, Central American, and South American cities, and Great Streets is seen by some as a *norteamericano* version of the same thing. There are even those who see Garcetti, the mayor of a city that's half Latino, and a man whose paternal grandfather was born in Mexico, as especially hospitable to that kind of streetscape.

I'm not sure they shouldn't also recognize that Eric Garcetti's other grandfather was a Russian Jewish immigrant, who took a similar route to America as the fathers and mothers in my own stick-ball-playing, street-peddler-welcoming neighborhood in Brooklyn.*

Los Angeles trying to look more like Brooklyn? Walter O'Malley must be rolling in his grave. Which is just one more reason to like Eric Garcetti.

>>>

Twenty-two hundred miles east of Los Angeles, and light-years away in climate, economy, and lifestyle, Columbus, Ohio, is joining the same street smart revolution.

Ohio's capital is also the state's most populous city, though that still doesn't crack the country's top ten. Home to about eight hundred thousand people in the city proper, with another million-and-a-half in the surrounding suburbs, Columbus is, in the words of one local business leader, "big enough to have scale, and small enough to do something with it." It's a prosperous and pretty place, with a dozen neighborhoods crisscrossed by half a dozen rivers and creeks, lots of local employment from large and small corporations, and, of course, Ohio State University. It consistently wins awards from magazines like *Forbes*, and organizations like Relocate America. And, for anyone who believes that active transportation is happening only in the usual suspects on either coast, Columbus is a powerful counterargument.

For one thing, Columbus has embraced the gospel of *Complete Streets*, an umbrella term for transportation policies that invert the old order that gave first (usually the only) priority in street design to the speed and convenience of automobile travel. Complete Streets

---

* It could be that a liking for pedestrian-friendly streetscapes is a heritable characteristic—except, of course, that just about everywhere we build streets that are as friendly to walkers as they are to cars, people embrace them, no matter where their grandparents came from.

are streets where the needs of pedestrians and cyclists are just as important as those of automobiles and buses. As with so much else in the world of active transportation, Oregon was the first state to pass a policy explicitly promoting Complete Streets back in 1971. Fifteen more states (and more than five hundred cities and towns) have followed. The basics of Complete Streets should sound familiar by now: sidewalks, crosswalks, curb cuts, traffic calming, dedicated bike lanes and bike parking, dedicated bus lanes.

In 2008, Columbus jumped into the Complete Streets movement with both—you should excuse the expression—feet. In fact, they were halfway there already, with extensive support for the city's smallest pedestrians through programs like "Walk Smart to School" and "Safe Routes to School," plus a bikeways plan, a repaving program for the city's sidewalks, curb ramps called "Operation Safewalks," and many others. Since then, they've been aggressively converting streets from one-way to two-way as part of the region's own road diet and improving both bikeways and pedestrian routes.

But the most interesting thing Columbus is doing to promote active transportation is the Columbus Healthy Places program, CHP for short.

CHP was established in 2006 explicitly to use the tools of active transportation to address Columbus's obesity problem—a substantial one, with higher levels of dangerous obesity than the US average, and far fewer than the average percentage of residents walking to work, or even walking at all. One source of the problem was the city's growth history. The old city, about forty-two square miles of dense, relatively walkable neighborhoods, started to annex surrounding land in the 1950s. As a result, most of its current 227 square miles are made up of cul-de-sacs, other low-density streets that don't connect, and even farms. One of the best-documented positive correlations in the world of public health is the one between sprawl and a higher average Body Mass Index—the number that measures the relative relationship between height and weight, a kind of Walk Score for obesity. Columbus was no exception. Growing larger led to, well, growing larger: 59 percent of the city's adults are obese or overweight, as are 38 percent of its third-graders.

CHP was created to increase active transportation in Columbus. The transportation and public health officials responsible for implementing it decided early on that the low-hanging fruit for Columbus walkability wasn't improving safety, so much as usefulness: the city needed to make it more practical to walk or bike to somewhere useful, and figured out a way to enlist the city's buildings department in the effort. They persuaded the department to grant them an opportunity to comment on all requests from developers to rezone a particular bit of land. They used that opportunity to propose that any new development that contained *trip generators*—shopping centers, bus stops, schools, parks, libraries, drugstores, or supermarkets—within half a mile of homes or apartments also include a suite of active transportation elements: bike racks, for example, connections to existing bikeways, and wider sidewalks connecting the trip generator to Columbus residences. And it worked. When the program began, only 7 percent of applications included active transportation structures before a Columbus Healthy Places review; afterward the number jumped to 64 percent. The greater the proximity of a desirable destination to an existing residence, the wider the sidewalks proposed. After sixty years of sprawl, Columbus is embracing density and promoting walkability.

And not just within the city proper. More than a thousand acres in the middle of Dublin, a suburb seventeen miles from Columbus, have been rezoned to create something called the Bridge Street district. In the middle of it is Bridge Street Park, which not only includes a pedestrian bridge across the Scioto River (cost: $14 million; value for pedestrian safety: priceless) but connects 150 condominiums and 650 apartments with two hundred thousand square feet of office space, ten restaurants, and sixty thousand feet of retail space, all within less than half a mile of one another, explicitly intended to persuade thousands of people to get where they're going on foot.

>>>

Using active transportation policies to combat obesity is the social version of all those individual health benefits from walking and cycling you got tired of reading about back in Chapter 4. In all industrialized countries, but particularly in the United States, the leading causes of death aren't infections or accidents, but non-communicable diseases like diabetes, stroke, and cardiovascular disease, which are responsible for something like thirty-six million deaths annually, and probably 80 percent of *all* preventable deaths. A sizeable chunk of those preventable deaths is due to inadequate exercise; that is, not achieving thirty minutes of moderate exercise a day.

Lots of things determine any *individual's* level of activity. One person might be a devoted runner, another a couch potato. Some families live in a climate where everyone spends most of the year outdoors; others are snowbound for months at a time. Some sixty-seven-year-olds spend two hours a day playing tennis and doing yard work (I just do the tennis); some teenagers spend six in front of a computer screen. But one thing that is almost certain to determine a *society's* level of activity is the kind of environment that it builds. As my friend and colleague Karen Lee puts it, "Individual decisions and society's choices are complementary."

She should know. Karen is about the smartest person I know on how what we choose to build affects our health. A physician and an epidemiologist with advanced degrees and scholarly research that take pages to list, she spent seven years directing New York's Built Environment Program, and is now senior advisor of Built Environment and Healthy Housing at the city's Department of Health and

Mental Hygiene. There she, along with Transportation Commissioner Janette Sadik-Khan, a bona fide transportation rock star, led the work on the city's 2010 Active Design Guidelines, which have become a model for designing buildings, roads, and neighborhoods that promote activity, especially active transportation.*

The guidelines should sound familiar by now, recommending, among other things, "accessible, pedestrian-friendly streets with high connectivity, traffic calming features, lighting, benches, and water fountains [and] developing continuous bicycle networks and incorporating infrastructure like safe indoor and outdoor bicycle parking." There is such broad consensus on these sorts of things that, as Karen Lee reminded me, "*not* doing anything is a contradiction of every bit of evidence we have."

The Guidelines don't limit themselves to urban design—those portions of the built environment in public spaces like roads, sidewalks, and bikeways. They also address the "micro" side of active transportation, which is something that transportation engineers tend to forget: the way we design the interiors of our buildings. Thus, the Active Design Guidelines also call for "providing a conveniently located stair for everyday use, posting motivational signage to encourage stair use, and designing visible, appealing, and comfortable stairs . . . [locating] appealing, supportive walking routes within buildings . . . showers, locker rooms, secure bicycle storage, and . . . exteriors that contribute to a pedestrian-friendly urban environment . . . [with] multiple entries, stoops, and canopies."

The document is as specific as a blueprint: in order to qualify for full credit—similar to the kind of LEED (Leadership in Energy and Environmental Design) credits for Physical Activity Innovation

---

* New York's success story is one worth spreading, which is why Karen founded Dr. Karen Lee Health+Built Environment Consulting, which advises local and state governments and other organizations on using environmental interventions and policies to address the global epidemics of obesity and chronic disease. See www.drkarenlee.com.

that builders get for environmentally sustainable elements like so-
lar panels—an Active Design Guidelines building should "position at
least one stair before access to elevators from the main building lobby,
along the principal path of travel [and] a maximum of 25 feet travel
and no turns should be required to reach stairs from the building's
main entrance." The Cable Building in New York's SoHo, where I had
my office for seventeen years, was a fine example: it had a grand wide
staircase just inside the entrance, but you had to walk to the back of
the building to find the elevators.

It's easy to make fun of the obsessive precision used in writing
any kind of design guidelines, but in this case they're really on to
something. In study after study, researchers have found that people
choose between stairs and elevators (or escalators) based on how easily they see them in their peripheral vision—or, as the academic research puts it, "the area of visibility in the horizontal plane opposite
to the direction of travel."* A systematic review of eleven different
studies on prompts for choosing stairs over elevators or escalators—
signs on the health or weight-loss benefits of stair climbing—showed
an average relative increase in stair use of nearly 50 percent everywhere prompts were used, from shopping malls to bus stations, airports, office buildings, and university libraries. It turns out that active
transportation doesn't just happen outdoors; it can be successfully
promoted indoors, too.

New York's success at promoting walking and biking wasn't
achieved without friction. This is New York we're talking about, after
all, though the action-reaction sequence is so universal that it's practically a law of transportation engineering. Step one: a pedestrian plaza
is proposed. Step two: local merchants and residents object, sometimes ferociously. Step three: the street is pedestrianized. Step four:
the merchants' businesses are not destroyed, but enhanced. Step five:

---

* The technical term for the space visible from a given point is the *isovist*. You have
now learned your word for the day.

hardly anyone can remember what the original objections were, and even fewer of them would willingly return to the status quo. It happens just about everywhere: before the sheepish smiles, the violent shouting. Like most things in New York, it just happened at a slightly higher volume.

Luckily, though, the shouters had a formidable voice responding to them.

In 2009 a colleague of mine, Charlie Komanoff, asked if I was jealous of Janette Sadik-Khan, the transportation commissioner appointed by then-mayor Michael Bloomberg. Without hesitation I said, "Damn straight, I am." She was doing things I had just dreamed about or had to abort: creating pedestrian plazas, adding physically separated bicycle lanes on Manhattan avenues (mine, implemented in September 1980, were ordered removed in November after Mayor Ed Koch, riding in President Jimmy Carter's limousine, watched as Governor Hugh Carey told the president to look out the window at the unused bike lanes, saying, "See how Ed is pissing away your money") and speeding buses through the densest parts of the city with a form of Bus Rapid Transit.* I swallowed my jealousy and helped and supported Janette throughout. And she needed the support.

Before her appointment in 2007, Janette had already spent fifteen years preparing for the job. She was a member of the Mayor's Office of Transportation during the administration of David Dinkins, had served as deputy administrator at the Federal Transit Administration, and as a globe-trotting executive for the engineering firm Parsons Brinckerhoff.

I knew we had something in common when she hit the front pages in 1993 for cracking down on UN diplomats over—what else?—

---

* The term is a little imprecise, but true BRT systems are distinguished from traditional bus lines when they feature some or all of the following: dedicated right-of-way, onboard fare collection, and priority at signaled intersections. In the best of them, stations are placed in the middle of the roadway rather than at the curbsides, and have raised platforms, level with the bus floors.

unpaid parking tickets. During her tenure as transportation commissioner she was an advocate for all forms of active transportation (building more than 285 miles of bike lanes, among other things) and for congestion pricing. Others have noted that she was generally regarded as a very capable public servant with a gift for abrasiveness, which doesn't remind me of anyone in particular. But it's her signature achievement that is closest to my heart. In 2007, she began the process of turning Times Square—Broadway between 42nd to 47th Streets—into a pedestrian mall.

It's impossible to overstate the level of vitriol leveled at this idea specifically, and Janette generally. Cindy Adams, the gossip columnist at *The New York Post*, started reflexively referring to her as the "wacko nutso bike commissioner." She was reviled as a Trotskyite and a Nazi. She had run-ins with the police commissioner, state legislators, and virtually every member of the New York City Council. Dire predictions piled up: Traffic congestion would reach nightmarish proportions. The theaters, restaurants, and shops on or near Times Square would be destroyed. Putting hundreds of thousands of pedestrians and tens of thousands of cars on the same half acre of asphalt at the same time would fill every emergency room in the city.

Instead, however, the disaster predicted for what both its supporters and opponents called "Broadway Boulevard" never occurred. Just the opposite, in fact:

- Traffic didn't slow down. It sped up. Cars traveling northbound through West Midtown (where the pedestrian plaza was) got where they were going 17 percent faster than they did when they tried the same trip through East Midtown (where the pedestrian plaza wasn't). Same deal southbound, eastbound, and westbound. Same deal for buses as for cars.
- Times Square didn't get more dangerous, but safer. A lot safer. Injuries to motorists and passengers dropped 63 per-

cent. Injuries to pedestrians declined by 25 percent, probably because a whopping 80 percent fewer pedestrians were
now walking in the Times Square roadway.

- Even so, pedestrian volume was way up. So were restaurant,
  entertainment, and souvenir dollars. So are rents. The Times
  Square Alliance surveyed its members, primarily the area's
  local merchants, and found that 74 percent of them said
  that the pedestrian mall improved the quality of life in the
  neighborhood.
- It definitely improved the quality of the air. The two pollutants most closely associated with automobile traffic—
  nitrogen oxide and nitrogen dioxide—were measured before
  and after Janette's pedestrian mall opened. Before, the con-
  centrations of the two pollutants were among the highest
  in the city. After? Nitrogen oxide levels fell by 63 percent,
  nitrogen dioxide by 41 percent.

But don't take my word for it. Tim Tompkins of the Times Square
Alliance is just one of "the employees and New Yorkers who are
here every single day, eighty percent of whom support the Broadway
plazas."

≫≫≫

My hometown may lead the way in using active transportation policies to address obesity (thank you, Michael Bloomberg and Janette
Sadik-Khan) but it's not alone. Another, even higher-profile attempt
to use transportation policy to combat obesity is under way somewhere wildly different from both Columbus and New York: Oklahoma City.

Mick Cornett took office as mayor of Oklahoma City in March
of 2004, but it wasn't until the end of 2007 that he put his entire

city, then ranked as the eighth most obese city in the country, on a diet. Literally. The website thiscityisgoingonadiet.com launched in early 2008, shortly after Mayor Cornett had lost more than forty pounds himself.

It was, as they say, only the beginning.

The mayor's signature program, announced in mid-2007, was MAPS 3, the third in a series of Metropolitan Area Projects that had previously included building a basketball arena, a fifteen-thousand-seat minor-league baseball park, a new library, and dozens of new school buildings. MAPS 3 was the same, only more so. And most of the "more so" was intended to promote active transportation. MAPS 3 included two new parks, one of forty acres, the other thirty, connecting downtown Oklahoma City with the Oklahoma River; between twenty-five and thirty-six miles of new sidewalks; and nearly thirty-five miles of bike paths and walking trails. And, while I'm not sure this actually qualifies as active transportation, MAPS 3 upgraded the banks of the Oklahoma River to accommodate both rowing and kayaking facilities.*

It also called for a state-of-the-art streetcar system running on five miles of rails through Oklahoma City's downtown, which isn't, strictly speaking, a form of active transportation. However, a meta-analysis—a research technique that combines multiple investigations, giving different statistical weights to each one depending on its findings—of fifty different studies found that one of the most important factors in walkability was connectivity: the ease with which walkers could get from one street to another. Streetcars that run regularly on routes perpendicular to walking routes make it a *lot* easier for pedestrians to get where they need to go.

One of the more satisfying things about MAPS 3—to me, anyway—is that most of it is being built on space that used to be occupied

---

* A stretch? Agreed. But kayaking is certainly transportation, and definitely muscle-powered.

by an Interstate highway, in this case the portion of I-40 known as the Oklahoma City Crosstown Expressway, which was built in the early 1960s and ran right through the city's downtown. When it was demolished and rerouted out of the city center in the 1990s, more than 750 acres were made available for remaking one of the most auto-centric cities in the country in a more pedestrian-friendly way— or, as Mayor Cornett told *StreetsBlog USA*, Oklahoma City was designed, perversely, as a city where no one ever has to walk anywhere. "In fact," he said, "you *can't* walk anywhere!"

Here's another thing about MAPS 3. Though Mayor Cornett is probably best known for promoting the active transportation features of MAPS 3 as an anti-obesity program, the way he actually makes the case to his mostly suburbanite constituents is telling them, "We're creating a city where your kid and grandkid are going to choose to live." He understands, as every mayor and city manager in the country is starting to discover, that if places like Oklahoma City—or Columbus or Portland—don't build the kind of city that Millennials want to live in, they're going to leave.

The same phenomenon is at work just about everywhere. In late 2014, I joined about five hundred people in Tampa at a group ride celebrating the inauguration of its bikeshare system, Coast Bikes. (Full disclosure: we are consultants to Coast.) After riding with Tampa's mayor, Bob Buckhorn—we'd met before, accidentally, while walking (of course) in downtown Tampa, before Bob was even a candidate for mayor—we chatted, and he told me that he wants his two daughters to remain in Tampa after they are grown, which is why he's making Tampa into the kind of city that is adapting to the Millennial generation. Whenever I'm brought into a mostly car-dependent community to improve transportation, this argument is my most powerful weapon. A few people in my typical audience seem moved by talk of a healthier city. Some—not too many—act like they care about clean air or the joys of walking and biking. But when I say, "I'm not here to get you to change your behavior. But, if you don't want to *lose your children* you had better change your town's streetscape," everyone wakes up. They don't applaud—this is scary—but they start to nod in agreement.

Which is why this is another place to remind ourselves that the relationship between active transportation and the built environment—all those sidewalks, traffic-calming measures, streetcars, parks, and even dense multiuse communities—is complicated. People still walk and bike in places that are dangerous and unpleasant, and they drive in places where they seemingly don't need to. Some Millennials can't wait to park their pickup trucks in front of a suburban house, and lots of their parents are moving to inner cities. But the greater the number of people choosing to live in more compact communities, the better for everyone. In the same way that the Oklahoma City suburbs are better places to raise children when downtown Oklahoma City is more attractive to young adults, the whole country enjoys a better quality of life when it improves the walkability of as many neighborhoods as possible.

>>>

Just as there's a science of walkability, there's a science of walking. If you thought people just put one foot in front of another, think again. There's a lot of empirical research on walking, and not just the way in which the thighbone is connected to the knee bone, a subject that was on my mind a lot after I had arthroscopic knee surgery in the summer of 2014. People have been measuring, analyzing, and modeling the way people walk ever since the original gurus of scientific management, Frederick Winslow Taylor and the husband-and-wife team of Frank and Lillian Gilbreth,* performed the first time-motion

---

* Yup: the same couple who inspired the original *Cheaper by the Dozen.*

studies to see how best to organize assembly-line work at the end of the nineteenth century.

Decades later, William H. Whyte—"Holly" to everyone who knew him—graduated from reporting on business organizations for *Fortune* and writing business bestsellers like *The Organization Man* (this million seller from 1956 is where the term *groupthink* was coined) to discover his true calling: describing the way people behaved and moved in public places. In the 1960s, under contract to the New York City Planning Commission, he ran something called the Street Life Project, eventually documenting his findings in two terrific books: *The Social Life of Small Urban Spaces* (1980) and especially *City: Rediscovering the Center* (1988).

Both his books, and the time-lapse photography that accompany them, are full of insights about walking. Twenty years of close observation, notebook in hand and photographic team alongside, produced familiar gems like what Holly Whyte called "the false goodbye," which is what happens when one person starts to leave an encounter, only to return to it (this is also known as "getting the last word in"), or the way people will start a stationary conversation in the middle of a busy sidewalk. One of Holly's disciples, a one-time urban geographer turned marketing consultant named Paco Underhill, made a huge name for himself advising retailers how best to organize the aisles of their stores, based on quantifying the results from dozens of Whyte-like hidden cameras (sample insight: "The faster people walk, the narrower their field of peripheral vision becomes").

Holly visited me quite a few times when I was traffic commissioner. He would show me slides of Fifth Avenue and Lexington Avenue. The photos showed congested streets with lots of pedestrians. It didn't look like much could be done about improving the avenues without sacrificing someone. Then he produced a graph showing people moved on foot versus people moved by car. The bar graph for pedestrians was several times higher than the one for cars even though the area for pedestrians was only a fraction of that reserved for cars. Then he pointed out that the curb lane was occupied by parked cars—all were of an official nature belonging to government, diplomats, or clergy. That number was a small fraction compared to the occupants in moving cars and paled next to walkers. It was obvious: there was a way for almost everybody to win. Holly said, "Get rid of the parkers, widen the sidewalks by the width of a lane and you still have the same number of moving lanes so the traffic moves as well or as poorly as before."

I took his advice to heart. I eliminated all the "free" parking on Fifth Avenue, including the military, a score of diplomats (which got me invited to the UN), some government workers, and a cardinal of the Catholic Church. This did not win me many friends. I planned to widen the sidewalks on Fifth and create a Champs-Élysées-like boulevard. Alas, my time at the NYC DOT ran out as a new mayor, David Dinkins, did not reappoint me.

At around the same time that people like Holly Whyte were applying the tools of anthropology to studying the way people walked, the world of transportation engineering took an interest. It was a long time coming, probably because people on foot are a whole lot harder to quantify than they are when in automobiles, buses, or trains. To this day, most of the engineering standards for foot traffic lead back to the work of a single guy, John J. Fruin, an engineer working for the Port Authority of New York and New Jersey, who wrote half a dozen books and monographs on pedestrian planning and design during the 1970s.

Almost everyone who followed Fruin used his numbers, both for pedestrian and walkway size. To Fruin, humans weren't complicated assemblies of trillions of highly evolved cells, but ellipses roughly thirteen inches deep by twenty-three inches wide. That dimension is why we need about two-and-a-half square feet of space to avoid unwanted contact, and prefer a bubble of personal space of between five and ten square feet. For the same reason, people in motion need

an additional seven inches of lateral space—thirty inches in total—
to allow walking abreast without touching, and between eight and
ten feet longitudinally. That is, if you're walking on an unimpeded
street and following a stranger at a distance of six feet, or alongside
at a distance of less than two-and-a-half feet, both of you will start
to feel uncomfortable.

Fruin also showed that pedestrians, when they don't have something in the way, move at between 150 and 250 feet per minute,
which means that walking at the preferred speed, all other things
being equal, demands around thirty-five square feet per person. This
is what we prefer, but isn't actually the maximum flow that a path
can carry. When there's only around five square feet per person,
we're forced into a staggering walk, moving at less than 100 feet per
minute—but there are so many of us that a sidewalk full of shuffling
pedestrians is moving at full, though uncomfortable, capacity.

This can be expressed in a fairly simple set of equations.[*] However,
they aren't just simple, they're simplistic. They assume that people on
foot behave like water in a hose. But uniform flow isn't the norm for
pedestrians. Stopping and queueing is inevitable. Swerving to avoid
collision is constant, as are the fits and starts caused by crosswalks
and traffic lights. Short-term fluctuations of flow—what engineers call
platooning, which is what occurs when pedestrians cluster either vol-
untarily (as in tour groups or school field trips) or circumstantially (as
when a bus discharges passengers onto a sidewalk)—can turn a nice
even flow into an unmoving crush.[†] Which is one reason that these

---

[*] The so-called fundamental equation (sometimes the fundamental diagram) for traffic flow is usually expressed as $f = s/a$ where f is the volume of pedestrians per square
foot, s is their average speed, and a is the area used by the pedestrians within the
traffic stream.

[†] Engineers who are hired to figure out how much space is needed in the real world
often use a different model, the time-space method, in which the supply of time and
space is divided by the time/space demand, that is, the total number of pedestrians using the space—for walking, waiting, window shopping, ticket purchasing, you
name it—in a given amount of time, such as fifteen minutes.

density equations are not just important but can be a matter of life and death. At some densities a mass of pedestrians becomes dangerous, even deadly. This wasn't just a matter of intellectual interest; "human stampedes" at places like soccer stadiums, train stations, and concert halls kill hundreds of people annually. As Fruin was one of the first to realize, when crowd densities are great enough to compress bubbles of personal space to something below about two square feet per person, a crowd of individuals is transformed into a solid mass, capable of transmitting shock waves that have enough compressive force to literally tear clothing off and even to kill, usually by asphyxiation. In April of 1989, for example, ninety-six people were killed (and nearly eight hundred injured) as tens of thousands of fans crowded into a tunnel during a soccer match at Hillsborough Stadium in Sheffield, England.

Calculating speed-density relationships for both safety and convenience is complicated. A bunch of people walking on a sidewalk is what physicists call a *self-organizing system*. Pedestrians in such systems can oscillate between chaotic masses and relatively organized "lanes" of foot traffic that are nearly as vulnerable to traffic jams as automotive roadways, depending on dozens of factors, including the composition of the pedestrian population; commuters, for example, walk at different speeds than tourists. People walk faster when they're wearing headphones, but slower when talking on cell phones (or smoking), and they are likely to stop traffic when they check their phones before entering a building. Even culture matters. Given the same density, Indians and Germans walking on the same sidewalks move at different speeds, probably because members of societies where no one minds bumping into another walker are untroubled by very high densities. This doesn't mean that it's impossible to model pedestrian behavior with any accuracy, but it does mean that it's not for amateurs.

One of the real pros, probably the world's best-known anthropologist of walking, is another of Whyte's followers, my friend Jeff

Zupan. Jeff has been one of the go-to guys on pedestrian behavior ever since he and his colleague Boris Pushkarev wrote a book entitled *Urban Space for Pedestrians* in 1975. If talking with Jeff is the best introduction imaginable to the nuances of pedestrian behavior, *walking* with him is a master class. The latest version of the *Highway Capacity Manual* of the Transportation Research Board tries to quantify so-called *shy distance*—a concept from the automobile world referring to the space between vehicles as they pass—in order to calculate the appropriate level-of-service for a properly designed sidewalk. (I said the engineers had finally taken an interest in walking.) According to the HCM, the proper shy distance on a sidewalk is between twelve and eighteen inches, and two-and-a-half feet should be allowed between a curb and an obstacle in order to let a pedestrian pass between them. But as Jeff demonstrates, people will start to swerve as much as seventeen feet before they are about to hit an obstacle. He can explain how many people will cross to a shady side of the street, or to a sunny side, depending on the temperature. Or how they will form a mass while crossing a street, and how soon they will disperse into lanes afterward. He knows how long a queue will remain organized without crowd-control stanchions. Jeff is, literally, a walking encyclopedia.

A few years back, some very smart computer types got the idea that the insights and knowledge inside the heads of people like John Fruin and Jeff Zupan could be turned into software programs that could analyze and illustrate the effect of different design choices on pedestrian behavior. As engineers, we use such programs to simulate everything from five hundred people arriving at a hospital to ten thousand people walking down a suburban street, from a hundred thousand people attending a football game to a million evacuating a city in the event of a disaster.* This is not an exaggeration: these programs can simulate a million pedestrians who remember previous

---

* Two very popular programs are Legion ("Science in Motion") and MassMotion ("Your Ideas Brought to Life").

routes, learn which ones offer the best compromise among directness, comfort, and speed, and adapt accordingly. They can assign individual tasks to (potentially) hundreds of thousands of animated "avatars." Some stop for a cup of coffee, or to check a smartphone. Some are fast, some slow; some have a preference for escalators, others for stairs (or elevators). Once our engineers input data on origins and destinations, thousands of avatars appear to decide on their own routes through multilevel landscapes like transit stations or sports stadiums.

They're as mesmerizing as any video game ever invented. And they're extremely effective in designing walkable environments. But, maybe even more important, they're a great way of explaining to the people who will be deciding on those environments how they'll encourage the best and safest pedestrian experience. As, for example, in the city of Chicago.

In 2011, Sam Schwartz Engineering was selected to be lead consultant on the Chicago Pedestrian Plan, a full-court press on active transportation in one of the world's largest cities, led by the Chicago Department of Transportation (CDOT). We began by recognizing that literally everyone is a pedestrian at some point during the day, and that they probably knew as much (or more) as we did about the pedestrian needs of the city. We conducted Walkshops™, which are combination workshops conducted as we walk a particular site. I find these to be invaluable, since they occur at the point that we, the community and the engineers, are seeing the same thing at the same time. And we, along with the CDOT, hosted seven neighborhood meetings at which we asked participants to let us know what they thought about the positives and negatives of being a pedestrian in Chicago. Ask and ye shall receive; in our case, more than five hundred ideas for improving the lives of pedestrians, from safer street crossings, to sidewalks that would permit pedestrian access to shopping centers without walking through parking lots, to more footbridges over the Chicago River.

We got to work. A year later, we had a plan.

Some of the sixteen tools that emerged for improving the safety and livability of Chicago's streets won't come as a surprise: refuge islands; pedestrian countdown clocks; marking crosswalks with painted bars or, where affordable, brick; road diets and skinny streets; horizontal traffic-calming tools like chicanes and traffic circles, and vertical ones like speed humps and speed tables. Others included changing the electronic signals that tell drivers when to stop and pedestrians when to go. We proposed adding something that transportation engineers call *leading pedestrian intervals**—walk signals that give pedestrians a head start by flashing "WALK" three to seven seconds before the accompanying traffic light turns green (with an accompanying prohibition on turns when the light is red). We recommended the installation of innovative signals and beacons, such as pedestrian-activated rapid-flash beacons that don't depend on timers. Pedestrians who want to cross a street where these beacons are installed just press a button or step on a pad on the sidewalk, and yellow lights embedded in the street flash on and off, alerting drivers to their presence.

Obviously, in a city the size of Chicago—really, anywhere—you don't just change the geometry of the streets overnight. The plan started, as they always do, with pilot programs. One of them—a traffic-calming plan for the densely populated Humboldt Park neighborhood on Chicago's west side, where fifty-six thousand people live in about three-and-a-half square miles—called for putting the neighborhood's main drag, Humboldt Drive, on a strict diet. The results weren't surprising, but they were extremely positive: traffic declined by a quarter, and, even better, the average traffic speed dropped by two mph, which doesn't sound like much, but reducing the average

---

* These were actually invented around 1982, when I was New York City's traffic commissioner, as we tried to solve a pedestrian-vehicle conflict at 59th Street and Third Avenue in Midtown.

speed from thirty to twenty-eight mph drops the median driver's "stopping sight time" from 197 feet to 178. This is, by any measure, a lifesaving distance.

However, as with Barcelona, Columbus, and Portland, safety was important but it wasn't everything (though, as you probably guessed, the more people walk, the safer they are, and not just from things like cardiovascular disease; as VMT declines, so do crashes). Our town meetings, observations, and algorithms told us that connectivity was equally significant: initiating programs that maintained space on sidewalks for pedestrian traffic by limiting the structures that block them, such as newspaper kiosks, tree pits, and sidewalk cafes. Or making it a lot easier to cross the 1,732 points where roads in the Chicago metropolitan area intersect railroads at grade, a heritage of the city's history as the center of America's freight network.[*] Or reducing the crossing distance of the city's many, shall we say, eccentric, intersections: diagonal streets that intersect north-south and east-west streets creating (deep breath) six-way intersections. The plan called for reconfiguring the city's parking lots to make them as safe and convenient for pedestrians as sidewalks, and adding digital wayfinding, such as interactive maps at transit stations and bus stops.[†]

Which was all good and necessary stuff. But sometimes it seems to me that we—and by "we" I mean not just engineers but everyone involved in transportation—assume that once we figure out how to make walking and biking safer and more useful, our job is done. This isn't quite accurate. Even in the most active-transportation-friendly neighborhoods of San Francisco or New York, or even Portland, we still walk and bike a whole lot less than demographically similar communities in Copenhagen or Amsterdam, or even Sydney, Australia.

---

[*] A 2002 study found that the railroads, by closing crossings to traffic for more than 1,500 hours on a typical weekday, delayed nearly half a million travelers an aggregate of more than 11,000 hours a day.

[†] For more on digital wayfinding, see Chapter 7.

After all, Americans are notoriously fond of not walking. One study that placed pedometers on people all over the world showed just how fond: the average Japanese adult walks 7,168 steps daily, and the median Australian an even more impressive 9,965. Americans: 5,117.

One reason, I think, is that we don't spend nearly as much time and effort making walkways and bikeways pleasant as well as secure and practical. We were determined not to forget this in the Chicago plan, which included quality-of-life elements like a "Make Way for People Program" that temporarily closes at least three streets each year to automobile traffic, and transforms them into public plazas: truly complete streets. It also called for placing original artworks—temporary (or permanent) outdoor galleries, video projections, and sound installations—on sidewalks and other walkways.

Even better: one of my favorite moments while working on the Chicago plan was the discovery that the Chicago Municipal Code of 1922—back in the days when the battle for the streets was still ongoing and hadn't yet resulted in complete victory for the automobile—actually provided for something called "Play Streets." This was a policy of regularly closing roads to cars so that kids could play in them. We added Play Streets to the plan, as well as three even more elaborate traffic-barring "Open Street" events for 2013.

Streets, it turns out—play streets, open streets, skinny streets: Complete Streets—are the answer to the question I posed earlier in this chapter, the one about the mismatch between the demand for walkability and the supply of it. A century ago we started building streets exclusively as machines for getting an automobile from place to place as quickly and safely as possible.* Sixty years ago, we kicked it up a gear, enlisting a generation of very skilled engineers and the most sophisticated tools of analysis and management in service of this goal. Because building a street is a very enduring decision, we've lived

---

* Safely for drivers and passengers, anyway.

with a huge number of consequences ever since. Like the narrator of Robert Frost's poem "The Road Not Taken," we chose a road without really knowing whether it would take us where we wanted to go or even if it would be any better than another choice.

As it turned out, the road we usually chose was the one that almost totally ignored the pedestrian. But unlike Frost's narrator, we have a chance to retrace our route and follow the road not taken. That's what's going on in Barcelona, and Columbus, and Pasadena, and Chicago. They're completing their streets, a critical step in encouraging more active transportation.

But active transportation is only one aspect of a street smart city. Making sidewalks and bikeways useful and connected is necessary, but not sufficient. Other modes of travel, and other ways of knitting them into a connected and navigable network, matter too.

UNLOCKING THE GRID

O N APRIL FOOLS' DAY 1980, THIRTY-FOUR THOUSAND OF NEW YORK City's bus drivers, subway operators, dispatchers, token clerks, and mechanics walked off their jobs.* Despite laws that made strikes by any public union illegal—they'd been on the books since 1966, the year of the *last* transit strike—Local 100 of the Transit Workers Union had hit the picket lines.

The reasons were straightforward enough. At a time when the US economy was going more than a little crazy—I know younger readers will think this is a typo, but the inflation rate in 1980 was nearly 14 percent, and banks were paying more than 12 percent interest on money market accounts—the transit workers had demanded a raise of 30 percent (this isn't a typo, either). The Metropolitan Transportation Authority offered 3 percent. This caused some hard feelings and, soon enough, a strike. Over the course of the next eleven days,

---

* In an unrelated job action, the trackmen of the Long Island Rail Road, the nation's busiest commuter line, also struck on April 1, returning to work two days later.

between overtime expenses incurred by the city's government and job absenteeism everywhere, New York's economy lost an estimated $1 billion.

I had been working on the city's response to a potential transit strike for months. Sure, there was lots of talk about it and the smart money had been betting on a strike, but I still didn't believe it when, at about 3 a.m. on April 1, my phone rang and Spiros Lambros, a department liaison with the other city agencies, said, "It started." The strike had been officially called at 2:05 a.m.

A waiting police car drove me from my Flatbush home to the Parade Grounds, a flat area of ball fields, just three blocks away—five minutes on foot, but less than a minute by car, and this was one time minutes mattered. There, I hopped on an NYPD helicopter and by 3:30 a.m. was flying over the Gowanus Expressway. I looked at the dark homes below, thinking, "They have no idea what's going to hit them when they wake up." In the distance I could see the headlights of drivers about to face the gargantuan task of getting in to work. I remember shuddering and thinking, "They are all counting on me."

Within minutes the chopper landed at One Police Plaza. I walked down one staircase into my new temporary office, the conference room of the police commissioner. One door led to the commissioner's office. The other to a wide expanse of desks, each with the nameplate of the agency represented: Fire, Education, Con Edison, Environmental Protection. By 5 a.m., every desk was staffed.

The mayor and the police commissioner made it clear to me: I had ten thousand cops, every city worker, every resource at my disposal, all of them looking to me for direction. After getting over the initial butterflies of opening night (actually dawn), I began barking orders.

I was well prepared. I had read everything I could on the strike fourteen years earlier, talked to cops and traffic engineers. I had concluded that it had been—mistakenly—treated as a police event when what it had really been was a scientific challenge: how to suddenly transport people away from their pods of subway trains and buses. My team did capacity assessments and sensitivity analyses, and used traffic engineering principles to move automobiles more efficiently. Our traffic signals had been prepped to take traffic primarily in one direction: inbound in the morning and outbound in the evening. If you were going against the flow, tough luck! Weeks before, we had manufactured hundreds of signs warning everyone that each car entering New York must have three or more occupants, and we had installed them at every major entrance to the city—and then covered them up. At 4:00 a.m. April 1, the covers were removed, the signals were activated, and the cops were posted. And Mayor Koch, along with several hundred thousand of his nearest and dearest friends, walked across the Brooklyn Bridge to work at City Hall.

As bad as the strike was, it had some good sides. Hotels never did better, as the employers of an estimated half a million commuters decided to keep them within walking distance of their offices. More than a hundred thousand people got out their bicycles and pedaled to work. And I added a word to the *Oxford English Dictionary*.

Though you'll find a slew of articles that say that the word *gridlock* was invented during the strike, this isn't really the case. Roy Cottam (the engineer in the Transportation Department who had reminded everyone about my strange habit of taking the subway) and I used it as shorthand to describe what the OED calls "continuous queues of vehicles block[ing] an entire network of intersecting streets, bringing traffic in all directions to a complete standstill." I used it in print for the first time in a 1980 memo titled "Grid-lock [I originally hyphenated the word] Prevention Plan" and Roy, who was paranoid about his name being associated with the term, gave me all the credit for originating it.

He was on to something. I'm pretty sure that the first line in my obituary is going to mention it, and way more people know me as

"Gridlock Sam" than as Samuel I. Schwartz, P.E. It's not quite "Ty-phoid Mary" but it does evoke some not-so-good emotions. Grid-lock is both common and *very* frustrating, which is why drivers who "block the box"—who enter an intersection but can't exit it before the signal changes—are supposed to be cited and given a very ex-pensive ticket. On the other hand, the reason that New York, and cities like it, are particularly vulnerable to gridlock isn't an entirely bad thing. To have gridlock, you first need to have a grid.

And grids aren't just good for transportation. They're great.

Even though, as we saw in the last chapter, active transportation has a huge number of attractive qualities, those qualities disappear for routes that aren't extremely short. Typically, transportation en-gineers assume that, for most trips, people will forgo traveling on foot for distances that are longer than a quarter- to a half-mile, or by bicycle when they have to travel more than two miles. This is a powerful argument for as much density as possible, in order to maximize the potential number of such trips, but it's impossible to imagine a transportation future in which *every* trip (or even most of them) will be short enough to be completed on foot or bike. Whether it's just for a weekly trip to a supermarket or a daily com-mute to work, for the foreseeable future, most people will need access to modes of transportation that are powered by something other than muscle.

But which modes? How many? And how organized? One way of answering these questions is to begin with the idea that all trans-portation systems have to maintain a balance between efficiency and flexibility. All other things being equal, by far the most efficient way to transport a lot of people is by collecting them in large vehicles that run on fixed routes at regular intervals. Bigger vehicles are more efficient than small ones, at least when they're full. Fixed routes are more efficient than those variable ones. The more predictable the times for departure and arrival, the more efficient it gets. This is why, as routes get longer, heavy rail is more efficient than light rail; light rail and streetcars are more efficient than Bus Rapid Transit; and all of them are more efficient—passenger mile efficient, that is, in terms of cost, energy, and any other way you can measure efficiency—than automobiles.

On the other hand, the private automobile, whether owner-driven or in the form of a taxicab, is the most flexible mode of non-muscle-powered transportation. Cars go anywhere streets are paved; with the right tires and transmission, they can even go lots of places where they're unpaved. They depart when travelers are ready, rather than when vehicles are. They're just hugely inefficient. A properly designed system needs the benefits of efficiency and flexibility, which means it needs to be, as we noted in the Prologue, what engineers call *multimodal*, offering many different ways of getting from place to place, and *multinodal*, with routes that incorporate the maximum number of connection points.

Whether small towns or megacities, the first key to multimodal/multinodal transportation is space: the two- and three-dimensional map of the transportation system—not just the roads and tracks, but the surrounding buildings and other structures and how they relate to one another. When the activities where people interact with one another—working, buying, selling, and so on—are largely in one place, the places where they live surround that one place, the center. When there are lots of places for interaction, when people work and shop in a variety of neighborhoods, clusters appear, scattered by history and circumstance to different areas. In a centralized system, the transportation nodes tend to concentrate in—no surprise—the center, and are linked in the same way that the outer edge of a wheel connects to the hub, by transport "spokes." In a city or town with a single downtown, a map of the highest-capacity linkages—streets and roads, for example—would look like a hub-and-spoke, since most trips are from the periphery to the center.

Many cities built before the late nineteenth century look a lot like this. But beginning with the growth of mechanized transportation, especially the first streetcars, cities started to adopt a grid pattern, in which streets meet at right angles. The reason is simple geometry: grids maximize accessibility and available space. In a grid, every part of the town or city is connected via a series of straight lines, which improves not just mobility but real-estate values. An urban environment with lots that are irregularly shaped is one in which the real estate market is relatively inefficient, like a supermarket in which the canned goods come in dozens of different sizes. One of the objectives (and criticisms) of the 1811 plan that transformed Manhattan's streets into the world's most famous orthogonal grid was to make large estates easier to subdivide into standardized lots. The plan's surveyor, John Randel, even defended his plan precisely because it facilitated "buying, selling and improving real estate on streets, avenues, and public squares."

But after the post–Model T battle for the streets (a battle the automobile won decisively) the streets themselves changed. The process really began in the late 1920s, when two English architects—Charles Stein and Henry Wright—transplanted their version of an English garden city to a town in Bergen County, New Jersey: Radburn, "a town for the motor age." There were some attractive things about the Radburn model: sidewalks were very safe, and none of them crossed scary arterial roads. Some were less so: residential "superblocks" of thirty or more acres where nothing but houses could be built, surrounded by wide and forbidding arterial roads that made leaving residential neighborhoods impossible except by car. Within the superblocks, connectivity—if you can call it that—was sabotaged by a curvilinear pattern of looping streets and, even worse, cul-de-sacs, which by definition are connected to nothing, with a single way in and the same way out.

The pattern was given the seal of approval in 1934, when the Federal Housing Authority published a series of technical bulletins that endorsed both superblocks and cul-de-sacs. The FHA's position thus established the model for suburbanization, mostly in America, but anywhere residential developments were built from the 1950s forward, and was one of the enablers of America's fifty-year-long mistaken enthusiasm for sprawl. Around the same time, the Institute of Traffic Engineers even published a standard entitled "Recommended Practice for Subdivision Streets" that discouraged grids, encouraged curvilinear streets, and even opposed building four-way intersections where T-intersections could replace them.

The Radburn plan, in all its incarnations, was well intentioned: an attempt to protect pedestrians from automobile traffic in the places where they lived. Its results, however, were the opposite of multimodal. In the Radburn version of the English garden city, the only way to get from your house to anywhere that wasn't your neighbor's house was by car. Access to any other form of mechanized transport, whether trains, trolleys, or buses, was severely compromised. Since straight lines are the shortest distance between any two points, all other lines are longer, which means that travel is considerably less efficient on curvilinear streets than on gridded ones. After more than half a century of forgetting the geometric advantages of right angles, America now has tens of thousands of miles of highly inefficient roads. Even the most successful suburbs organized around curvilinear streets can be transportation deficient. The planned community of Columbia, Maryland, built by the Rouse organization in the 1960s, which is consistently ranked as one of the most livable communities in America, has never been able to support a decent public transportation system. Moreover, none of its ten bucolic villages has a Walk Score that exceeds 36.

Connectivity has become an even more acute problem in the twenty-first century than in the twentieth, since fewer and fewer urban areas are truly concentrated enough to take advantage of the transportation efficiencies of a hub-and-spoke system. Though millions of commuters will continue to commute from outlying suburbs to Manhattan for a very long time, clustering is far more prevalent than centralizing. Whether within a medium-sized city like Columbus, or a megalopolis like Los Angeles, travel is just as likely to occur between the northwest quadrant and the southwest, as it is from either to the center. More walkability can't make that kind of connection work. Many if not most routes will remain too long for foot or bike, no matter how much we improve walking and biking access to employment, shopping, and entertainment. Given the increasing inefficiencies and costs of automobile dependence, those routes need to be accessible by public transportation.

Which brings us back to grids, which are the (relatively) simple solution to the classic transportation problem: how to minimize route distances at the lowest possible cost. In a grid, every intersection of perpendicular lines is reachable by a short walk from another intersection. What makes it work for routes too long for foot or bike is that every one of those intersections is a potential transit node: a place where a bus or streetcar can collect and discharge passengers. In practical terms, every intersection doesn't have to have a bus stop or transit station. Generally, it works perfectly fine to have transit arteries laid out on parallel lines separated by a half-mile, or even three-quarters of a mile, which puts transit nodes within walking distance of one another. Even cities that were laid out in eras before the street-based grid of the streetcar era have created their own rail-based grids that run underground. This is why maps of the Paris Métro and the London Tube are far more gridlike than the respective city's street maps.

And then there's Vancouver, the seaport city that is at the center of Canada's third most populous metropolitan area.

No one writes more eloquently about the geometric advantage of grid-based transit than planning consultant Jarrett Walker, who calls Vancouver's system the "almost perfect grid." As he points out, not only are the parallel arteries used by the city's bus and rail system spaced between a half-mile and six-tenths of a mile apart, but they were explicitly designed to solve another problem of efficient transit design, the seemingly unavoidable fact that a bus or streetcar traveling through a zone with the same population density throughout is only using half its available capacity. A trolley that starts at the north end of Main Street and runs all the way through town to the southern end is going to be empty at the origin and empty again at the terminus, with maximum use right in the middle of the line. Fifty percent of the train or bus goes to waste.

The way to solve this is by anchoring the ends of a transit route at *really* popular destinations, so streetcars and buses will be just as full at the beginning and the terminus as they are in the middle, thus reducing all that waste. Which is exactly what TransLink, metropolitan Vancouver's transportation network, does. It's not that the planners of TransLink were more skilled than their colleagues in other cities, but rather that they had history and geography on their side—both human geography and the natural kind.

Vancouver was established in the middle of the nineteenth century, first as a seaport, then as a logging center, and finally as the western terminus of the Canadian Pacific Railway. Apparently because of nothing more than great luck, it is the only major city in North America without a single limited-access freeway entering it. This means that when, in the 1970s, the city's planners started pushing back against automobile-first policies, they weren't obliged, like San Francisco, to stop existing freeways from being completed, or to tear down those that were. The original street map, laid out for streetcars, was the only template they needed to concern themselves with.

That, and the city's natural outlines. On a map, Vancouver resembles a hitchhiker's hand. At the base of the thumb that sticks out into Vancouver Harbour is the city's downtown, occupying the northernmost part of the Burrard Peninsula. That's where the original 1870 settlement, Gastown, was built. Rebuilt after the Great Vancouver Fire of 1886 (but with the original cobblestones in place), it's now the center of a complex of upscale and funky stores, nightclubs, traditional office space, and high-tech startups. And every one of Vancouver's north-south transit lines converges on it, full of tourists, residents out for dinner, software engineers going to work, and artists to their studios, all the way to the end. In the same way, the city's western border, the hitchhiker's middle knuckle, is occupied by the University of British Columbia, which pays TransLink directly so that its forty thousand students and nine thousand faculty and staff ride for free, thus anchoring the west side of all the system's east-west routes. In the south is Vancouver's International Airport, and in the east, the gateway to half a dozen suburbs with what are, by North American standards, extremely high population densities. In fact, while the city of Vancouver houses six hundred thousand people in only forty-four square miles—fifty-five thousand people per square mile; by comparison, Manhattan has sixty-seven thousand—metropolitan Vancouver isn't exactly sprawling. With more than 2.4 million people packed into a square roughly thirteen miles on a side, its density is exceeded in all of North America only by New York and San Francisco, which, not at all coincidentally, likewise grew up on limited land around great deep-water seaports.

If Vancouver's transportation policymakers were fortunate in having population and employment centers grow up on its periphery, rather than in its center, they were still very smart in how they turned it to their advantage. Servicing multiple clusters efficiently also requires a lot of transportation modes, and Vancouver has 'em all. SeaBus, TransLink's ferry system, carries four hundred passengers every fifteen minutes (during rush hour, anyway) from terminals at the downtown waterfront to Lonsdale Quay on the other side of Burrard Inlet, connecting the city with dozens of different bus routes servicing North Vancouver. Two different kinds of Bus Rapid Transit technologies are on offer as well: electric trolleybuses* on the north-south arteries, diesel-powered on the east-west lines that terminate at the University of British Columbia. The city's monorail system, SkyTrain, the world's largest system of fully automated—that is, driverless—metro trains, is composed of three (soon to be four) different lines running from the base of the hitchhiker's thumb that is Vancouver's downtown, one running due south, across the Fraser River on the SkyBridge, the world's longest cable-supported, transit-only bridge. The other two run south by east, up the hitchhiker's forearm. But while Vancouver is regularly cited for its highly photogenic and reliable trains (and buses and ferries), the most valuable lesson from the success of TransLink is the importance of its geometry, which may be the most important element in any successful transportation network.

The other lesson is that transportation networks aren't built from scratch. They accommodate themselves to both geography and history, the choices that put certain neighborhoods, or business districts, or shopping areas, or schools, in particular spots. The folks who planned and built Vancouver's TransLink had some built-in advantages, but the planners of *any* transportation network benefit whenever they can incorporate a similar combination of multiple transport modes and nodes.

How do they do it? Once goals are established and problems identified, professional transportation planning is usually a four-step process. First comes an estimate of the number of trips that begin or end in a particular geographic area: what engineers call *trip generation*. Residential areas are said to "produce" trips, while everything else—stores, businesses, and so on—"attracts" them. Attractors are then subdivided into different buckets: work, school, shopping, and socializing.

---

* Because traditional trolleys (sometimes called streetcars or trams, depending on the venue) have metal wheels that run on tracks, rather than rubber tires on pavement, they can be powered by a connection to overhead wires using a single pole, with the conducting metal of the track itself closing the electrical circuit. Trolleybuses need two wires and two poles in order to do the same job.

The equations that appear in models can be extremely complicated but the concepts aren't. The number of trips at the producer end is a function of the number and type of households—apartments versus single-family homes, for example—and the number, income, and age of the people living in them. On the other hand, the number and type of jobs and retailers (and the competition among them) and their accessibility are among the factors at the attractor end. The model is then compared with observation of a (hopefully) representative sample of people traveling in real life.[*]

The second step takes the total-demand curves and refines them into destination choices: matching origins and destinations into a table. In yet another example of the physics envy that made me a fairly bright star among my classmates in engineering, traffic planning uses equations from a fundamental piece of classical mechanics—Newton's Law of Universal Gravitation—and transposes them into the world of transportation. There are even textbooks that describe a simplified "law of retail gravitation," which calculates a "point of indifference" between two potential destinations: the point at which a potential moviegoer, for example, is equally likely to see the latest blockbuster at one of two different multiplexes. A bigger attractor will (like a bigger planet) have a stronger attraction even at a greater distance.

You probably already saw step number three coming: once planners have a sense of the total number of trips, and have matched origins to destinations, they have to account for the kind of transport modes people will use to get from one to the other. Here, the most popular modeling technique isn't derived from hard sciences like physics, but behavioral disciplines like economics and psychology. Perversely, this didn't make the math easier, but harder. The "Logit

---

[*] Putting together all the inputs, planners use an intimidating-sounding statistical method, *ordinary least squares regression*, which squares the differences between predicted and actual numbers. Since those differences can be positive or negative, squaring them turns them all into positive numbers, making it easier to fit the observed and predicted results to nice smooth curves.

Model" (which won economist Daniel McFadden a Nobel Prize in Economics) is another statistical tool that estimates the way people value different travel alternatives. In theory, if you knew precisely how travelers—collectively and individually—valued their time, the cost of gas, parking, the enjoyment of driving or of sleeping on a bus or train, and everything else, you'd be able to predict their mode choice: walking versus biking, for example, or taking the car versus taking the train. Unfortunately, though, as all those predictions about increasing VMT from the early 2000s showed, you can use incredibly sophisticated models, with hundreds of precisely calculated variables, to arrive at completely wrong conclusions.

Once you know how many trips will connect origins and destinations, and the modes that will be used for the trips, the final step of the system calculates the routes that will be taken, along with variables that estimate the flow and capacity on any link in a transportation network at any given time. If all the t's have been crossed and the i's dotted during the planning process, an optimal network of transportation modes and nodes should emerge. Sometimes it actually does.

This doesn't mean that a grid like Vancouver's is always going to be the best solution. Another kind of route map that maximizes modes and nodes isn't based on perpendicular connections, but radial ones.

Not this:

But this:

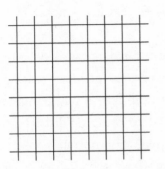
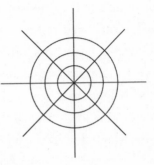

David Smucker (Sam
Schwartz Engineering).

The second version, which resembles a spiderweb, with radiating spokes, is generally less efficient than the first. Spoke routes have geometry on their side. As the Pythagorean theorem demonstrates, diagonal routes are always shorter than traveling around two legs of a right triangle, which is what grid systems require. However, the cost of creating a system with a sufficient number of uninterrupted spokes is high, which means that, the further travelers are from the center of the web, the more indirect their routes tend to become. Moreover, the trains, buses, and streetcars will inevitably be filled only as they converge on the web's center, and be empty at the periphery.

There's another reason traffic engineers don't like radials. They often create *multiple phase intersections* when they cross a grid. A typical, two-phase, perpendicular intersection forms an ×, so a simple traffic signal stopping traffic in one direction at a time is all that's usually needed. But, introduce one of the diagonal streets common to radial systems—something like *—and another signal needs to be introduced to let the traffic on the additional street stop and go. So if the traffic signal repeats on a cycle one hundred seconds long, each movement in an × intersection averages fifty seconds, which is reduced to thirty-three seconds in an * intersection. This is part of the brilliance of Janette Sadik-Khan's plan that closes a section of Broadway, which runs at an angle through the otherwise perpendicular Manhattan streets, to cars. The vehicular pattern changed three-phased signals into two-phased signals. So closing a street to traffic actually improved traffic!

However, attractors often got concentrated decades or centuries before contemporary planners started work; the planners don't get to choose where attractors go. Lots of cities still have a traditional, single, prime destination—usually the original central business district, as with Boston, Massachusetts—and can satisfy many transportation needs with a traditional hub-and-spoke system. Paris, whose twenty *arrondissements* are laid out in a spiral, is a prime example of a radial spiderweb. Within the city's core, the Metro lines circle the hub, while the city's eight tram lines orbit the core—the T3 tramway alone carries riders on thirty million trips annually—and intersect inbound transit spokes.

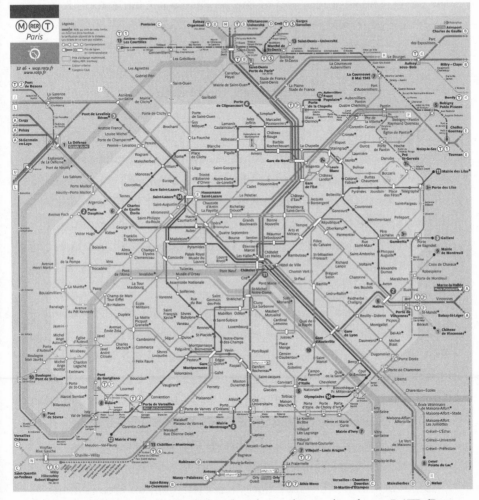

The Paris Metro: A modern radial grid underneath a medieval city. *RATP (Paris Transport Authority). All rights reserved.*

Paris, Boston, and even Vancouver are well-known examples of the importance of preexisting geography in planning a multimodal system. But the same lesson is on display in less familiar places as well, such as Charleston, South Carolina.

If Vancouver resembles a hitchhiker's hand, thumb up, Charleston looks, on a map, like a foot trailing in the waters of Charleston Harbor, with the Ashley River on one side and the Cooper River on the other. The southern end of the peninsula is Charleston's historic heart: a downtown composed of buildings dating back to the eighteenth century. It includes destinations that attract nearly two million visitors annually: the Broad Street shopping district, the City Market, and the South Carolina Aquarium, to say nothing of the Fort Sumter National Monument out in Charleston's harbor. The College of Charleston and the Citadel, the Military College of South Carolina, between them have more than fifteen thousand students and three thousand faculty and staff. At the northern end of the peninsula, the city—or, rather, the Charleston Area Regional Transportation Authority, or CARTA—is building a state-of-the-art transportation hub, the North Charleston Intermodal Transportation Center, which will connect local transit, like buses and taxis, with both Amtrak and the Southeastern Stages intercity bus network.

Charleston has a strong and growing economy. The Port of Charleston remains one of the country's busiest, and in 2011, Boeing built a new assembly site for their Commercial Airplanes division in North Charleston. Ten years before that the Charleston Digital Corridor ("18th-century architecture. 21st-century technology") began actively attracting dozens of telecom, IT, and software companies to the city, in designated neighborhoods like the Gateway District in the north of Charleston's peninsula, and the University and Wharf Districts in the south. The Charleston metropolitan area is home to around seven hundred thousand people, and is expected to grow to nearly a million over the next ten to fifteen years. Their challenge is supporting this kind of growth without choking to death on automobile exhaust. Like so many other places, the city is carved up by highways. Interstate 26 terminates in Charleston its subsidiary highway,

I-526, loops it; and ten other limited-access highways curve around and through it.

In August of 2014, I met with Tim Keane, director of Planning, Preservation, and Sustainability for the city of Charleston, to discuss a future for the city that would allow it to grow using advanced alternatives to the automobile. Historically, as Tim reminded me, Charlestonians have always expected that "they will have a parking space wherever they work and live. But that can't work anymore; we just don't have the room."

On the other hand, they do have a beautiful and untouched urban environment, one that's older than the steam engine, much less the Model T. Walking around Charleston is a little like walking through a set built for a movie that takes place during the era of America's founding, only it's real. It's not an accident. When Charleston passed the nation's first preservation law in 1931, the city was already 261 years old. The law, which made it impossible to tear down much of anything, therefore also made it impossible to build anything either, so the core of Charleston has escaped most kinds of development-driven sprawl.

Charleston's fundamental transportation need isn't too hard to figure out. With the Intermodal Facility and Boeing to the north, and most of the Digital Corridor, the universities, and the tourist destinations to the south, the peninsula has two potential anchors for a multimodal, multinodal system. CARTA already operates a traditional, fixed-route, motor bus system both in the peninsula and the surrounding areas, and, downtown, it runs a trolleybus system known as DASH, for the "Downtown Area Shuttle": three different lines circulating along loops through the southern end of Charleston's peninsula, with stops at the Broad Street shopping district, the City Market, the aquarium, and both colleges. What Tim envisions, though, is a fully operational, north-south trolley, running the entire

length of the peninsula. And, he adds, it "must be wonderful" to attract a car-oriented public.

>>>

Vancouver and Charleston need different networks because they
have different histories and different geographies. What they all *want*,
though, are the same things: reliability and frequency. The last parts
of network planning—the route maps—are the real determinants for
the frequency of service along each of the routes: how many trains,
buses, or streetcars, and how often they will stop to pick up and discharge passengers. This is always managed as a series of tradeoffs, since
more stops means more access, but slower speed. Even the question
of whether stops should be located at intersections[*] or mid-block is
a tradeoff, since intersections offer more access, but mid-block stops
pose less potential for conflict with other transport. If the first measure of a network is how it handles space, the second has to be how
it manages time.

Just as varying travel distances favor different travel modes—a five-
block walk to the corner drugstore, versus a three-mile-long car trip
to the supermarket, versus a thirty-mile commute by train—different
travel purposes require different frequencies. Though every few years
some company experiments with staggered work hours (and most
of the time, they turn out to be pretty happy with the results), the
efficiencies of consolidating work in the traditional 9–5 portion of the
day are hard to overcome. Rush hour is with us for the foreseeable
future, which determines transit frequencies in the peak mornings
and evenings.

However, for all other travel, a usefully frequent network is one
that stops at a convenient transit node at least every fifteen minutes,

---

[*] Or even on the near or far side of an intersection.

and ideally even more often. The advantage of this, of course, is that no one really needs to know a transit schedule to use such a system; you just get yourself to the transit stop, and hop on. Creating such a frequent network isn't a trivial task. But it can be done, even in some of the most auto-centric cities in the country. Such as Houston, Texas.

Houston isn't just the biggest city in Texas, it's the fourth largest city in the entire country, and one of the most sprawling. The city alone has 2.16 million people scattered across more than six hundred square miles, while 6.3 million people live in the *ten thousand square miles* that comprise the ten counties of the greater Houston metropolitan area. As a region that not only grew up during the automobile age, but whose economy was built on the fossil-fuel business, it's not much of a surprise that Houston is what you might call automobile dependent. Before the Metropolitan Authority of Harris County— METRO, for short—started its light rail service in 2004, Houston was by far the largest city in the country with no rail transit at all, which is why nearly 90 percent of its residents drive to work—one person to a car, of course—on nearly six hundred miles of limited-access freeways. The road system is organized in a classic spiderweb, with a series of beltways and interstates looping around the city, but it's hard to call it a very efficient one. Houston is the fourth most congested city in the country, and the average resident spends fifty-eight hours a year stuck in traffic.

With the very modest ambitions of METRORail—only thirteen miles are currently operational, and it will be many years before the seventy-three miles on the drawing board are built out, if ever—the bus system offers the only potential transit alternative to the automobile. But it's also one of the least attractive, an option used mostly by Houstonians too poor to own automobiles. It's probably too much to expect METRO to change that anytime soon. But they have identified, and have produced a plan to repair, the mass transit system's biggest deficiency, which has been its lack of frequency.

If a decently frequent system is one in which most people live within a quarter-mile of a transit node where a bus (or streetcar) stops at least every fifteen minutes, Houston wasn't doing so well. By those criteria, barely five hundred thousand people qualified, even during peak weekday travel times, and fewer than half of them did so on weekends. A new system, which METRO calls the "frequent network," would allow 1.1 million Houstonians to board a bus within twenty minutes of leaving home: a five-minute walk, followed by, at most, a fifteen-minute wait. That's nearly three-quarters of Houston's transit users, and they would receive the service fifteen hours a day, seven days a week.

Did I mention that the "frequent network" provides this level of service at exactly the same cost as the old system? Designing it was an exercise in good transportation planning basics, going back to the four steps described above, with an added twist. This analysis compared two different transportation goals: *patronage*, a measure of the number of riders the system could carry, how far, per dollar spent; and *coverage*, a calculation of service availability: whether every part of town, or every segment of the population, got its "fair share."

The two goals aren't necessarily in conflict, but neither are they always in harmony. In Houston, especially, the old system offered far more coverage than patronage, which made the existing route structure a long way from optimal. The existing bus map had largely mimicked Houston's early-twentieth-century streetcar routes,* and therefore had a lot of stops in places without a significant number of transit riders, and a lot of transit riders in places with no stops at all. This made for a huge amount of waste. The old system had less than half its resources in places with high ridership, while the new one devotes 80 percent of the bus lines to them. The "frequent network" replaced the meandering routes that converged on downtown (now

---

* Yes, even Houston had a system of nearly ninety miles of streetcar and trolley lines. And, yes again, it was one of the systems bought up and put out of business by National City Lines.

home to less than 25 percent of the region's employment) with a high-frequency right-angled grid that gets most transit riders to an employment cluster with a single transfer, at most.

They may never get there. Transportation planning in Houston is more like religious warfare than engineering. It's not that the city has no advocates for walkability, density, and transit availability. Tom Lambert, METRO's head, says, "Rail used to be a negative word around this town. It's not anymore." More than half of Houston's residents, according to the Kinder Institute's Houston Area Survey, want to live in a mixed-use community that isn't completely dependent on the automobile. However, there's the other half, Houstonians who believe themselves under attack from anti-car zealots who want to turn their city into—horror of horrors—Portland. Vocal and powerful local groups don't just hate the existing light rail system, but fight the expansion of it as if the train stations were porn shops in which plague-infected crack was being sold to schoolchildren. They dislike buses and loathe trains, but they love, love, love their cars. These are the folks who chose to spend $2.8 billion, twice the cost of the entire METRORail system, on widening a twenty-eight-mile-long segment of I-10 known as the Katy Freeway from eight to—wait for it—*twenty-six* lanes. As of this writing, METRO's new multimodal, high-frequency grid may be allowed to improve the lives of a million of Houston's residents. Or not.

Either way, Houston isn't going to look like Zurich anytime soon.

>>>

Houston and Zurich are both what have come to be known as "global cities": places that occupy critical positions in the world economy.[*]

---

[*] Dozens of different groups of geographers and economists rank such cities annually. As of 2012, according to *Foreign Policy* magazine, Zurich is number 31 on the list of global cities, with Houston at number 36.

Both have a lot of extremely wealthy residents, and both have a powerful aversion to taxes. And that's pretty much where the points of comparison stop. Houston was founded in 1836, Zurich in 15 BCE. Houston is flat as a pancake. Make that flat as a crepe: the entire city is between sea level and forty feet above, with a famously steamy climate. Zurich sits on the Swiss Plateau, between 1,300 and 2,800 feet above sea level, with the Alps towering above. The average temperature of the coolest month in Houston exceeds that of the warmest month in Zurich.

To a transportation engineer, all that is just background noise. Zurich is probably the most transit-friendly city in the world.

Zurich is Switzerland's largest city, with about three hundred thousand people (that's the city proper; the metropolitan area is home to 1.8 million) tucked into a little more than forty square miles on both sides of the Limmat River just north of Lake Zurich.

Just reciting the options available in Zurich requires taking a very deep breath. The city's tracked streetcar system operates nearly three hundred trains on fifteen different routes, running on more than a hundred miles of track set flush into the pavement, and carries more than 200 million passengers a year. Nearly eighty trolleybuses, running on six lines that parallel and supplement the streetcar network, add another thirty-four miles to the system, and another 54 million trips. In acknowledgment of the value of a grid system, two of the trolleybus lines run on north-south routes, two on east-west, and two are radial. Not enough? The transit system also runs 180 motor buses on sixty routes, 18 of them within the city of Zurich, for another 37 million trips annually. The Zürichsee-Schiffahrtsgesellschaft (Lake Zurich Navigation Company) operates seventeen passenger ships—two of them renovated early-twentieth-century paddle steamers—that travel from the Bürkliplatz dock at the city's south end across Lake Zurich and up the Limmat River for another 1.2 million passenger trips annually on short ferry rides—90-minute round-trips to Erienbach, for example—and cruises that can take seven hours. Five additional ferries carry both automobiles and passengers on a ten-minute trip across the lake at a point seven miles south of the city, allowing drivers to avoid nineteen miles of driving, for another 2.2 million people, and more than a million cars and trucks, every year.

If you're counting—and I know you are—that's well over 300 million trips on public transit annually, in a city with three hundred thousand residents and a metro area with fewer than two million. And I haven't even mentioned the S-Bahn, 240 miles of commuter train tracks that knit together the entire canton of Zurich.

Then there are the funiculars. I have a special place in my heart for funiculars, those cable railways that climb up and down slopes too steep for traditional trains that depend on friction to keep them on track. They are a cross between a train and an elevator. Something about looking up or down those tracks evokes memories of Coney Island's legendary Cyclone roller coaster—my favorite. Zurich has two of them: the Polybahn funicular railway carries two million passengers annually on a 135-foot climb from Zurich's Central station to the terrace of the Swiss Federal Institute of Technology. And the Rigiblick funicular does the same thing for the six hundred thousand passengers in the city's northern suburbs, only higher: 308 feet, at an average grade of 25 percent.

Of course, Zurich isn't the envy of the transportation world just because of quantity. Quality matters, too. And Zurich does even better on those measures. The entire fleet of clean, comfortable, and remarkably easy-to-use vehicles combines the world's best on-time performance—Switzerland isn't the watch capital of the world because the Swiss don't care about punctuality—with frequencies that are almost incredible. Virtually no one standing at any transit node, whether for streetcar, trolleybus, or motor bus, waits more than three minutes before a vehicle stops at it. It isn't just that Zurich designed a well-integrated schedule and then forgot about it. When you have a schedule that depends on streetcars meeting trolleybuses within minutes either way, a cyclist changing a tire in the wrong place can disrupt the entire system. The only way to keep the system operating at expected frequencies is by constantly fine-tuning it, which is why a network of more than four thousand sensors monitors all traffic, and high-speed computers using intelligent algorithms change signaling within the city on the fly. As vehicles—cars, motorbikes, trolleybuses, motor buses, or streetcars—approach any of the city's nearly four hundred intersections, detectors buried in the pavement recalibrate signaling times, giving priority to streetcars and trolleybuses. The combination of a dense grid and literally split-second coordination of each different mode and route means that even the longest edge-to-edge trip can be completed in less than thirty minutes—most are less than twenty—even when they require transfers, either from one streetcar to another, or from a streetcar to a trolleybus.

All this shouldn't be cheap, but it actually is: the equivalent of $30 a month for full use of the entire system. And it's solvent. Once again, this is Switzerland, and they understand finance even better than they understand clocks. Fares pay nearly half the operating *and* capital costs for the system, which is far more than in a typical American system.

The reason is that it is so heavily used. According to the 2010 transport "microcensus" performed by the Civil Engineering Office of the City of Zurich every five years, 32 percent of Zurich's residents use streetcars and trolleybuses regularly, while only 26 percent depend on cars (and motorcycles/motorbikes). Fewer than half the city's households even own a car or motorcycle. In addition, while "only" 15 percent of all trips are *intermodal* (that is, involving two or more modes for the same trip), nearly 60 percent of the city's residents are *multimodal* (that is, they use different modes for different trips depending on their daily needs and schedules).

And they haven't forgotten active transportation, either: 36 percent of all trips in Zurich are made on foot, and another 6 percent are by bicycle.

It would be easy to conclude that Zurich's extraordinary transportation network was the residue of historical good luck. Because of its size and age—some of the city's streets were laid out by the Romans in the first century CE—Zurich never had to cope with the auto-centric design of newer American cities. Such a conclusion would, however, be a mistake. Zurich is what it is because it decided, not so very long ago, to end its dependence on, and addiction to, the automobile.

Or, more accurately, addiction to parking.

Though parking is a lot less flashy than automated electric trains, or interactive signs that help in finding routes, it's hard to overstate its importance in building a successful multimodal transportation system or, for that matter, turning streets back into livable places. Back in 1997, Donald Shoup, then at the Department of Urban Planning at UCLA, wrote one of the most cited papers in the entire transportation literature, "The High Cost of Free Parking," which demonstrated the flaws in setting minimum parking requirements for every land use—for every house, or store, or office building—based on peak demand. The problem with such minimal requirements is that the users of (almost) all such parking got all that parking at either zero cost or at well below the price they were willing to pay for it. Constructing all of it was costing "more than ten times the impact fees"—these are the fees that local governments charge for the public costs of private development, such as water treatment, sewers, but also additional police and fire department costs, even school expenses—"than all other public purposes combined." Nor was street parking the answer, even if it wasn't free. Whenever more than 85 percent of curbside parking is taken, significant numbers of drivers cruise looking for a space, causing immediate and paralyzing congestion. In study after study, dating back to 1927, an average of 30 percent of the cars in America's congested downtowns are cruising for a curb parking space; in Brooklyn, researchers found a whopping 45 percent.

Both problems were part of Zurich's experience. Prior to the 1990s, Zurich had parking regulations comparable to those in most other European and American cities. For every square foot of new construction, whether residential or commercial, some minimum amount of parking would likewise be required. In 1989, though, the city changed from a parking *minimum* to a parking *maximum*. And the maximums weren't very maximal. For every 1,333 square feet authorized by a Zurich construction permit, developers were allowed to supply only a single parking space. In the United States, a comparable permit would require *at least* three spaces for the same amount of square footage.

Then, in 1996, Zurich passed a statute requiring that virtually every new parking space be built underground, and that they be priced to what the market would bear. Even more important, they placed a ceiling on the total number of parking spaces in the city. This meant that for every new parking space built underground, at least one parking space on the city's streets had to be eliminated, until the total amount of parking in the city equaled the amount available in 1990.

The result has been dramatic, and dramatically effective. As of 2014, the maximum parking allowed in Zurich's city center is 0.08 spaces for every 1,000 square feet of new construction. In the employment and shopping clusters at the city's periphery it's not much more generous: 0.5 spaces for every 1,000 square feet. For the 750,000 square feet of commercial space in four new buildings constructed above the city's Hardbruecke Train Station—one of them thirty-six stories—the city allowed only 250 parking spots. A similar complex in the United States would require at least 2,000 spaces.

Restricting the number of street parking spaces opened up the streets to other uses. Half a dozen streets that until 1996 offered parking (frequently on both sides of streets that were less than twenty-five feet wide) are now fully pedestrianized districts. Rennweg, for example, the main street in the medieval old town of Zurich. Maybe even more tellingly, the Bahnhofstrasse—the Fifth Avenue of Zurich—and the Limmatquai promenade that runs along the Limmat River were major auto thoroughfares ten years ago. Now they're pedestrian and transit parks.

In my practice I routinely advise my clients to apply for variances that would permit them to provide less parking than required. Many are supportive, not because they hate cars, but because it costs less, and in places like Manhattan, a lot less, since most parking has to be underground, which is *very* expensive. Fewer square feet for parking also frees up space for other uses: more labs and classrooms for Columbia University's new campus or more retail acreage for the IKEA home furnishings store in Brooklyn.

One problem with restricting parking, all other things being equal, is that it forces even more vehicles to cruise for longer periods of time looking for space. It would scarcely have helped Zurich's or Brooklyn's streets (and, especially, the reliability of the streetcars and trolleybuses that use those streets) if the same number of cars were entering the city, with even fewer places for them to park. Zurich's answer, one of the best-known aspects of its transit network, is a system of in-pavement sensors like the ones that regulate traffic signals inside the city, but located at municipal boundaries. Those sensors automatically calculate the congestion index for the city at any moment in time. Once a given number of cars have entered the city, the system's algorithm uses traffic signals to halt automobile traffic on the main roads into the city until congestion falls back to a manageable level.*

---

* I used a crude form of this during the 1980 New York transit strike. On April 9, 1980, a day that shall live in traffic lore infamy, the skies opened up and unleashed a torrent of rain and wind. Midtown traffic was paralyzed. I ordered traffic stopped for vehicles entering Manhattan and turned as many lanes as I could outbound, kind of emptying the bathtub of Manhattan of cars. A few years later, I wrote an award-winning paper on the concept, titled "Metering High Density Sectors."

For a lot of people, like those fighting the Houston METRO Rail, this is evidence of Zurich's powerful aversion to the automobile. To be honest, a lot of the city's most fervent advocates would probably agree. Many people, including a lot of those I speak to and work with, see transportation in very black-and-white terms: either you believe the automobile is the devil's handiwork, and that cars have no place at all in a virtuous future, or you believe that riding a bicycle to work, or liking public transit, is evidence of something un-American. Both are half right. Which means that they're both all wrong.

The key to understanding what's improving mobility and quality of life in Vancouver and Zurich, and may start to do the same in Charleston and even Houston, is that no single transportation mode is ideal. That's how we got in this mess in the first place, believing that the personal automobile had achieved a kind of perfection in transportation, the ideal way to shop, commute, and socialize. But arguing that the automobile has *no* place in a properly designed transportation system is as wrong as maintaining that nothing else has *any* place. Even in transit-happy Zurich, more than a quarter of the population uses a car on a daily basis. Every task that requires moving from place to place has an appropriate solution(s), just as every destination has an optimal route.

But which mode was the most appropriate one? Which route was optimal? These are questions that frequently have simple and elegantly modeled engineering solutions. But no matter how cleverly planners add modes and route choices to the environment, no matter how many new nodes are created, no matter how sophisticated the trip generation models, the real test of a multimodal system is whether its users can navigate it efficiently. In even a medium-sized city, that means that transportation success is a function of millions of decisions made by hundreds of thousands of people every day. Shall I take this route to work, or that one? When do I have to leave the house to make it to the airport in time? Should I drive, or take the bus? If I drive, what are the chances I'll be able to park my car when I arrive?

Even when definitive answers to these questions theoretically existed, most transportation systems provided no practical way for people to find them, no way to unlock the transportation grid, at least in an acceptable amount of time. Over-engineering the system by simply adding modes and route choices doesn't make the problems easier to solve. It makes them harder. And it makes it particularly hard on users who might otherwise be inclined to use public transit: if it takes longer to figure out whether it's cheaper or easier to take a bus or train, or faster to take the express or local, than it does to just get in the car and start driving, people will put away the transit schedules and reach for the car keys.

But, on the other hand, what if it got so cheap, easy, and fast to answer those questions that anyone could do it in a matter of seconds?

WHAT MAKES A SMART CITY?

I N 1973, JUST A COUPLE OF YEARS AFTER I BEGAN WORKING FOR THE NEW York City Traffic Department, the US Department of Defense initiated the project that became the NavStar Global Positioning System, or GPS for short. The original idea was to standardize the systems that the US Navy and (sometimes) the US Air Force were already funding in the hope that satellite technology would revolutionize navigation. The satellite technology was very new; remember, this was only sixteen years after Sputnik, and barely a decade after Telstar, the first communications satellite.

If they only knew. The original idea behind GPS was to launch satellites into orbit around Earth at a distance of about eleven thousand miles, each of them carrying radio transmitters with the most precise time measurement equipment ever invented, accurate to within trillionths of a second. Since the speed with which radio waves travel is the speed of light, if you knew the precise location for each orbiting transmitter, and the time of transmission, and time of arrival for each signal, you could closely calculate the latitude, longitude, and altitude for any receiver on the planet. It took a while to turn theory into practice, not just increasing the world's computing power by several orders of magnitude but putting twenty-four satellites into orbit (there are now thirty-two) in order to ensure that the entire globe was covered by four at any one time.* But in April of 1995, the system, which had cost somewhere between $10 and $12 billion, became operational, first as a military-only network and five years later as the first precise and practical navigation system for civilians.

In 2000 I purchased my first GPS-enabled car. Ten years later, in 2010, I bought my first smartphone. It came with what was rapidly becoming a standard feature: its own GPS navigation system.

Any number I quote about the number of people with a working GPS receiver will be obsolete by the time you read this (actually, it will be obsolete by the time I finish writing this sentence). In 2010 alone, just under 110 million were sold, more than three every second. By 2013, not even counting standalone GPS units—for some quirky markets; ever since 2006, the USGA has permitted "distance-measuring devices, including GPS-based systems," for improving the performance of America's golfers—and the ones built into cars like General Motors' OnStar system, more than 150 million smartphone users in the US were carrying a built-in GPS receiver, along with a mobile connection to the Internet, pretty much everywhere they went. The implications for what transportation engineers call *advanced traveler information systems*, or ATIS, are, literally, impossible to exaggerate.

ATIS is more than handheld devices or even the Internet, of course. A whole category of ATIS builds the "I"—the information—into the traveler's route, rather than the traveler's pocket or purse. Familiar ex-

---

* In case you've forgotten all that spherical geometry you studied back in high school, here's the reason four satellites are needed: Each signal is deciphered by a satellite as the surface of an imaginary sphere. When two spheres overlap, they intersect as a circle; when that circle intersects a third sphere, it does so at two points. The fourth signal, the final sphere, eliminates one of those points, leaving the actual position.

amples include the time-and-distance signs along many limited-access highways, the ones that read, "8 Minutes to Route 110 Interchange" or "George Washington Bridge: Upper Level 8 minutes, Lower Level 12 minutes." The mass transit versions of these route-based ATIS are the countdown clocks on train platforms and bus stops that show the time until the next departure or arrival, or their routes.

These kinds of systems are really just dynamic versions of traditional signs. What makes them "advanced" is that the information they provide is both accurate and easy to understand, two things that even the best fixed maps don't do especially well. A map of the New York City subway system is posted in every car and on every platform, and it's a pretty good one, of its sort.

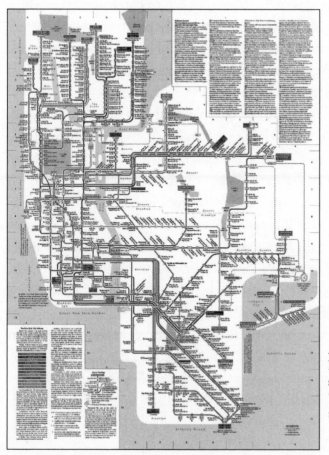

A thing of beauty: New York subway system map. *John Tauranac. Reprinted with permission.*

But like the equivalent bus map, it contains both too much information and too little. Travelers who want to get from Rockefeller Center to downtown Brooklyn don't really need to see every train or bus that will get them to Yankee Stadium. Meanwhile, for what they *do* want to know—"When is the next train leaving, and how long will it take to get there?"—the map is useless.

This affects different travelers in different ways—important ways. The most important of those differences is familiarity. Because most trips are familiar ones, whether it's the daily commute to work or the weekly trip to the supermarket, they're taken on automatic pilot—by the people who take them regularly. We all know not just the shortest driving route for picking up kids at school, but the best places to park, how to avoid the especially dangerous intersection, and even which streets could use a new repaving. All that information makes the familiar trip much easier for you than the unfamiliar one, but the inverse is also true: your familiar trip is someone else's first experience with it, with all the anxieties and inefficiencies you'd expect.

Don't take my word for it. Go to any large transit hub like 30th Street Station in Philadelphia, or Union Station in Chicago, and watch how travelers behave. Commuters know where to stand, when the train announcements are made, how much time they have to use the restroom or get a cup of coffee. Tourists, on the other hand—easy to spot, if only by the luggage—are anxious. You can almost hear the questions running through their heads: Do I need to show my ticket to the conductor as I board? Is this an express, or a local? When I arrive, will I be able to catch a bus to my next stop? A cab? When is my train actually going to get here?

It's like this in every city in the country. One class of travelers knows every stop on the Muni Metro, or the CT1 bus, or the Route 36 streetcar—in San Francisco, Boston, and Philadelphia, respectively— and another one feels like it's trying to find the way out of a corn maze:

intimidated, anxious, and unsure whether to look down at the maps they're carrying or up at the arrival and departure signs.

Unfamiliarity is always intimidating to the traveler, but the intimidation factor is a bigger obstacle to mass transit use than to driving, since when you're behind the wheel of your car, at least the vehicle is familiar. It's even more forbidding for transit that requires the multiple transfers needed to take advantage of the multimodal networks described in the last chapter.

Or, I should say, it used to be. The combination of thirty-two satellites and a couple of hundred million GPS receivers has changed two critical aspects of transportation. First, it has dramatically increased the value and appeal of existing public transit systems. And, second, it has created an entirely new category of transportation options.

In 2010, Next City, a nonprofit organization aimed at improving the sustainability and livability of cities, and a team from the research firm Latitude performed a study of how new technologies like mobile Internet and GPS could improve public transit, both quantitatively (getting people where they want to go faster and more conveniently) and qualitatively (in ways that improve the experience itself).

The program was what is known as a *deprivation study*: researchers recruited regular drivers twenty-four to fifty-one years old, who agreed to forgo—to be deprived of—driving for a week. The program's participants stopped driving, but they didn't stop traveling. Virtually all of them replaced their cars with buses, streetcars, biking, and walking; the average participant used five different modes during the deprivation week (94 percent walked, 89 percent took buses, 61 percent biked; only 6 percent used a scooter). And, because they were unfamiliar with their respective city's transportation options, they did so using mobile transportation apps. Lots of them.

One reason is that the study was done in two cities where apps of all sorts have a lot of appeal, and where the transit systems are, by American standards, anyway, very high-end: Boston and San Francisco. In addition to the by-now-ubiquitous Google Maps and MapQuest, Boston features dozens of local transport apps, such as Transit Spy, Nextime, Nexmap, and Open MBTA. The San Francisco equivalents—Bay Tripper, iCommute, SFMuniApp, Pocket MUNI—are, if anything, even thicker on the ground. Though the drivers selected for the study weren't users of anything except driving-specific mobile tools, they had no difficulty finding lots of excellent ones for navigating public transit systems, for choosing safe and efficient bike paths, and even the best routes for walking.

Before and after their week of auto deprivation, the study's participants were interviewed in depth about their experiences. Two-thirds of them reported that the absence of a car exposed them to new experiences. They felt more connected to their communities. Many felt literally claustrophobic when they returned to driving after the deprivation experiment.

There's more. The results confirmed that a perceived "experience gap" separating driving from public transit explains a lot of the resistance many travelers have about transit in general. And the biggest chunk of that gap wasn't the feeling of ownership they got from their cars, or the greater comfort of driving. It wasn't even status. Though Americans, especially those Millennials, still derive status from their consumption choices, they're now more likely to do so from the services they choose, rather than the products they own: Netflix and HBO, not DVDs. Spotify, not CDs.

So, if not comfort or status, then what? Autonomy. Travelers feel helpless and dependent when they have to rely on public transit, independent when they're behind the wheel of a car. Specifically, most respondents tend to think that boarding a bus or train makes them hostages to an inflexible system. They believe, with some justice, that they can make in-the-moment decisions when driving that aren't possible on a streetcar, train, or bus.

They have a point. You can't reverse a bus because you forgot your purse at home, or stop a streetcar because you have a sudden hunger pang that strikes you as you pass a barbecue joint. From scandals like National City Lines' purchase of dozens of urban streetcar lines in order to shut them down, or political decisions like the GI Bill's preference for suburban construction, or the Interstate Highway System's subsidy for limited-access roads, it's tempting to conclude that the automobile never had any intrinsic appeal at all, that it triumphed over public transit in a rigged game. But that turns out not to be completely true. The dice were loaded, all right, but even if they hadn't been, the private automobile would still have been a very attractive choice for most people. There was always a lot of autonomy in the automobile.

This appears, at first glance, to be an obstacle for a multimodal, active transportation future. But I choose to see it as inspiring. What the research shows isn't that travelers want *cars*, but rather that they want *freedom and control*. If technology can make them feel free and in control, if it can liberate them from, for example, the tyranny of cars, such as the need to find a place to park them, they're going to like it. A lot.

Overall, the reactions of the deprivation-study drivers to a week of being walkers, bikers, and smartphone-wielding passengers were nearly all positive. But, as is often the case, the more they got, the more they wanted. Most especially, they wanted (and needed) a comprehensive information resource that showed *all* possible travel choices, with comparative data on time, availability, and cost.

It's not there, not yet. But the reason it's getting closer all the time is the other reason that San Francisco and Boston were chosen for the study. Both cities are pioneers in what's known in the app business as "open data." While the municipal transit agencies in both places produce half a dozen different user-friendly components of an intelligent transportation system, they don't make them all. They don't need to. They just need to give away the information they're already collecting. Just a few years ago, according to Richard Davey, general manager of the Massachusetts Bay Transportation Authority, "providing riders with real-time information would have required the installation of costly signs at bus stops throughout the system." Now, though, all they have to do is to make the data freely available, and wait for third-party developers to step into the breach and create apps; in Boston as of this writing, there are more than thirty just for the trains and buses of the MBTA.

Open data is making things happen in systems all over the country, some of them a lot more surprising than San Francisco and Boston.

- In America's mountain West—the "Greater Yellowstone Region," which hosts more than three million visitors annually—transportation providers in twenty-seven rural counties in Idaho, Wyoming, and Montana have formed, through a member co-op, the LINX system, a web and mobile app that allows users to book and confirm tickets for transit throughout the region. LINXComm—still testing, as of this writing—offers online ticketing, GPS location information, and Wi-Fi service on the region's buses.
- In the mid-sized city of Chattanooga, Tennessee—170,000 people live in the city proper, half a million in the metropolitan region—the Chattanooga Area Regional Transportation Authority's SmartBus program allows users to connect to vehicles on the sixteen lines within the system by using cell-

phones and Wi-Fi access on buses. Automated announcements from CARTA send texts and messages to mobile devices advising of bus delays, arrivals, and route changes in real time.

Real time is real important. A survey of Chicago-area commuters unsurprisingly concluded that awareness of, and experience with, real-time transit information increased ridership, especially among infrequent users of the transit system. A lot of people who tended to avoid transit because of earlier experiences with an opaque system were lured back once it became clearer. Another study, this one of the King County system of Seattle/Bellevue, Washington, showed something even more important, at least for anyone interested in persuading more people to choose transit. It turns out that riders without real-time information consistently report their *perceived* wait times as longer than the *actual* time they experience. Time always seems longer in the absence of a known end point, and not just for transit; if you're asked how long you've been watching a particular movie, you're far more likely to overestimate the time when you don't know when it will end. The same is true for transit. When riders were given accurate information about wait times for buses—King County's OneBusAway system provides next-bus countdown information by website, text message, and smartphone apps—it not only decreased their *actual* wait time (because they were able to arrive closer to true departure times) by nearly two minutes, but decreased their *perceived* wait time by an additional 13 percent. That's made for lots of happy (or, at least, happier) bus riders in King County.

Not as many as in Salt Lake City, though.

The geography of Salt Lake City, the biggest city in Utah—and the biggest city in the huge and sparsely populated portion of the

United States known as the Intermountain West—makes it a surprisingly promising place for building a workable transit system. The city itself has the advantage of decent density, with 190,000 people living in about 110 square miles, but the real advantage is the topography of the metropolitan area. Mountain ranges and lakes pack the 2.3 million people who live along the Wasatch Front, a string of cities connecting Salt Lake with Ogden to the north and Provo to the south, into a space that's 120 miles long but nowhere more than about 18 miles wide. The Wasatch Front can't really sprawl.

Basin-and-range geography made building a world-class regional transit system possible in Utah. It didn't require it, though. That's something Salt Lake City chose for itself. In 1997, after the city was picked to host the 2002 Winter Olympics, politicians, business leaders, and farmers' associations from the four-county area surrounding Salt Lake recruited environmental and urban planning experts to host a series of public meetings that they named "Envision Utah." The idea was to accommodate both the surge associated with the Olympics and the predicted long-term growth of the region, to do so in a way that preserved the natural environment that made it so attractive in the first place, and to keep Salt Lake City attractive to the next generation of transit-happy Millennials.

The hallmark of Envision Utah was what its creators called a strategy of "quality growth": an explicit commitment to less sprawl and more density. Less reliance on cars, more on walking and transit.* Step one was the TRAX light rail system—multiple-car trolleys powered by overhead electrical wires—that opened with seventeen miles of track and twenty-three stations in 1999. It was an immediate success, so much so that the crowds soon rivaled those of Tokyo subways at rush hour. By 2006, the Olympics were long gone, but the Utah

---

* And biking. Salt Lake City is in the process of building eighty-seven miles of bike paths.

Transit Authority, or UTA, had expanded the system to accommodate virtually the entire Wasatch Range metro area. It added twenty-eight miles of new trolley track, forty more stops, and the FrontRunner, which carries passengers on eighty-eight miles of heavier commuter rail running from Ogden through Salt Lake all the way to Provo. The University Line, to the University of Utah and Medical Center, was opened between 2001 and 2003, taking daily student ridership from 1,500 a day to more than 10,000.* A new Green Line connected the city with its airport, the Red Line with Amtrak's California Zephyr train to Chicago, and the Blue Line with the FrontRunner to Provo. The Blue Line also connects with Salt Lake City's Sugar House Line, which serves one of the city's oldest neighborhoods with another fixed-rail system powered by overhead wires, but one more like a streetcar. The Sugar House Line runs more slowly than the rest of the city's trolleys, stops more frequently, and uses single cars rather than multicar trains.

With its combination of traditional buses, bus rapid transit, street-cars, and light and heavy rail, Salt Lake City may have the most multimodal transit system in the United States. It might even be the best large public transportation system in North America. That's what Michael Melaniphy, president of the American Public Transportation Association, said when APTA named Utah Transit Authority 2013's "outstanding public transportation system," though he couldn't have been very surprised. It was the fourth time that UTA had been recognized by the association.

But while UTA gets a lot of deserved applause from the professional engineering community for building such an extensive system

---

* According to Hal Johnson, UTA's manager of Project Development, campus parking—ten thousand total spaces—was at 96 percent capacity in the fall of 2001. By 2013, that had dropped to 70 percent, entirely because of the number of students using the University Line.

so rapidly—in the five years from 2008 to 2013, UTA completed seventy miles of rail line—and from Salt Lake City's taxpayers for doing it for $300 million less than was budgeted for it, the system wouldn't be very popular with riders if none of them could figure it out. And it's definitely popular. Annual ridership is closing in on forty-five million, with nearly twenty million trips on UTA's 130-plus bus routes. The routes include the MAX, a limited-stop bus with dedicated lanes, credit card ticketing, and traffic signal priority, which UTA calls "light rail on rubber tires." As MAX buses approach intersections, the lights turn green, which is the reason that they enjoy an unheard-of 97 percent on-time performance. TRAX generates more than eighteen million trips and the FrontRunner is closing in on four million, with a few million more trips via streetcar, vans for the disabled, and so on.

This kind of arithmetic is impressive, but it's also daunting. Salt Lake City is an emphatically multimodal system, which means that a very high percentage of trips require a transfer from one route to another, and frequently between modes. It's hard to see how this could work with nothing but a traditional map.

Luckily, it doesn't have to. As far back as the 2002 Olympics, when the Federal Highway Administration commissioned a study of what even then was Utah's state-of-the-art intelligent transportation system, the state's transportation agencies have been leaders in getting information to travelers. It's not much of a surprise, then, that UTA has embraced mobile information systems as enthusiastically as any system in the country. On its own, it operates mobile and web-based apps like Ride Time, UTA Pro, TRAX Tracker (this one includes countdown times for the next three trains), and UTA Tracker (with a special version for students at the University of Utah, more than a third of whom are commuters who get to classes using UTA). UTA also allows third parties access to its data, which means that riders throughout the Wasatch Range can use apps like

GeoUTA, a GPS-driven app tracking UTA buses; iTransitBuddy Lite for train schedules; Roadify Transit for real-time arrivals and departures for multiple transit choices; SmartTransit; and Moovit, which uses UTA-supplied open data but supplements it with anonymous crowd-sourced information.

It's not just Utah, of course. CityMapper (the "Ultimate Transit App") provides point-to-point routing plus real-time departure information on every available form of public transit for San Francisco, Chicago, New York, Washington, DC, Boston, London, Paris, Berlin, Madrid, Barcelona, Milan, and Rome—and, with a single stroke, will plan a "get me home" route, as well. TransitAPP uses its software platform and the GPS locator in any mobile device to show a similar menu of transit options and departure times, plus the availability of bikeshares, and any service advisories in real time for eighty-seven cities (and counting) in the United States, Europe, and South America. The "directions" panel from Google Maps, of course, does the same thing for everywhere Google Maps has a map, which is, of course, everywhere, including the floor of the Atlantic Ocean, a region with fairly limited transit options.

Apps don't just make travel faster or more efficient. Though less known than Google Maps or CityMapper, a bunch of mobile apps with names like Random GPS, Serendipitor, and Drift generate routes for dérives (French for "drift," or aimless strolling—and, yes, I know how silly this sounds). One team of researchers from the University of Torino and Yahoo Labs created a mobile mapping algorithm that didn't find the shortest routes, or even the most meandering, but the most pleasant—the ones with the greenery and the Victorian houses—using an algorithm that ranks every route choice along three criteria: beauty, quiet, and happiness. As you might guess, quantifying this wasn't the easiest thing in the world. The researchers used the online votes given to 3.7 million photos of London street scenes, and another 1.3 million from Boston, loaded on the photo-sharing site Flickr to compute the elements that resulted in the highest vote totals. The "psychogeography"—yes, this is actually a thing; it's been part of the world of academia since the 1950s—algorithm generates four different paths from London's Euston Square to the Tate Modern: the shortest, the quietest, the prettiest, and the happiest.

I suspect that apps like these have barely scratched the surface of what all that information and computing power can do. It's not entirely accurate to say that smartphones have made us smarter, but in a way they have. Give me an iPhone and a broadband connection and I could probably fight Ken Jennings to a draw in a mano-a-mano game of *Jeopardy*. With the same tools, even a first-time visitor to New York might beat me in a subway race from Bensonhurst to Lincoln Center.

This phenomenon illustrates, as well as anything I know, what the Street Smart program is all about. Until very recently, nearly everyone made travel decisions—Shall we walk or ride? Depart this morning or this afternoon?—using a very limited number of tools that were mostly just a combination of habit and guesswork. In many parts of the world, that's still the case.

In smart cities, though, these limits don't exist anymore. In them, giant oceans of information about schedules, prices, and routes are easily navigated by just about everyone. It's not that smart cities are filled with nothing but smart people (though it may be that they're the first to realize the advantages of living in them). It's that you don't have to be a genius to get the most out of smart buses, smart streetcars, smart sidewalks, and, of course, smart streets.

>>>

In August of 2014, I used the car service known as Uber for the first time. I had been at the annual Sam Schwartz Engineering Coney Island Afternoon, which gives folks in our New York office the chance to blow off some steam riding the (very scary) Cyclone wooden roller coaster, which has been terrifying riders since 1927; to take the swinging car on the Wonder Wheel; and even to experience the thrill of being shot into the air from gigantic slingshots, which is where I, at least, draw the line. After, and I stress *after*, the rides, we have a picnic-style dinner of hot dogs, hamburgers, and fries.

By the time dinner was done, the August sun had set. We had all taken the subway from our Manhattan office to the last stop in Brooklyn, and I intended to return the same way. But after a few beers and feeling really good, I thought, "Why don't I try Uber?" I had read enough about it to know that how popular it had become, and had, months before, downloaded the app to my smartphone, but there's nothing like doing it. I logged in, punched in my request, and was told that a car would pick me up in three to four minutes. It even showed the car on a map and I could see it was pretty close. After five minutes, though, the car wasn't any closer. I was confused. Like all first-timers with a new toy, I thought I had done something wrong, though I discovered, soon enough, that the driver wasn't actually in his car but relaxing at his apartment when he got the message, and it took a few minutes before he dressed and hopped into the car.

I now use Uber with some frequency and have had nothing but good experiences. It is reliable, safe, and not too expensive. I do worry, however, what a fleet of cars transporting one passenger at a time means if it continues to grow at the pace of Uber. Think of a building the size of the Willis Tower in Chicago in which everyone gets to ride in his or her own elevator, alone. This is a reason that my firm is working with VIA, a company that solves part of the problem by using a single vehicle to transport up to eight people with eight different origins and destinations efficiently through the use of very complex algorithms. Though I have to admit that another part of the reason I find VIA, Uber, and their ridesharing competitors so fascinating is that so many of the people who are now working on these kinds of complex traffic problems are, like me, lapsed physicists, using sophisticated mathematics to improve the world of transportation. (In fact, my professor brother, forty years after rejecting me as a physics has-been, invited me to a physics PhD candidate's defense of her thesis, which mathematically described the flow of traffic on highways. Now who's the scientist?)

Actually, although Uber is often described as a ridesharing company, the "sharing" part is a little disingenuous. In fact, the only sharing that applies to most of the trips taken by travelers using Uber or Lyft (though not VIA) comes from the drivers sharing their cars with passengers. What these companies actually do is *ride-matching*.* The basic structure of the business is fairly simple. Drivers pass background checks (of themselves and their cars; in some places, like New York, they are also required to have a specialized license). They are given either dedicated phones or apps for their existing phones. Whenever they're online, they get messages telling them when an order has been placed for service within what a GPS-driven algorithm concludes is a reasonable distance away. Meanwhile, a customer who has an account with the service requests a ride, is told the price, and confirms. After the ride is complete, the customer's credit card is charged, with some percentage going to the ride-matching service and the rest to the driver, who is responsible for gas and tolls. Most of the services also oblige drivers and customers to rate one another. Which is why, even more than state-of-the-art apps for public transit, they are creatures of the age of mobile GPS.

Very young creatures, at that. Uber is, as I write, the largest and the oldest of the ride-matching companies, though it began as a service offering limos and SUVs in San Francisco only in 2010. (A few earlier

---

* At Uber, ridesharing—people traveling from roughly the same origin to about the same destination, while splitting the cost of the trip at a discount—is rare enough that it has its own name: uberPOOL.

incarnations confuse matters, but that's when the mobile app at the center of the service, which handled reservations, payment, and driver ratings, went live.) At the time, the base fee was $8 plus $5 a mile and a $15 minimum. Two years later, the company launched the UberX program which expanded the service to offer "sharing" for essentially any driver who could pass the background check and owned an acceptable car.

That was when things started to heat up. Competitors like Sidecar (launched January of 2012) and Lyft (founded summer of 2012 as an extension of an earlier city-to-city ridesharing service known as Zimride) noticed the potential upside for a business that could extract revenue from travelers without actually investing in anything as expensive as buses, trains, or even cars; all that they needed were software algorithms and marketing. Though the California Public Utilities Commission, under pressure from existing taxi services, shut them all down, it allowed them to reopen the following year as what the state of California now calls "Transportation Network Companies."

Uber, by far the biggest kid on the ridesharing block, expanded to Paris, Toronto, and London in 2012, and hasn't looked back. By 2015 you could download the Uber app to your smartphone and request an Uber pickup in more than two hundred cities in forty-five countries.* This kind of growth attracts all sorts of attention. *USA Today* picked Uber as their "tech company of the year" in 2013, and venture capitalists have invested so much in the company that, as of the end of 2014, it had a valuation somewhere north of $40 billion.

Not all the attention was positive, however. None of the original San Francisco–based companies, or newer arrivals such as the Israeli startup Gett, have figured out how to avoid controversy for more than a week or two. The backlash against Uber specifically, and ride-matching companies generally, was as rapid and ferocious as the

---

* Lyft, the Avis to Uber's Hertz, operates in a third as many markets.

business's own growth. In general, the complaints came from one (or more) of four categories:

- Objections from existing taxi businesses and competitors either because companies like Uber threatened their monopolies or because, as unregulated competitors, the ride-matching companies enjoyed an unfair advantage.
- Objections from consumers, mostly over the Uber-specific policy of *surge pricing*: raising fare prices by up to 500 percent during times of high demand.
- Objections from other ridesharing services about abusive business practices.
- Objections from their own drivers.

All of them have their points. I can understand why taxicab drivers, who paid hundreds of thousands of dollars (or in New York, more than a million dollars) for what they were told was an exclusive franchise, might be upset to learn that it wasn't nearly as valuable in 2015 as it had been in 2012. In Chicago and New York, during the two years after those app-driven fleets appeared, the price of an exclusive taxi medallion fell 17 percent (for a New York City taxi medallion, this represented a decline of nearly $180,000). In Boston, it fell 20 percent. I also get the bad feelings engendered by surge pricing. Though I believe in raising tolls on bridges and tunnels to transit-rich areas like Manhattan to reflect the real demand for them, I also understand why charging a hundred bucks for a twenty-block ride just because it's snowing and it's Valentine's Day can tick people off.

The concerns about business practices, which include threatening journalists and making false reservations with competitors to limit their performance, aren't really in the same category. It's not that they're not important, but that they're not integral to the ride-matching business model. Complaints that come from drivers are a little different. So long as Lyft and Uber and the others are in competition with one another, they're going to be under pressure to cut prices, which inevitably comes out of the pockets of their drivers. And so long as they're able to offer such great service by saturating neighborhoods with cars, they're not just competing with other companies. Uber's own drivers are, inevitably, competing with one another, and a significant number of them are working for what amounts to a little above minimum wage. In Los Angeles, the largest US market for the most popular service, uberX, drivers average less than $17 an hour before gas and tolls.

However, even these aren't the biggest concerns. If the goal is to improve mobility for city dwellers—to replace automobile dependency with active and multimodal transportation options—then it's difficult to see how ride-matching can ever be more than a small part of the solution. That's because the defining characteristic of the Ubers and Lyfts of the world (and of their very vocal cheerleaders) is hostility to regulation.

For decades now, regulation has been getting very bad press, and not just from conservative politicians and libertarian economists. Everyone has a list of silly bureaucratic rules that have long outlived their usefulness, and I'm no exception. One of my favorites is the requirement that a car's registration sticker be to the left of the inspection sticker or you'll get a ticket. Wait, I think it might be the other way around. Actually, I'm not sure whether it applies when you're in the car or facing the car. But, after spending a lifetime studying the subject, one of the few unarguably true things I've learned about transportation networks is that access to them can't be efficiently allocated by an unregulated free market.

The first problem with eliminating, or strictly limiting, regulation of these new and exciting services is consumer protection. Because ride-matching isn't a regulated business, the relationship between drivers and riders—all that "sharing"—is governed by contract law.

When you download an app and take a trip in a car you summoned, the contract you accepted is between you and your driver, not with the company that created the app. Uber isn't responsible, for example, if one of their drivers attacks you, or runs you down. That's why they insist that the drivers carry liability insurance of $1 million. The company's terms and conditions include the following (the capitalization is theirs, not mine):

YOU ACKNOWLEDGE THAT UBER DOES NOT PROVIDE TRANSPORTATION OR LOGISTICS SERVICES OR FUNC-TION AS A TRANSPORTATION CARRIER. UBER'S SERVICES MAY BE USED BY YOU TO REQUEST AND SCHEDULE TRANSPORTATION OR LOGISTICS SERVICES WITH THIRD PARTY PROVIDERS, BUT YOU AGREE THAT UBER HAS NO RESPONSIBILITY OR LIABILITY TO YOU RELATED TO ANY TRANSPORTATION OR LOGISTICS PROVIDED TO YOU BY THIRD PARTY PROVIDERS THROUGH THE USE OF THE SER-VICES OTHER THAN AS EXPRESSLY SET FORTH IN THESE TERMS.

UBER DOES NOT GUARANTEE THE SUITABILITY, SAFETY OR ABILITY OF THIRD PARTY PROVIDERS. IT IS SOLELY YOUR RESPONSIBILITY TO DETERMINE IF A THIRD PARTY PROVIDER WILL MEET YOUR NEEDS AND EXPECTATIONS. UBER WILL NOT PARTICIPATE IN DISPUTES BETWEEN YOU AND A THIRD PARTY PROVIDER. BY USING THE SERVICES, YOU ACKNOWLEDGE THAT YOU MAY BE EXPOSED TO SITUATIONS INVOLVING THIRD PARTY PROVIDERS THAT ARE POTENTIALLY UNSAFE, OFFENSIVE, HARMFUL TO MI-NORS, OR OTHERWISE OBJECTIONABLE, AND THAT USE OF THIRD PARTY PROVIDERS ARRANGED OR SCHEDULED US-ING THE SERVICES IS AT YOUR OWN RISK AND JUDGMENT. UBER SHALL NOT HAVE ANY LIABILITY ARISING FROM OR

IN ANY WAY RELATED TO YOUR TRANSACTIONS OR RELA-
TIONSHIP WITH THIRD PARTY PROVIDERS.

Uber clearly has no legal exposure whatever. But the real problem
with an unregulated market in ride-matching, where the number of
smartphone-dispatched cars is limited only by the number of willing drivers, isn't a lack of liability. It's a surplus of VIM: Vehicles in
motion.

The VIM problem isn't a new one, but then, once you strip away
the GPS and smartphone apps from ride-matching services, they're
not entirely new either. What they resemble, more than anything else,
are old-fashioned radio-dispatched limousines, a subject with which I
have some history. Back in 1982, when the number of taxi medallions
in New York City—at that time, 11,787, which was the same number
issued in 1937, although since then it's been allowed to increase to
13,347—seemed inadequate to the demand, a guy named Bill Fugazy,
who owned the Fugazy Limousine Company, announced that he was
prepared to put six thousand brand new limousines on the streets
of the city, each of them just a phone call away from anyone with a
credit card.

The number actually didn't sound too daunting. More than thirty
thousand vehicles enter Midtown Manhattan each hour, two hundred
thousand a day. Manhattan's bridges and tunnels were handling more
than one million daily. What could be so difficult about handling another six thousand? The mayor was for it. The City Council was for
it. The voting public was for it. The only people who saw any red flags
were cranky transportation engineers. Such as me.

What we knew was this: at that time, the number of vehicles in
Manhattan's Central Business District at any one time was between
139,000 and 181,000. But we also knew that not all of them were
actually moving. Many if not most were parked. I figured that the way
to calculate the true number of vehicles in motion for any given hour

required knowing the miles traveled—yes, our old friend VMT—during that hour divided by the speed, in miles per hour.

Simple algebra. And simple geometry. Knowing, for example, that the core of Manhattan's grid comprised segments of eleven avenues, each segment 1.19 miles long, I was able to calculate that, during the morning rush hour, between the hours of 8 and 9 a.m., only a few more than 5,200 vehicles in the core were in motion, and the maximum number that would allow any movement at all was less than 9,000. Which meant that if only a third of those radio-controlled limos-of-the-future were to operate in the most desirable part of New York at any given time, they would increase traffic density by at least 20 percent. The result? Total gridlock.* As I wrote at the time, all those limos would be stopped dead, with their only purpose to provide seating space on Manhattan streets at $25 per hour.

It's not just a New York problem. Every city on the planet has a measurable VIM maximum. It's a different number for each city. In Manhattan, it's a little more than seven thousand cars. Each car above that critical number on the streets results in fewer total miles traveled. Nor is it like an on-off switch. Mobility starts to degrade long before complete gridlock occurs.

This doesn't mean that there's no place for ride-matching services in a Street Smart city. Not only are they hugely convenient, they make the decision to live without a personal car possible, even attractive. I applaud the technology that created them, and expect that they will continue to supplant existing taxi companies, or to convert those existing companies to a service that looks a lot like Uber: cabs that can be summoned to a particular location using GPS, and paid for using smartphones. But to the degree that their appeal depends on increasing the supply of cars to the point that no one is ever more than a

---

* I'm considering trademarking the term: Total gridlock^{TM}.

few minutes away from a roving driver waiting for a smartphone to put driver and rider together, the model is fundamentally unsustainable. Long before enough smartphone-carrying drivers hit the streets, the VIM tipping point will be reached. Beyond that point—that is, beyond the maximum carrying capacity of a particular city's streets—the numbers won't add up to more mobility, but less.

This is an unavoidable fact of life. No matter how sophisticated the technology becomes, public streets will remain a public resource with finite capacity. When ride-matching services like Uber and Lyft treat city streets as a free good, they're just repeating the same conceptual mistake that the original champions of motordom did during the 1920s—the argument that, while streetcars and trains were responsible for maintenance of "their" right-of-way, streets were free for everyone. Smart cities shouldn't insist on stupid regulation. But that doesn't mean they can do without regulation at all.

>>>

On Alice's second trip through the looking glass, she meets Humpty Dumpty, who tells her that the word *glory* means the same thing as "a nice knock-down argument." When she objects, he tells her, "When I use a word, it means just what I choose it to mean—neither more nor less."

Smart city is like that. Ever since the term *smart cities* started appearing in the early 2000s, it's been used in a dozen different senses, from describing the sort of place that attracts creative industries like publishing, design, R&D, and advertising* to one that is able to adapt to changing circumstances, to one that offers a more sustainable quality of life. Smartness, in one definition, is anything that results in better public services and lower energy use. Cities are said to have

---

* If you're thinking that *creative industry* is another Humpty Dumpty phrase, you're right.

smart infrastructures, smart governance, and smart healthcare, and each category is foggier than the last.

For transportation, though, it's a lot clearer: A smart city uses information to improve mobility and access for its residents and visitors. The more it uses information, the smarter it is.

In the same way that widely distributed and accessible information is changing consumption choices from products to services, it's transforming the components of mobility from the physical—vehicles, tracks, roads, fuel—to the virtual. This isn't just the Millennial-led revolution in work, entertainment, shopping, and socializing, all of which are now activities that can be done, at least some of the time, without leaving home. It is a shift in the kind of infrastructure that can now be built for when we do leave home.

Think of it this way: Ever since the architects and builders of the first cities started roughing out their plans on clay tablets or papyrus scrolls, they've faced the same kind of problem, which is that their transportation corridors, whether roads or rails, needed to be built to accommodate peak demand. By definition, therefore, during every time of the day or year when demand was below the peak, the systems had a lot of surplus capacity, what we in the trade call *over-engineering*. As cities grew, so did peak demand, and, for a long time, the only way to satisfy that demand was by increasing capacity: More (or wider) roads and rails. More over-engineering.

Lots of people have heard of the "Report Card" on America's infrastructure prepared annually by the American Society of Civil Engineers. (Full disclosure: I'm not only a member of the society but have served on the New York Committee on America's Infrastructure, which is responsible for assigning grades.) The Report Card gives a grade to sixteen different categories of America's infrastructure, from aviation to ports to schools to inland waterways, and if you've heard of it at all, you probably know that our overall GPA is currently a pretty pathetic D+. That same report estimates the investment needed to bring us up to a passing grade by 2020 at $3.635 trillion—that's tril-lion, with a "T." The largest single component of that number, $1.735 trillion, is surface transportation: roads, highways, transit, and bridges.

However, when you dig a little deeper into the way in which that number was calculated, here's what you'll find.

In the "Roads" category, the biggest reason that the ASCE gives America's four million miles of public roadways a grade of D is the costs of congestion. But as we've seen, congestion isn't always what it appears. The congestion paradox—that more congestion is correlated with higher prosperity—would seem to argue that spending hundreds of billions of dollars in road construction to alleviate it might not be the best way to improve the average American's bank account.

Even better—or worse, really—the ASCE Report Card on roads also makes some unpersuasive assumptions about future driving hab-its. This is a direct quote from the 2013 Report Card:

> While VMT has been decreasing over the last few years [that is, from 2004 to 2010, which is the last date available for the ASCE numbers] due to continued congestion and the recession, the trend is not likely to continue for a long period of time.

This is an assumption backed up, literally, by nothing. My col-leagues at the ASCE even backtrack a bit in the same report, pointing out that "our nation's roadways can benefit from significant perfor-mance improvements without adding new highway lanes . . . includ-ing wider use of performance pricing, variable speed limits, and more efficient signal timing." Unmentioned, for some reason, are other applications of the newest tools of the information revolution, ones that make it possible, for the first time, to redistribute demand across different times, modes, or routes, allowing the same infrastructure to carry more people from place to place quickly, safely, and efficiently. This is actually good news. It turns out we can improve many, if not most, of the deficiencies of American roads for a whole lot less than a trillion dollars. Smart cities are using those technologies for managing peak transportation demand in the same way that a modern power grid automatically reroutes electricity. And for the same reason: they save money.

The comparison between the power grid and the transportation network is a pretty good one. From the time the first power grids were built at the end of the nineteenth century through the 1960s, power companies had a similar peak-demand problem as the same era's roads and rails: if you build for peak demand, you find yourself with a lot of expensive and redundant capacity, like "peaking power" generators that were turned on only when July heat waves caused millions of air conditioners to work overtime. The reason was the same for power generation as for transportation: since electric utilities could measure power demand only in limited ways, they had to over-engineer the system.

Now, though, what is known as a "smart grid" has the ability to collect huge amounts of data from devices like automatic meters that provide continuous real-time information. With access to so much information that it is measured in exabytes,[*] and the computer capacity to analyze it instantaneously, the system becomes highly dynamic. Some devices, like air conditioners, now have the ability to adjust their cycles when the grid is working its hardest. Like the old-fashioned grid, a modern smart grid can shunt power to different portions of the network automatically, but it can also manage consumption.

There are dozens of analogies for this kind of data collection and management in a smart city's transportation grid. The four-thousand-plus sensors that Zurich Public Transport uses to manage automobile and streetcar traffic are one of them. Like an electrical utility adjusting the cycle of an industrial air conditioner because the system is oper-

---

[*] One quintillion bytes. And, yes, I had to look it up.

ating at peak demand, Zurich allows only as many cars into its center city as can be accommodated without congestion. Just as important, though, for a smart city's transportation system is the ever-growing network of hundreds of millions of GPS-enabled smartphones. Those mobile devices aren't just providing travelers with maps, turn-by-turn directions, and the occasional restaurant review. They're also populating the network itself with information about the phone users' location and speed. The data they send up the line is why the information that returns—when your bus will arrive, for example—is ever more precise and useful. Better data in, better data out. The city of Dallas and the US Department of Transportation have built what they've named the "511DFW system," essentially a public website, a phone-enabled travel line, and an Interactive Voice Response system that consolidates sensor data, smartphone GPS signals, and real-time information on road closures and collisions, to guide users to optimal routes by any combination of travel modes.

Lots of similar systems are the creations of public transportation systems themselves. Some are general, others very specific. The French national rail company, SNCF, uses a sophisticated algorithm to predict, based on time of year, weather, disruptions, and so on, how many people are likely to be traveling on any particular train, up to providing an estimate of the likelihood of getting a seat, and on which car. SFpark, a project of the San Francisco Municipal Transportation Authority, uses sensor data from parking meters to offer real-time information about available parking, a nontrivial aspect of transportation management, since, at any given time, 30 to 50 percent of the VIM in a city consists of drivers looking for parking spaces.

Not all the information permeating the system is created by public agencies, or even by private companies using public data. The private software-and-data company INRIX collects trillions of bytes of information from nearly two hundred million smartphones and other mobile devices (like fleet vehicles with GPS locators), analyzes it, and sends it out in the form of real-time traffic information to, among others, Google Maps and the navigation device manufacturer TomTom. A thousand different ways to smarten up transportation systems are already in operation, and ten thousand more are probably gestating in the brains of software designers and app builders.

Data, algorithms, and smartness are the missing ingredients required for building a new kind of transportation network. Without them, the best-designed multimodal transportation network imaginable, one with precisely the right number of routes through exactly the right neighborhoods, one with high density and well-designed walking paths and safe roads, one with the most diversified and comfortable assortment of trains, streetcars, buses, cabs, and private automobiles, is still deficient. Remember those two classes of travelers in our hypothetical transit hub? The ones who were comfortable with the system and, well, the other ones? What separated the two wasn't native intelligence but familiarity, which is really just another word for easily accessible data. Linking those thirty-two satellites to a billion (and counting) smartphones is the key ingredient putting the "smart" into Street Smart.

The impact of this is already enormous, and its potential is even greater. It's more than encouraging tourists to take subways and buses when visiting new cities. It's more than supplying transportation departments with the ability to balance supply and demand for mobility in real time, and definitely a lot more than enabling thousands of Uber and Lyft drivers to race one another to the same traveler standing on the same corner. The real value of pouring all that information into the system is that it gives the same sense of autonomy to transit users as the old system did to automobile drivers. This, as we'll see, is critical. Though easy-to-access information is, indeed, the missing ingredient for a modern multimodal transportation network, such a network still won't survive long-term unless it attracts the widest possible customer base. A Street Smart system needs to be useful.

CHAPTER 8

TUXEDOS ON THE SUBWAY

Transportation Anywhere, Anytime, and for Everybody

MORE THAN FORTY YEARS AGO, WHEN I WAS IN GRADUATE SCHOOL AT the University of Pennsylvania, my mentor and advisor, Vukan Vuchic, often compared the state of transit systems in the United States with those in European cities. I especially recall his vivid description of the subway system in Moscow—not just the efficiency of the trains, but the beauty of the stations, which featured chandeliers hanging from the ceiling as if they were lighting nineteenth-century ballrooms.

Even more vividly, I remember Professor Vuchic saying that, in Moscow, it was common to see formally dressed couples on the subway: women elegantly turned out in long dresses, men in tuxedos, on their way to the opera or the theater. "Can you imagine," he exclaimed, "someone riding the New York City subway wearing a tuxedo?"

In 1969, when I first heard Professor Vuchic on the subject, he had a point. It was two decades after the subway fare was doubled from a nickel to a dime, beginning a vicious circle of regular fare hikes and worsening service, and more than five years before the financial crisis that would mark an even steeper decline in New York's transit system—and in just about every aspect of life in New York. Subways and buses weren't exactly the first choice for the city's more affluent residents. In a very smart 2014 column in the *New York Post*, Nicole Gelinas reminded readers that as far back as 1953, Esther, the poorly paid magazine intern who is the heroine of Sylvia Plath's novel *The Bell Jar*, took cabs everywhere in order to avoid the smelly, dirty, not-for-nice-girls subways, especially when dressed for an evening out. Thirty years later, the heroes of Jay McInerney's *Bright Lights, Big City* were, if anything, even more repelled by New York City's public transit. By then there was plenty of dressing up and revelry, but the subways are mentioned only a few times, and never positively: "At the subway station, you wait fifteen minutes for a train [until] a local, enervated by graffiti, shuffles into the station."

But thirty years after that? In the spring of 2014, I left a black tie affair at the Waldorf Astoria on Park Avenue and 50th Street, walked four blocks to the subway station at 53rd Street, and was home in fifteen minutes. Me and my tuxedo and my wife dressed to the "nines." On the subway.

The point of this story isn't to advertise my virtue, or to give a shout-out to the investments made in my hometown's public transit system over the last thirty years. It's not even to demonstrate how a great public transit system—one that operates not just everywhere, and all the time, but *for everyone*—builds social cohesion. Not exactly, anyway. It's this: because great public transportation systems are expensive, they only get fully funded when they're used by both the well-to-do and the not-doing-so-well.

This is one of the sad but true aspects of transportation, one that they don't teach in engineering school. No matter how well laid out the sidewalks and bike paths of a city's active transportation network, no matter how cleverly designed its multimodal grid, no matter how easily its residents can get real-time interactive directions, if the city's public transportation becomes a system only for the less well-off, it's in trouble. It's the same phenomenon that hamstrings public hospitals and public education: unless every socioeconomic group in a particular city feels invested in the system, it starves. As much as anything else, this fact explains why, despite all the well-documented problems with our dependence on private automobiles, road building continues to have first call on transportation budgets. Streets and highways really are used by everyone. Whether we're talking eighteenth-century streets like Bedford Avenue, or Houston's hypertrophied Katy Freeway, roads are just as likely to carry a brand new Mercedes-Benz as a ten-year-old Chevrolet Impala. Buses and streetcars, on the other hand, are the opposite of economically diverse. In the United States, 63 percent of the users of small transit systems, 51 percent of users of medium-size transit systems, and even 41 percent of riders in the largest transit systems are at or below the poverty line.

Even worse, the tendency of public transit systems to be perceived as the choice of travelers who can't afford something better is vulnerable to what engineers call *positive feedback*: small pushes in one direction (either good or bad) tend to accelerate movement in that same direction. It can become a vicious circle: the more transit becomes dominated by less affluent people, the more it becomes associated with poverty. And the more it gets associated with poverty, the less appealing it becomes for the affluent. Equity declines.

You'd be forgiven for thinking that transportation had been at the front line in the struggle for equity in the United States for more than a century, though not always in the way that I've used it above. The term appeared prominently in the names of two vast multiyear federal transportation bills in the last two decades: the 1999 "Transportation Equity Act for the 21st Century" and its 2005 successor, the "Safe, Accountable, Flexible, Efficient, Transportation Equity Act

[SAFETEA]."* In both cases *equity* is used to describe a fair, or at least not too unfair, allocation of federal highway funds among the states.

Those multiyear transportation bills are all about something often called *return-to-source* or *horizontal equity*: a bit of jargon that describes a point at which states, municipalities, and even individuals, in the words of Todd Litman of the Victoria Transport Policy Institute, "get what they pay for, and pay for what they get." SAFETEA, for example, guaranteed that each state get back between 90 and 92 percent of its residents' contribution to our old friend, the Highway Trust Fund.

Redistributive or *vertical equity*, on the other hand, has a different definition of fairness. This kind of equity recognizes that since some groups are advantaged, others must be disadvantaged, and, to balance the inequalities of the private sector, the disadvantaged should be favored in public transportation policies. Offering discounted fares to less affluent riders, or increasing bus routes in poor neighborhoods, for example, corrects for the fact that not everyone starts life in an affluent family. Investing in buses that can accommodate wheelchairs balances scales that are out of kilter in another way.

A lot of the equity discussions today, as above, are concerned with the competing demands of relatively well-off drivers and less affluent transit riders. But even within the world of public transit, scarce resources have to be allocated either horizontally or vertically. In fact, long before the automobile transformed travel, there were still pretty pointed debates about the allocation of public transit resources—usually between rich and poor, even more frequently between black and white. The battle for civil rights in America was famously fought out in streetcars, trams, buses, and trains.

---

* These are popularly known in the transportation racket as "TEA-21" and "SAFE-TEA." They were succeeded, in their turn, by the "Moving Ahead for Progress in the 21st Century" bill in 2012, abbreviated as MAP-21. I have occasionally wondered if congressional staff members are tested for their talents at acronym forming at their initial job interviews—and whether the people who get hired are the ones who score the lowest.

In 1892, a black man named Homer Plessy* bought a ticket on the East Louisiana Railroad and took a seat in the "whites only" car, thus deliberately challenging the state's Separate Cars Act. After Judge John Ferguson ruled that Plessy had to pay a fine for his presumption, the appeals that followed ended up in the US Supreme Court. When the Court handed down its decision in *Plessy v. Ferguson*, it upheld the constitutionality of "white" and "colored" sections, enshrining the concept of "separate but equal" facilities for whites and African Americans for the first half of the twentieth century. Five decades later, Rosa Parks refused to take a seat in the back of a public bus in Montgomery, Alabama, igniting the yearlong boycott that was ended by another Supreme Court decision, this time desegregating the city's buses and consequently public transit throughout the United States.

Over and over again, access to public transportation and the promotion of social equality have been joined together at the hip. This isn't just some vague Progressive liking for diversity for its own sake. Smart streets are diverse, but it's not a cost: it's a benefit. Neglecting this is one reason that the streets of so many planned communities, from Radburn, New Jersey, to Columbia, Maryland, aren't as smart as their designers had hoped. Smart streets are more than just paths through well-designed theme parks, and they're the opposite of exclusive. In order for a community to be vital—to be *alive*—its streets have to welcome the widest variety of people, precisely because that's what makes the streets interesting and appealing in the first place. Transportation policies that segregate people by income or education aren't just unfair, they're self-defeating.

For most of American history, the challenge of fighting that kind of segregation was simple, though demanding: assuring access to the disenfranchised. Today, however, transportation planners have to balance two interests that aren't always in sync. On the one hand, we're

---

* Actually, Plessy had only one African American great-grandparent, but according to the enlightened laws of Jim Crow Louisiana, that made him black.

obliged by every measure of decency to provide access to the people who need public transit the *most*, but on the other hand, we have to make it an appealing option for the people who need it far less.

The first objective is clear enough. Poor people generally need and use public transit far more frequently and intensively than anyone else. The nation's poorest families spend more than 40 percent of their take-home pay on transportation, including cars. African American and Latino poor families spend most of that 40 percent in subway turnstiles and bus fare boxes.

The fact that less affluent families allocate their transportation budgets differently from the more well-to-do is mirrored in the ways that the state, municipal, and national governments allocate their budgets. This makes for a lot of racially tinged transit policies, all of them costly to poor people. Almost eighty cents of every federal transportation dollar already goes to highway building and road maintenance, which obviously discriminates against people who aren't affluent enough to own cars. Even the remaining 20 percent—billions of dollars—spent on public transit isn't distributed very equitably. Over the last thirty years, attorneys representing black and Latino plaintiffs have won dozens if not hundreds of lawsuits alleging discriminatory funding practices, in places as far apart as Los Angeles, Macon, Atlanta, Houston, and Boston (particularly the disproportionately black suburbs of Roxbury and Dorchester). Frequently, these transit policies robbed the bus systems used disproportionately by poorer, urban families in order to subsidize the train lines used by affluent suburbanites: Robin Hood, only backwards.

Different access to government funds isn't the only form of bias faced by the less affluent (and less white) segments of society. Private businesses engage in different but no less costly forms of discrimination in their attempts to keep the wrong sort of people away. As a planner and engineer I've encountered all kinds of ways that retailers in shopping malls, for example, try to deter bus riders from visiting, up to and including lobbying municipal governments to prevent city buses from stopping anywhere conveniently close. Even when the shopping malls "allow" buses, they generally send them to the back of the mall parking area, behind the buildings. Buses that once relegated people of color to rear seats are now themselves forced to the back of parking lots.

When the Swedish furniture emporium IKEA planned to open a store in Brooklyn, I advised them to try something different from their traditional footprint, which was that of a very large store surrounded by an even larger parking lot. It was a precedent that had worked well for them, and seemed impossible to change, since their retailing model depended heavily on customers who could transport hundreds of pounds of flat-packed wooden furniture from store to home. However, I reminded them, they were trying to sell their goods in a market in which fewer than half the households owned cars. "How about giving the buses the preeminent spot, right in front of the store?" I suggested.

To my delight they agreed. Today, not only do two New York City bus lines stop right at the front of the store, so does an IKEA-financed free ferry to and from Manhattan, as do free buses from nearby subway stations. The result is a little discombobulating: a hugely successful branch of IKEA has a parking lot that is always half empty.[*]

The IKEA story, though, remains an unusual one. Discrimination against public transit is still endemic. Sometimes, it's also deadly. In 1995, Cynthia Wiggins, who lived on the largely African American east side of Buffalo, New York, took the Niagara Frontier Transportation Authority's Number Six bus to her job at the suburban Walden Galleria Mall. However, since the mall management had promised

---

[*] From the Department of Unexpected Consequences: not only did the expected traffic congestion never appear, but so many Brooklynites used the free ferries as an easy way to travel to Manhattan that IKEA now charges $5 to any rider without a receipt. Others use the esplanade that IKEA built for its water taxis as a park.

its tenants that no inner city bus would be allowed to stop at the upscale mall, Cynthia's bus dropped her more than a quarter-mile away. On December 14, she was hit and killed by a dump truck while trying to cross a seven-lane highway lined with eight-foot-high barricades of snow.

Then there's Atlanta.

Atlanta doesn't, of course, get anything like Buffalo's annual allotment of snow, which is probably a good thing. On Tuesday, January 28, 2014, a snowstorm that would have been laughed off in Buffalo—maybe two inches of powder and wet snow—paralyzed Georgia's capital. Thousands of flights were canceled, and more than two thousand kids spent the night in schoolrooms and police stations, unable to get home. Two weeks later, the city hit the nation's front pages again, when another storm, this one of ice, did it again, only worse. A city of six million, held hostage to an accident of weather. Or so it seemed.

However, Atlanta's Snowpocalypse wasn't the result of bad meteorological luck, but bad transportation policies, policies that were a predictable result of what a charitable person might call racial—or at least class-based—Balkanization. In the same way that a map of Vancouver reveals how geography can support a healthy transit network, a map of Atlanta shows how it can cripple one.

The big difference is that Vancouver's transportation geography was determined by natural boundaries, but Atlanta's was manufactured. The Atlanta metropolitan region comprises (depending on who's doing the counting) as many as two dozen separate counties. Within those counties are more than *sixty* municipalities. That's sixty mayors, or city managers, or city councils, all with slightly different ideas about how well they want to play with the other mayors, city managers, and city councils. The result is that the city of Atlanta became, in large part, a commuting destination for people who live in Atlanta's suburbs, and a lot of them moved to those suburbs precisely in order to avoid paying for the schools, police, and—especially—the transportation network used by the people they had left behind. When they travel to Atlanta, on business and pleasure trips, most of them do so along one of the most congested parts of the entire Interstate Highway System, a so-called downtown connector made up of a confluence of I-75 and I-85, which not only did to neighborhoods like Mechanicsville and Summerhill what the Cross-Bronx Expressway did to East Tremont, but produces some of America's worst traffic jams, even when the weather cooperates.

The downtown corridor is the overwhelming choice for Atlanta's millions of commuters because it's essentially the only one. While the Metropolitan Atlanta Regional Traffic Authority is the country's eighth largest, it serves only the city of Atlanta itself, and two of the region's counties, Fulton and DeKalb. Everywhere else, MARTA is forbidden to travel. (A clue why: a widely used version of the authority's acronym is "Moving Africans Rapidly Through Atlanta.") It wasn't an accident of weather that made millions of people hostage to the most weather-sensitive form of transportation. It was a self-inflicted failure of understanding. Public transportation works only when it's used by every segment of the public. When it's equitable. When it's transportation for everybody.

>>>

As traditionally understood, no transportation policy (much less any real-world transportation system) can both return benefits to each community commensurate with that community's own contributions and restore fairness to disadvantaged communities. Most fail to do either. Resources are finite, the argument goes. Transportation everywhere, anytime, and for everybody is, like equality itself, a noble-sounding goal, but in the real world must give way to a series of compromises.

This is true as far as it goes. You can't spend the same transportation dollar twice, which means that planners frequently have to limit service in one area in order to provide it in another. This is what the designers of Houston METRO's "frequent network" did when they chose per-dollar patronage—the maximum number of riders the system could carry for a given amount of money—over providing an equal number of buses and bus stops to every part of the city.

As we saw back in Chapter 6, the frequent network is a very well thought-out response to a very difficult set of problems. But it isn't the only route to transportation equity. Even if resources are finite, they aren't fixed. When they can be increased, it makes it a whole lot easier to improve equity; it's easier to slice a larger pie evenly than a smaller one. That's the philosophy of what has to be the world's most inspiring municipal leader on the subject of transportation equity, Enrique Peñalosa, the former mayor of Bogotá, Colombia.

Sometimes transportation equity is best studied in a place where inequality of all sorts is off the charts. That certainly describes Colombia's capital city, whose seven million residents suffer from the greatest disparity between rich and poor in all of South America.

Differential access to transportation is, of course, not the only reason for the gap between Bogotá's rich and poor, which was in place from the time of the city's sixteenth-century founding as the capital of the New Kingdom of Granada on a narrow plateau bordered by the Andes Mountains on the east and the Bogotá River on the west. It certainly hadn't improved much by the time Simón Bolívar liberated the Spanish crown colony in 1819. However, from the time that the city's first transit system was opened, in 1884, transportation policy conspired to exaggerate Bogotán inequality. That system was a mule-drawn tramway that connected the city's central square, the Plaza de Bolívar, with Chapinero, in the northern part of the city—not at all coincidentally where Bogotá's most affluent residential and commercial districts were to be found, then and now.*

Unless it is carefully managed as a public resource, mass transit follows money. So when the old streetcar system was replaced in the 1940s by buses owned by private companies, the result was predictable. The best neighborhoods got the best service: relatively luxurious buses known as the *ejecutivo*, which prohibit standing riders. Everywhere else got the less expensive *corriente*. Even worse, the thousand-plus buses operated by the private companies did what competing companies do: they competed, which in Bogotán terms meant they frequently disrupted one another's service. Since, by long tradition, the city's sidewalks were regarded as extensions of the automotive arteries, they became parking lots for thousands of buses and, eventually, more than a million private cars.

Even so, from the 1950s through the 1980s, Bogotá continued to grow, not always for the best possible reasons. As the center of the Colombian drug trade, the city became notorious throughout the world not just for financial instability and inequality, but for crime. In 1993 alone, the city recorded more than four thousand homicides, which made it one of the most dangerous large cities in the world.

Then, in the middle of the 1990s, two successive mayoral administrations turned the city around, partly by improved policing and security, partly by better financial administration, but also by rethinking the city's transportation system. The list of transportation innovations begun by Antanas Mockus when he was elected Bogotá's mayor in 1995, and expanded by his successor Enrique Peñalosa from 1998 to 2001 (Mockus would, in turn, succeed Peñalosa, and serve until 2003), is nothing if not impressive.

---

* The original tramway was electrified in 1910 and ran until 1948, when Bogotá, like so many other cities in North and South America, eliminated its streetcar system.

The most significant, in terms of passenger miles, was the Bus Rapid Transit system known as the TransMilenio, a network built around a thousand 160-passenger articulated vehicles that covered the city's longest and most traveled avenues on dedicated busways with elevated stations placed on road medians, with bus and station floors at a level for both convenience and safety. Tickets for the TransMilenio buy a full day's travel, while the feeder routes for the BRT system are served by smaller buses on perpendicular roads to the main grid—and they are free, in order to make certain that the city's less affluent are able to benefit from it. Small wonder that the system now carries nearly two million passengers per day, which is one of the highest usage rates in the world.

The TransMilenio, to be perfectly honest, is simultaneously a good news and a bad news story, both of which are instructive. The system's biggest problem at the moment is overcrowding—bad enough that riders frequently can't even exit the bus at their preferred stops— which is a reminder that the demand for public transit in Bogotá still exceeds supply. This is true even though the TransMilenio's all-day fare—currently 1,700 Colombian pesos—is a very pricey option for low-income Bogotáns, who frequently earn less than 5,000 pesos daily. Even with the high fare structure, though, the system is severely underfunded. Though the TransMilenio was built as a private-public partnership, it still receives no subsidies from the municipal government.

In addition to shaky finances, the TransMilenio is a victim of poor execution. Like any Bus Rapid Transit system, it depends on decent roads, and the main artery used by the buses, the Avenida Caracas, was designed badly and maintained even worse. And, just to pile on, the system was also built without much in the way of state-of-the-art traffic engineering, which means that the schedules are the opposite of reliable, when they even exist (the system's private bus systems have no published schedules at all).

Some of Bogotá's other transportation innovations have been more successful. Mockus and especially Peñalosa were determined to make Bogotá a paradise for cyclists, and they very nearly succeeded. When Peñalosa took office, he immediately rejected a proposal to build what his engineers told him was the highest priority for the city's infrastructure, an elevated highway costing some $600 million. Instead, out of a conviction that active transportation was not only more sustainable, but equally popular with every level of Bogotán society, he spent a fraction of that money on the *ciclorrutas* system: 234 miles of permanent bike paths separated from automobiles by curbs and the short posts known as bollards. Less useful for commuting, but even better loved by the city's residents, he expanded the city's *ciclovías*, which close seventy-five miles of Bogotá's streets each Sunday and transform the temporarily car-free streets into plazas full of street entertainers, group exercise classes, and of course walkers and cyclists. It gets even better: ever since 2000, on the first Thursday in February, the entire city, rich and poor, goes car-free.

Peñalosa went further still. Those sidewalks that had been commandeered as de facto parking lots by the city's traditional buses and cars? Peñalosa ordered them cleared, and then built a network of curbs and bollards to keep the vehicles off them permanently. He widened the sidewalks where he could—"skinnying" up the streets—and reduced the available street parking. To further discourage driving in the city center, and so attract more affluent riders into the city's transit system, Bogotá restricted the number of private automobiles permitted during rush hour by 40 percent. You read that correctly. Depending on the last number of your license plate, four cars in ten were prohibited from Bogotá during peak travel times.*

---

* Some argue that this has had an unforeseen consequence: wealthy Bogotáns purchasing additional cars (with different last numbers on their license plates) to evade the restriction.

The former mayor is now the president of the board of directors of the Institute for Transportation and Development Policy, and is rightly regarded as one of the world's most articulate promoters of transportation equity. In an interview after a talk at Canning House in London (and again in his TED talk), Peñalosa observed, in words that I'd be proud to have on my own tombstone, "An advanced city is not one in which the poor can get around by car, but one in which even the rich use public transport."

>>>

Penalosa's goal is laudable but it's a long way from assured. Although the revolutionary era that began when the first Millennials entered adulthood as car skeptics shows no signs of changing direction, and the pace of innovation in sustainable, active transportation is, if anything, accelerating, the road ahead is nonetheless still under construction, and some obstructions are predictable.

The first is political. Like everything else in this feverishly partisan era, transportation policy is a blood sport for both self-described progressives and conservatives. As Houston has proved, once a fairly straightforward decision about infrastructure gets turned into a proxy debate about competing myths about America, rationality flies right out the window. I am guilty of this myself. I am inclined to assume, for example, that knowing how frequently someone uses public transit or rides a bike tells me what that someone thinks about gay marriage, climate change, and gun control.

It's not that this kind of thinking is completely wide of the mark. Bill Bishop in *The Big Sort* describes how Americans have been grouping themselves into like-minded communities for generations now, and how one of the key markers for almost every political choice is where they choose to live. Or, more accurately, the density of the communities they choose. During the 2012 presidential election,

98 percent of America's most densely populated counties voted for Barack Obama and 98 percent of the country's least densely populated counties voted for Mitt Romney. It works at almost every level of granularity: until a community—a county, a city, a town, or even a voting precinct—reaches a density of about eight hundred people a square mile, it's as reliably Republican as Fox News. Once it exceeds that number, though, the voting patterns do a somersault. Anywhere under eight hundred people a square mile, there's a two-thirds chance that a randomly selected voter went Republican; above it, that hypothetical voter pulled a Democratic lever two-thirds of the time. As the political prediction machine Nate Silver of 538.com tweeted in 2012, "If a place has sidewalks, it votes Democratic."

It's not totally obvious whether people vote a certain way because of where they live, or whether they move to places where everyone votes the way they do. What is obvious though is that *all* the elements of a Street Smart transportation system depend on density. At first glance, this would appear to be a giant advantage for a Street Smart future, since every demographic indicator shows that America and the world are headed for a much more urbanized future. Between 1970 and 2000, the world's urban areas grew by about 22,300 square miles, but in the three decades between 2000 and 2030, they are expected to grow by *590,000* square miles, and house nearly one-and-a-half billion more people than today. All those Millennials and Boomers migrating to big cities are just the leading edge of an avalanche.

On the other hand, all that action is causing a powerful reaction. When Enrique Peñalosa lost his bid for reelection in 2000, he was followed by three successively more conservative administrations, and it's not too much to describe what they've done to some of his signature transportation initiatives as sabotage. In the United States, the reactionaries pushing back the hardest on urban public transportation systems are led by the billionaire brothers David and Charles Koch, and their umbrella advocacy organization, Americans for Prosperity. Perhaps that's not surprising. In September 2014 Tim Dickinson in *Rolling Stone* described what the brothers' businesses were: "Koch-owned businesses trade, transport, refine and process fossil fuels."

This book is way too short to document all the silliness and conspiracy-mongering funded by AFP. But no matter how much time they spend on climate-change denial, repealing the Affordable Care Act, or attacking Agenda 21, the nonbinding United Nations blueprint for sustainable development, AFP and the Koch brothers–funded Reason Foundation always seem to find a few idle hours each day to oppose public-transit investment. In 2014 alone, they spent hundreds of thousands if not millions of dollars undermining a program of dedicated transit lines in Nashville; forbidding the city of Indianapolis from even studying a light rail system; fighting—and, happily, losing—battles opposing the Washington Metro's expansion into Loudon County, Virginia, and Los Angeles's Exposition Line rail system; and killing Florida's plans for a high-speed rail system, which had been overwhelmingly approved by the state's voters. Urban populations may be growing, but they're going to have to fight for improved public transit so long as the Koch brothers can continue writing checks.

On the other hand, the partisan divide between transit-loving liberals and car-adoring conservatives may not be as wide or as deep as it first appears. It's true that polls consistently show substantial differences in transportation and housing preferences between liberals and conservatives. In a 2012 Pew Research Center study, three-quarters of self-described consistently conservative voters said they would opt to live where "the houses are larger and farther apart, but schools, stores and restaurants are several miles away," while only 21 percent of consistent liberals said the same. Meanwhile, 71 percent of liberals (but only 22 percent of conservatives) would choose communities where "the houses are smaller and closer to each other, but schools, stores and restaurants are within walking distance." Conservatives like big lawns; liberals like walkability.

And they vote accordingly. Just about every big city in the United States consistently votes Democratic. Even in Republican states like Missouri, more than 80 percent of the electorate in a city like St. Louis votes Democratic.

However, the exceptions to this rule are the really interesting ones. Two of the biggest cities that voted for Mitt Romney in the 2012 presidential election were Salt Lake City and Oklahoma City. Despite that, as we've seen, both cities recognize the critical importance of building the elements of a Street Smart transportation system, from walkable downtowns to multimodal grids. Ideologically driven politicians and think tanks can fulminate all they want about the creeping dangers of European-style urbanism in the land of the free and the home of the brave. But mayors and city managers all over the country, whatever their political affiliations, can't afford to see transportation policies in those terms. They know that the *only* future that will keep their cities vital and attractive to Millennials and the generations that will follow them isn't reachable without streetcars, sidewalks, and bike paths. As a result, I'm not terribly worried about the increasingly desperate tactics of the reactionaries to disrupt the ongoing revolution in America's transportation networks.

Nor am I concerned too much about the price of oil, which spent the second half of 2014 behaving like a skydiver with a bowling ball strapped to his back instead of a parachute. In six months, the price of a barrel of oil fell from $115 to less than $60, and was forecast to stay somewhere under $70 for at least another year. This is a very big deal in a lot of ways. It puts a huge amount of pressure on big oil-exporting nations, from Saudi Arabia to Russia to Venezuela. It will probably cause a reassessment of hydraulic fracking and nuclear-power-plant construction, and is a gigantic bonus for almost the entire US economy.

One thing it is not, though, is something that is likely to change the direction, or even the slope, of all those graphs showing a decline in annual vehicle miles traveled. When the really sharp decline in VMT began in 2004, the price of a barrel of oil was less than $40 a barrel. Five years later, when the VMT decline had become obvious to every transportation planner in the country, it was about $44.*
That price didn't last, but then there's little reason to believe this one will, either. For a little while, at least, car owners are going to be paying less for every mile they drive, but it's hard to see why they'll be putting too many more of them on their odometers. In addition, the average driver pays about $9,000 a year to own a car. Saving a few hundred bucks a year on gas won't change the financial decision tree much.

That doesn't mean there's no risk of any bad outcomes. Given the difficulties most of us have with distinguishing between short-term appetites and long-term good sense, there's a chance that lower oil prices will lead to some poor decisions on infrastructure investment.

Even if the price of oil doesn't distort investment decisions, it's not as if we were making the most efficient decisions on infrastructure before. Though there is actually a lot to recommend in the American Society of Civil Engineers' analysis of the sorry state of all aspects of the country's infrastructure—we really *do* need to upgrade our waste-water treatment plants and our internal waterways—the Report Card makes some serious errors in urging greater investment in big parts of the transportation system. Spending hundreds of billions of dollars on expanding and restoring roads when Americans are driving fewer miles each year is a very expensive exercise in nostalgia, one that could easily turn our fifty-year-long mistake into one lasting decades longer.

This is especially true when the words *deficient* or *obsolete* are used to describe elements of the transportation infrastructure. Most

---

* In both cases, even the inflation-adjusted numbers are about 20 percent lower than the price at the end of 2014.

people believe that when a professional organization of civil engineers says that more than sixty-five thousand American bridges—11
percent of the total—are "structurally deficient," they mean that they
are in imminent risk of collapse. Few actually are, though. Most of
the structural deficiencies are part of normal wear and tear, and simply indicate a need for rehabilitation of one or more components.
(There is a class of structurally deficient bridges that does worry me:
the ones that are *fracture critical*. These are spans—some eighteen
thousand of them, all built more than forty years ago—designed
without what engineers call *complete redundancy*; this means that
if just one critical beam or a single connecting joint fails, the entire
bridge can collapse.)

The bigger problem, though, is the more than eighty thousand
bridges that the ASCE calls *functionally obsolete*. This is another engineering term that just means a particular bridge isn't wide enough,
or robust enough, to carry the maximum amount of traffic, including
the biggest trucks, under conditions approaching free flow. This was
the argument made by the federal government during the tug-of-war
over the Williamsburg Bridge. Had we decided to replace the bridge,
New York would have had to spend three-quarters of a billion dollars
on a bridge whose primary effects would have been to destroy existing neighborhoods on both sides of the East River and put even more
cars and trucks on Manhattan's streets.

This doesn't mean that we shouldn't be urgently repairing needed
bridges, or roads, or railroads. The key is recognizing which ones are
needed, and which not. And how much we have to spend to do the
right repair.

The last bit is critical. More than forty years of participating in the
political process by which we allocate transportation investment has
taught me that it's far easier to secure money for new infrastructure
than for maintenance of the stuff we already have. Some of the reasons are found in human nature: everybody loves a ribbon-cutting,

and mayors and governors are a lot happier seeing their names on the congratulatory signs that accompany a new bridge than on ones about repainting the understructure of an old one, even though the bang-for-the-buck equation almost always favors the latter. Other reasons are statutory. When I was responsible for New York City's 840 bridges, the annual budget that came with the job was around $400 million, almost *all of it for capital expenditures*. That is, I had the equivalent of the entire municipal budget of a city the size of Spokane for *building* bridges, but next to nothing for painting or repairing them.* It's not exactly unknown for manipulative city budget analysts to force an agency to forgo maintenance of infrastructure for exactly this reason.

If there is a lesson from all the preceding chapters in this book, it's that a transition to a Street Smart transportation infrastructure isn't just aligned with the changing preferences of young, and not-so-young, Americans. It's that the transition doesn't need to cost any more than our current resources allow, and probably a whole lot less. Unbuilding, as with the West Side Highway or the Embarcadero—or, even better, never building—is far cheaper than building and then maintaining forever. There is reason for concern that we haven't yet learned that lesson completely, but also reason for hope that the next generation of transportation professionals understands that their primary objective will be improving access and mobility, not increasing capacity. If they do, the costs of new infrastructure will be a lot lower than anyone expects, and far lower than staying on the path we've been traveling for the last fifty years.

More concerning to me is a very specific kind of technology, that of autonomous driving. In 2014, a team of researchers from the Rudin Center for Transportation Policy and Management at New York University tried to imagine the impact of technology on the mobility in four US metropolitan areas—Boston, Atlanta, Los Angeles, and

---

* One of my smaller triumphs as a public servant was getting things like paint classified as a capital expense.

northern New Jersey—in the year 2030. They used an approach for describing alternate futures originally developed at the University of Hawaii in the 1970s, one that assumes that all possible future narratives take one of four basic shapes:

- Present trends continue on the path they're at, either growing exponentially or linearly.
- Things collapse. Critical systems fail and others deteriorate because of predicted and unpredicted events.
- The future runs into a wall. Limits on key resources place a constraint on growth, and a sustainability model of slower or zero growth takes its place.
- An unpredictable transformation occurs. Some disruptive technology appears, changing the direction of, well, everything.

In transportation, the ultimate disruptive technology may well be upon us: driverless cars. Though it may not be correct to call it unpredictable. As far back as the 1920s, a radio-controlled car from the now-defunct Achen Motor Company navigated its way through downtown Milwaukee. In 1940, Norman Bel Geddes, the same architect and industrial designer hired by Walter O'Malley to imagine an Ebbets Field of the future, anticipated that the cars of 1960 would

> have in them devices which will correct the faults of human beings as drivers. They will prevent the driver from . . . turning out into traffic except when he should. They will aid him in passing through intersections without slowing down or causing anyone else to do so and without endangering himself or others.

For the next five decades, companies like RCA, General Motors, Mercedes-Benz, and others worked to bring Bel Geddes's vision to life. For most of that time, autonomous vehicles were conceived as part of a system that traveled on dedicated roads or tracks, rather than streets, and went by the name of *Personal Rapid Transit,* or PRT.

PRT is generally used to describe a network of small, driverless electrical vehicles—pod cars—traveling on elevated guideways* containing sensors and switches that can, in combination, offer point-to-point travel nearly as flexibly as an automobile, but as safely and efficiently as a subway or streetcar. PRT has had a number of champions over the last fifty years (although more detractors), and a few fairly successful small-scale systems have even been built. One of them, at London's Heathrow Airport, uses eighteen vehicles traveling on two-and-a-half miles of track to transport travelers among three terminals. The Morgantown campus of the University of West Virginia has a similar system, and others are planned from Korea to Sweden. Still more remain under consideration in Mountain View, California, and Boston.

However, the scalability problems of PRT seem almost insuperable. Princeton's Alain Kornhauser, one of the technology's earliest and most articulate proponents, calculated the requirements for a PRT system that could actually replace the twenty-five million daily trips taken each business day by private automobile in the state of New Jersey. The numbers are staggering: 215,000 electric vehicles traveling among more than eight thousand interconnected stations, at an initial capital cost that would exceed $200 *billion.*

By far the largest part of that enormous price tag comes from constructing the elevated guideways on which the system depends: for New Jersey alone, Kornhauser's system would require more than ten thousand miles of them, a quarter the length of the entire Interstate Highway System, which makes me think the $200 billion price tag is still way too low. For a long time, such guideways seemed absolutely necessary for segregating driverless vehicles from existing streets and

---

* One system currently in development in Masdar City, just outside Abu Dhabi, will run underground.

so avoiding the danger of collision. If a way could be found, though, to run driverless vehicles just as safely on existing streets, the system's cost starts to become affordable, not least because, unlike a traditional PRT network, driverless cars can share the road with traditional automobiles. That would mean that a system using them wouldn't need to be fully built out before it becomes useful.

That was the idea behind the Autonomous Land Vehicle project, which was initiated in the 1980s by the US Department of Defense Advanced Research Projects Agency, who enlisted a hundred different university engineering departments in a contest to produce a robotic vehicle. Some came very close. Navlab 5, one of a series of vehicles developed at Carnegie Mellon University, drove from Pittsburgh to San Diego, a journey of 3,100 miles, more than 2,900 of them driverless.* By 2005, the ALV program gave way to a new DARPA initiative, the Grand Challenge, won by "Stanley," a car created by Stanford University and Volkswagen's Electronics Research Laboratory. Like the sophisticated GPS signaling and open-access transportation data that make both multimodal transit systems and car ride-matching services like Uber and Lyft viable, the newest generation of driverless cars combine incredibly precise real-time mapping algorithms with remote sensing systems that use radar, sonar, and lasers to "see" other vehicles as well as obstacles.

By 2010, every major automobile manufacturer was heavily invested in autonomous driving technology that could be used on existing roads. Part of the enthusiasm for the technology is that components of the technology required for a truly driverless car are valuable on their own. Adaptive cruise control, for example, a system that can detect distance between one car and another and modify speed accordingly, is already available on a number of luxury automobiles. So is autonomous steering, which can do the same for lane keeping,

---

* More or less. The car steered itself, but humans controlled throttle and brake, out of a perfectly reasonable concern for safety.

as are systems that can drive a car into a multistory parking structure and ease itself into a space directed by a smartwatch rather than a driver, and even solve the bugaboo of drivers everywhere, parallel parking a car in a space only ten inches or so longer than the car itself. In the view of former PRT advocate Alain Kornhauser, who is now convinced of the practicality of street-useful driverless cars, the beauty of these technological improvements is that, because they increase driving safety, they even have the potential to be self-financing: so long as collision avoidance and other autonomous driving modules cost less than the potential liability from future accidents, it will be in the interest of automobile insurance companies to pay for them. Even better: so long as more autonomy equals more safety, there is no point where the cost of the technology exceeds its added value.

The most prominent player in the world of autonomous driving, though, isn't Allstate or Geico. It isn't Mercedes-Benz or Ford, or even Tesla. It's Google.

The Google Self-Driving Car is a project that the Internet giant saw as a natural outgrowth of its existing mapping software, particularly the technology from Google Street View, which stitches together panoramic photos of more than five million miles of roads in more than forty countries. Google's versions of the driverless car—refitted Toyotas, Audis, and Lexuses—combine real-time access to all that data with a laser rangefinder that creates and refreshes three-dimensional maps of the area immediately around the car. It has so far succeeded in a dozen different road tests, comprising more than seven hundred thousand autonomous miles without a single self-caused problem (one car did get rear-ended; not, one hopes, by another autonomous vehicle). Though the company admits to a number of limitations to the existing technology, including bad weather, the Google car has done a spectacular job promoting the potential of autonomous driving. For people who believe in the never-ending bounty of digital improvement it seems only a matter of a few years before Google solves the remaining technical obstacles in the path of truly autonomous driving.* (At that point, Google, which invested more than $250 million in Uber back in 2013, will be able to launch its new subsidiary, which I call Goober.)

Lots of people are sold. I'm not sure who first pointed out that predictions are difficult, especially about the future,† but whoever it was had a point. Here are a few popular notions about the likely consequences of autonomous driving technology:

In 2012, the Institute of Electrical and Electronic Engineers predicted that driverless cars will account for "up to" 75 percent of the vehicles on the road by 2040. (You have to love the way two little words like "up to" can cover the asses of so many engineers.) Alberto Broggi, a member of IEEE and professor of engineering at the University of Parma, believes they will be capable of speeds "*up to* one hundred miles an hour by 2040" (emphasis added).

Meanwhile, the marketing consultancy Navigant Research predicts that by 2035, annual sales of autonomous vehicles will be more than 95 million. At the other end of the spectrum, Columbia University's Earth Institute calculated, in 2013, that, by combining the Internet, advanced propulsion systems, vehicle sharing, and driverless cars in Manhattan alone, nine thousand driverless cars could replace thirteen thousand cabs, with both shorter wait times and faster travel, all at a per-mile cost of one-tenth of that incurred by present-day cabs.

The consulting and accounting firm PwC goes even further, predicting that the number of traffic crashes occurring in the United States every year could drop from 10.8 million to 1.1 million (just switching from driving to transit also achieves a better than 90

---

* As of this writing, another technological behemoth, Apple, is rumored to be developing an automobile that may be self-driving.

† It's been attributed to everyone from the Nobel Prize–winning physicist Niels Bohr to Yogi Berra, and is almost certainly the only time those two giants of the twentieth century have been confused with one another.

percent reduction in crash probability on a per-person per-mile basis), that congestion-based "wasted fuel" could fall from 1.9 billion gallons annually to 190 million gallons, and that the privately owned US vehicle fleet could collapse from its current level of 245 million to only 2.4 million. Not to be outdone, the prognosticators at Morgan Stanley predict that the United States would save $158 billion annually in fuel, $563 billion from reducing automobile crashes, and $422 billion in productivity improvements (from allowing people to do useful work while traveling in their driverless cars), for a net addition to the American economy of more than $1 trillion a year. With all that, it's not too surprising that many advocates for driverless cars argue that *any* investment in old-fashioned, capital-intensive transportation infrastructure is foolish, given the very real possibility that such investments would be obsolete before they were even operational.

I hate to be a killjoy. But there are a few speed bumps (sorry) in the path of those predictions.

First, while Google Maps and Google Street View are both incredible pieces of software, the level of data collection—and especially the updating requirements—required of maps needed by the computer operating a Google car is at least an order of magnitude more complex. All those successful test drives have been performed using a dedicated vehicle that preceded the autonomous car on the route in question, uploading every physical object on that route into the car's memory immediately before the journey. This isn't quite as big a con job as a mentalist who has confederates checking out marks before a performance, but neither is it a system that can be scaled up for real-world use. Remember: we're talking not just roads, but driveways, parking lots, ferry terminals, and basically anywhere a car can already travel.

Then there's the uncomfortable reality that the map is not the territory. No matter how frequently it is updated, no mapping software can keep up with every new lane marking, or pothole, or construction site, or utility truck blocking a road. As I write this, most street markings in the Northeast are covered by snow and ice, and snow banks often require driving illegally into lanes reserved for oncoming traffic. (By the way, who gets the ticket if a driverless car breaks a rule and how does it know to pull over for a cop?) If an autonomous vehicle doesn't know a traffic light is in the road, it can't obey it—and temporary portable traffic lights are moved to new intersections every day. And that's without even mentioning the so-far-untested ability to distinguish between a piece of newspaper in the road and a rock; a police car's flashers and a turn signal; or—and this is the scary one—a deer, a dog, and a five-year-old child.

Nonetheless I am convinced the driverless car will be safer overall than those driven by even more fallible humans. However, it might not be the most efficient way to keep people out of the hospitals, or the morgues.

More than eighty years ago, a cartoonist named Rube Goldberg became famous for his drawings of needlessly complicated gadgets that performed the simplest tasks in the most convoluted ways imaginable, using levers, cranks, balls rolling downhill, and balloons rising upward to pour a glass of milk, for example. In a way, driverless cars seem like a Rube Goldberg approach to getting from here to there. For short trips, walking and biking are safer and healthier than Google's most ambitious vehicle; for many longer ones, so is transit. Not only does switching from driving to transit also achieve a better than 90 percent reduction in crash probability on a per-person per-mile basis, it also costs energy—in a good way. Transit riders use more than 20 percent more calories than drivers on a per-trip basis, which gives buses, subways, and streetcars a giant health advantage over cars. In fact, after five years of taking transit, the obese percentage of a given population—those with a Body Mass Index greater than 30—drops by more than half.

And, as long as cities create plazas and piazzas where cars are banned but not people, self-driving cars offer no advantage, even without recognizing the mathematical impossibility of moving thousands of people through a city center in single-occupant vehicles. This doesn't mean there isn't a place for cars, with or without laser-rangefinders and GPS mapping. In less dense parts of cities, suburbs, and rural areas, all the safety aspects developed by automated cars make sense.

In some ways, the driverless car is a natural next step following all the technological and demographic changes that contributed to the original Millennial-led driving revolution that is the subject of this book, especially the information oversupply that made smartphones into a tool for transportation planning. Driverless cars are also, in their way, a new army on the battlefield over which the original war for right-of-way was fought nearly a century ago, in which roads were transformed from multipurpose commercial and social real estate into single-use arteries for automobile travel. Driverless cars are unarguably transportation anywhere, and anytime. And, to the degree that driverless cars will be available to all levels of society, they're transportation for everybody, too. They can even coexist, peacefully and profitably, with streetcars, commuter rail, bike paths, and subways.

Still, it isn't clear whether that new army of driverless cars is a Street Smart ally or opponent. There are any number of potential benefits to be found in a world dominated by driverless cars, including the possibility of turning nine out of every ten vehicles currently on the road into planters. As hardly needs underlining, the environmental and social benefits of taking 90 percent of existing cars off the streets are almost incalculably high. Moreover, given that some 93 percent of the six million automobile crashes in the United States every year are at least partly due to human error, that's something like thirty thousand deaths that might be prevented by getting human beings out of the business of driving. But because driverless cars are possible only insofar as they use existing streets and roads, they are still subject to the same hard cap of the vehicles in motion calculus described in Chapter 7. Because a computer's reflexes are better than yours or mine, autonomous vehicles can pack roads more efficiently than traditional ones; the cap is higher, but it doesn't disappear. The rosiest scenarios for autonomous driving, the ones that forecast a precipitous drop in the number of cars on the road, assume that most of those cars won't be personal vehicles but part of fleets of what we might call A-taxis. This means that virtually all of them will be in motion, virtually all of the time. In cities, particularly the densest parts of cities, driverless cars may be a recipe for constant gridlock.

However, even if driverless cars can, theoretically, reduce traffic delays because more of them can travel safely on a given stretch of road, this doesn't mean that they will. One reason for the anticipated appeal of driverless cars is that they are expected to mimic travel by train: smooth enough for reading, or working, or Internet gaming. But in order to do this, they would have to also mimic the (slower) acceleration profile of trains—and when they do, according to a recent simulation by a group of researchers at University College London, they don't improve travel times. They increase them. A group of simulated driverless cars negotiating a typical urban intersection at the same (slow) acceleration of a commuter train increases the time needed to cross the intersection by anywhere from 36 percent to more than 2,000 percent. If you want to browse the Internet while commuting, and still want to get to work on time, trains look like a much better option.

There are other reasons to be suspicious of the brave new world represented by Google's self-driving cars and others of similar ambition. On a purely personal level, I'm a little taken aback by the promise that autonomous vehicles will be able to collect you at your front door and deposit you at the front door of a supermarket or shopping mall—or even at your desk or workstation—without your feet ever touching the ground. In the Disney movie *Wall-E*, spaceship-bound refugees from an Earth destroyed by environmental catastrophe are so well cared for by their robot transportation devices that hardly anyone even stands up anymore, with the result that the universe's entire remaining population of *Homo sapiens* is morbidly obese. This, it seems to me, is not a particularly utopian future—one in which fewer people die from crashes, but more get hypertension and diabetes at ever-younger ages. Also, virtually all the really dramatic predictions about the benefits of driverless cars assume an entirely driverless network—one in which no one drives, and for which virtually driving is done autonomously. This is a nontrivial point: a system that is "only" driverless on expressways, for example, isn't going to change behavior in large ways, since most trips are less than ten miles in length. And don't get me started on trying to figure out who gets sued in the event of a collision between autonomous cars.

Maybe more plausibly, others have wondered whether autonomous cars, by reducing the pain and misery associated with driving, will therefore make it more appealing—so appealing, in fact, as to reverse the centripetal phenomenon that is now drawing more and more people back into densely populated cities from the sprawling suburbs that attracted their parents and grandparents after the Second World War. In that scenario, a new generation of commuters will be so happy to enter a driverless vehicle—one that allows them to watch movies, read books, or catch up on e-mail without ever having to worry about other drivers, traffic jams, or even missing that exit on Route 124—that they will be quite content to accept commutes that run into hours each day. Why not? It's not torture anymore but a chance to binge watch all those episodes of *The Sopranos* on your high-definition tablet. Sprawl would be a natural and inevitable consequence.

It depends, I think, on whether we believe that the revolution in driving behavior ignited by the Millennials is largely a reaction to the costs of automobile commuting in terms of money, time, and discomfort. If that's the case, then anything that removes or lessens those costs does indeed have the potential not just to adjust the curve but to reverse it.

But I'm unpersuaded. I believe that the behavioral changes we're seeing are less a matter of the pain and misery of commuting by car than they are about the pleasures of living in a walkable, accessible community. If that's the case, then autonomous cars would be exactly the kind of beneficial technology that could actually help us to return to the kind of human-scale, livable transportation system that existed before we decided to subsidize sprawl and penalize density.

Only better. While I'm personally nostalgic for the kind of streets on which I grew up, I also know it's important not to sentimentalize them too much. The streets of late-nineteenth-century Brooklyn or early-twentieth-century Los Angeles were walkable, but they were also dirty, overcrowded, and unsafe for both vehicles and pedestrians. It's worth remembering that the Brooklyn Dodgers were originally nicknamed the "Trolley Dodgers" in 1895, by which time electric trolleys were killing between thirty and fifty Brooklynites annually. One of the beauties of the Street Smart program is that it uses groundbreaking new technologies to upgrade the transportation systems—roads and rails, sidewalks and bikeways—in ancient, or at least centuries-old, cities.

But there's another advantage to smart streets. Smart street principles—narrower, traffic-calmed thoroughfares; enough density to promote walkability; Internet and GPS-enabled wayfinding; and multiple choices for both transportation modes and connections—can be economically and successfully applied anywhere.

This is more important for transportation equity, even for democracy, than is generally understood. The neighborhoods and cities that are leading this particular revolution have been, in general, wildly successful, but one consequence of that success is that the cost of living in them has increased dramatically. The demand for walkable, street smart neighborhoods with good public transit is, at present, far exceeding the supply (and it wasn't as if homes in San Francisco or Manhattan weren't already in great demand). To the degree that we smarten up neighborhoods in places where Millennials, in particular, already want to live, we run the risk of making them unaffordable to all but the most prosperous of them. If the revolution were simply to promote more active transportation and easier-to-use transit in the wealthiest American and European neighborhoods, it will have fallen short of its promise.

That's why the preceding chapters made a point of visiting places like Charleston and Columbus and Oklahoma City. Density is just as prized in the upper Midwest as it is on the East Coast. Houston can benefit from a rebuilt and walkable downtown just as much as Pasadena. Most of all, the digital systems that make bus routes, rail lines, and even ride-matching car services transparent to their users work just as well in the cities of the Wasatch Range as in Northern California. The Street Smart revolution truly is everywhere, all the time, and definitely for everybody.

EPILOGUE

Flatbush and Atlantic

I N JANUARY OF 2006 I GOT A CALL FROM THE OFFICE OF ONE OF NEW York City's most prominent and ambitious developers, Forest City Ratner, itself a subsidiary of an even larger Cleveland-based real-estate behemoth. Bruce Ratner, who was the CEO of the development company, had been the city's consumer affairs commissioner around the same time I headed the Traffic Department. Despite his pedigree—four of his uncles had founded the multibillion-dollar family corporation in 1920—he was a down-to-earth, unassuming guy.

A year before, Forest City Ratner had received the go-ahead from the relevant city and state authorities to start work on redeveloping the two dozen acres that had been designated the Atlantic Yards Urban Renewal Area, specifically the Long Island Rail Road yards between Atlantic Avenue and Pacific Streets.* The Atlantic Yards project

---

* This, rather than any proximity to the ocean on the other side of the continent, is why the development, then known as Atlantic Yards, has been renamed Pacific Park.

called for a complex of residential and commercial buildings, but its centerpiece was to be a basketball and hockey arena, Barclays Center. Bruce had bought the NBA's New Jersey Nets in 2004 and had spent the following two years planning to move the team to a new arena by the time he called on Sam Schwartz Engineering to design a transportation plan for it.

The two years probably felt like twenty, what with vitriolic opposition from community activists about everything from affordable housing set-asides, to the proper use of eminent domain, to conflict-of-interest accusations, to the environmental strains that the new development might put on the sewer system. One of the biggest concerns was that the arena was going to be a traffic nightmare, since it was sited at the intersection of the street grids of three densely populated Brooklyn neighborhoods—Fort Greene, Park Slope, and Prospect Heights—with Flatbush Avenue running a diagonal through all three. Even worse, Flatbush, Atlantic, and Fourth Avenues each carry enough traffic volume that each would be the main thoroughfare of most cities. On a good day, traffic was bottled up; on a bad day, three grids were locked.

No sane traffic engineer would have designed anything like it. And no sane engineer did. Instead, half a dozen different planners from the dozen different towns that made up nineteenth-century Brooklyn created their own street plans, long before it became a single city, and eventually merged with New York City just before the turn of the twentieth century. As I am forever being reminded, roads are forever; changing the grids was unthinkable.

The prevailing wisdom was that the only kind of person who would consider building a major sports stadium at such a location would have to be even crazier than the original street designers. Bruce Ratner, however, wasn't the first team owner to go a little crazy about the acreage between Atlantic and Flatbush. Atlantic Yards was precisely where Walter O'Malley wanted to build a stadium for my beloved

Dodgers, and was the *casus belli* in the war between O'Malley and Robert Moses, the one that ended with the demolition of Ebbets Field, the end of major league sports in Brooklyn, and—more or less for the same reasons—the suburbanization of America.

As the song says, everything old is new again. A major-league sports team was returning to Brooklyn. However, this didn't change the challenge of getting their fans to join them. Atlantic Yards was just as much a traffic nightmare in 2006 as it had been in 1956; or it would have been if O'Malley's original idea about fans traveling to games overwhelmingly in private automobiles was accepted as a given. But if you were prepared to question that idea, then Flatbush and Atlantic was not only a reasonable location, it was a terrific one. Nine subway lines and one railroad sat just belowground at that intersection. Two other subway lines were just blocks away. The carrying capacity of a dozen different railroads dwarfed that of any possible street grid.

The challenge was to change the behavior of a fan base that had been used to driving to Nets games. Which was pretty much everyone, ever since the Nets had moved to New Jersey in 1977. We made a few assumptions. First, the team would be drawing fans largely from Brooklyn, Queens, and Long Island, since it stood to lose a fair bit of its ticket-buying base from New Jersey, and the Knicks remained Manhattan's favorite team. This particular assumption had history on its side: whenever new teams—baseball's Mets, football's Jets—had entered the New York market and had been compelled to play in the shadow of more established franchises—the Yankees, the Giants—they had drawn most heavily from the parts of the metropolitan area east of Manhattan.

The Mets and the Jets, then and now, play in stadiums surrounded by giant parking facilities. Given the impossibility of shoehorning a seven-thousand-vehicle parking structure into Atlantic Yards, we had to solve not just engineering challenges, but legal and political ones. The Environmental Impact Statement required by New York State law obliged the development to minimize air pollution, noise, and neighborhood impact, all of which were tied directly to traffic congestion. Transportation demand surveys calculated that, while the default percentage of people arriving at Nets games by private automobile would be about 50 percent, we had to guarantee that no more than 28.6 percent of fans traveling to basketball games at Barclays Center would do so.

No one had ever achieved such a low car-share anywhere in the United States, not even Madison Square Garden, smack in the middle of the pedestrian and transit paradise that is Midtown Manhattan. We had to get the overwhelming majority of eighteen thousand basketball fans to leave their car keys at home and ride public transit.

A dozen focus groups, and fifteen thousand completed surveys later, we had confirmed who the fans were. And we had confirmed that a considerable proportion of them were nearly as car-dependent as any families in America. Long Island doesn't sprawl quite as much as Oklahoma, or Texas, or Florida. But it wasn't going to be easy to get thousands of them to travel to basketball games—or concerts, or anything else—in anything but a car.

Nonetheless, we asked them what might induce them to use transit instead. We suggested free subway and bus fares as part of the ticket to a game. We proposed discounts on team merchandise. We even offered free food. Nothing changed the minds of more than 1 or 2 percent of our respondents.

Nothing except information. More than 20 percent of the potential Nets fans who planned to drive to a game would switch if they knew which train to take there, when it left, and when it arrived.

This we could do. We could build wayfinding tools along the routes from Brooklyn, Queens, and Long Island. We could offer maps, interactive signs, and proprietary online tools. And we could rely on open data apps, from the Metropolitan Transportation Authority and the Long Island Rail Road, to supply the rest. Every ad for the arena emphasized transit. I spoke at news events warning of the nightmares of driving. We were confident enough to recommend that the development build fewer than half the on-site parking spaces allowed in the Environmental Impact Statement, only 541 spaces for an arena with more than eighteen thousand seats (though we also proposed reduced-price parking for cars carrying three or more passengers, and half-price parking at five remote parking facilities served by a free shuttle bus, and a bicycle parking lot able to accommodate four hundred bikes).

Did it work? I was biting my nails (figuratively) as we waited for the big test: opening day on November 1, 2012, which featured a game between the Nets and their subway rival, the New York Knicks.[*] All eyes in New York would be focused on Barclays, which meant that we were looking at the equivalent of a Broadway opening night, when a single bad performance can sink a show forever. A week before, we had held our final planning meeting with the representatives from the Metropolitan Transportation Authority, the city's Department of Transportation, the New York City Police Department, and a dozen others. We planned to have more than forty people measuring traffic, assessing transit, and actually controlling traffic through our company's Pedestrian Traffic Managers. We prepared for everything.

Everything except Hurricane Sandy.

Sandy hit New York City on October 29, which gave us just two days to prepare. We were still set to go as late as Halloween but the city wasn't. Game one versus the Knicks was cancelled. The arena finally opened for regular season play against the Toronto Raptors. I savored those first few moments when I heard a major-league PA announcer say "Brooklyn" for the first time since the Dodgers left. (My dog is also, unsurprisingly, named Brooklyn.) I rejoiced at looking up

---

[*] Barclays Center actually hosted its first game on October 15, 2012, a preseason game between the Nets and the Washington Wizards.

at the scoreboard and seeing Brooklyn versus Toronto. F-U O'Malley and Moses. "Brooklyn's in the House!" I said, under my breath.

Even though many of the city's transit lines were still underwater—they don't call them subways for nothing—my colleagues, along with a team from the MTA and the DOT, were out in force making sure all went well. There was no paralysis at Flatbush and Atlantic. The media were impressed. There was joy in Brooklyn.

By March of 2013, we knew that we hadn't hit our targets. We had exceeded them. Our goal was to have no more than 28.3 percent of fans arrive by private automobile for weekday games. Barely 25 percent actually do. In fact, so few people arrive by car that the on-site parking has never filled up. Out of 160 events surveyed—not just basketball games but concerts featuring acts as varied as Barbra Streisand and Mumford & Sons (to say nothing of the ever popular Disney on Ice)—not one came close to occupying the 541 spaces that had been built. Only eight events needed even half of them, and the average number of parking spaces used was only 120. Getting that many people out of cars and into walking, biking, and taking transit is great for the environment, and great for the community's mental and physical health. It's also not exactly a financial sacrifice for anyone: in 2013, Barclays Center was the highest-grossing venue in the United States for concerts and family shows, and second in the world only to London's O2 Arena.

Not long ago, I attended a basketball game at Barclays. At 6:45 p.m., I checked my smartphone for the various route choices. By car, Google Maps predicted a twenty-nine-minute trip via the Manhattan Bridge to Brooklyn. Or, I had the option of three different public-transit choices, the longest of which was only twenty-three minutes. Had I wanted, I could even have walked for an hour and nine minutes over the Manhattan Bridge, down Flatbush Avenue, with the phone giving me turn-by-turn directions.

In the event, I took the simplest option: walking two blocks to the number 1 subway line, changing to the number 2, and exiting at the Atlantic Avenue/Barclays Center stop. The trains, each of which had been preceded into the station by an alert on a countdown clock, had been occupied by suit-wearing executives, stroller-pushing parents, backpack-wearing students, and dozens of Nets fans wearing baseball caps. The only uniform missing was a tuxedo.

Ah, well.

I walked under the open-to-the-sky oculus in the arena's main plaza and through the turnstile to my seat, fifteen minutes before tip-off. And it occurred to me, as I settled in, that I was, at that moment, roughly halfway between the apartment in which I grew up and the one where I live today. Nearly sixty years after Walter O'Malley broke my heart, and forty years after starting a lifelong education in urban transportation, I was part of another revolution.

Felt pretty good.

ACKNOWLEDGMENTS

BILL ROSEN HAS BEEN MY CO-CONSPIRATOR THROUGHOUT THE WRITING of this book and is just about the best-read and most intelligent person I've ever met. I'm convinced Bill can pick up almost any topic and become an expert in just a few months.

Marisa Cortright, my colleague at Sam Schwartz Engineering, provided illumination into the world of Millennials and has been a member from the start of the triad who put this book together.

David Gurin was in effect my teacher of "walking" and cities when we worked together at NYC DOT. His review of an early draft of this book helped affirm the tenor of the book and his criticisms were well-taken.

Cristina Roman finds doors I don't see and provided a perspective I wouldn't have realized on my own.

Many people deserve thanks for rounding out this book: Lloyd Ultan, the Bronx historian, for background on the Grand Concourse. Alain Kornhauser, from Princeton, for his cutting-edge take on self-driving cars. Karen Lee, a medical doctor with the goal of making us all healthier with the best medicine of all: walking and becoming active. David Bragdon for his research on the latest trends in transportation. Adria Civit, commissioner of mobility in Barcelona, who explained the secret to safe streets. Ranjani Sarode and David Smucker for great help with graphics. Gabrielle Lewis helped in fact checking. Thank you, John Tauranac, for sharing the very best subway map of New York City.

Many others helped on background, history, and insights. I apologize to those I may have overlooked. In no particular order: Andres Pazmino, Eric Shabsis, Jon Gerlach, Charlie Komanoff, Joe Iacobucci, Morgan Whitcomb, Mark de la Vergne, Danny Garwood, Ben Rosenblatt, Dan Schack, Jeff Smithline, Fred Cannizzaro, Larry Kallman, John Reinhardt, Joan Verbon, Mateu Hernandez Maluquer, Art Cueto, Scott Kubley, Janet Campbell, Jae Kang, and "Uncle" Joe Cortright.

The Perseus PublicAffairs team was terrific in first reaching out to me after a glowing op-ed appeared in the *New York Times*, especially Clive Priddle and Susan Weinberg, for supportively challenging me to form this book from the myriad ideas and experiences I had in my mind. Maria Goldverg for fine-tuning the book. Rachel King, Melissa Veronesi, and Melissa Raymond for all their hard work seeing the book through production. My publicity team: Jaime Leifer, Chris Juby, and Kristina Fazzalaro. David Steinberger, Perseus's CEO and my old colleague at DOT—it has been great working together again. Special thanks to my agent Carol Mann for her input and guidance throughout.

And to my wonderful parents whom I miss greatly, David and Frieda Schwartz, for raising me in Brooklyn and not succumbing to the lure of the suburbs.

NOTES

PROLOGUE: BEDFORD AND SULLIVAN

x   one the *New York Times* called "grandiose": (*New York Times*, 1952).

xi   "three worst human beings who ever lived": (Golenbock, 1984).

CHAPTER 1: MOTORDOM

1   built in Somerset in 3807 and/or 3806 BCE: (*New Scientist*, 1990).

1   still used in parts of Europe: (Flaherty, 2002).

3   explicitly "providing roads for automobility": (Norton, 2008).

3   "a radical revision of our conception of what a city street is for": (Norton, 2008).

3   "it is impossible for all classes of modern traffic to occupy the same right of way at the same time in safety": (Norton, 2008).

3   "Suggest that the driver of the motor-car be lynched": (Norton, 2008).

4   "a burdensome tangle of restrictive legislation": (Norton, 2008).

4   and the head of the National Automobile Dealers Association: (Norton, 2008).

5   1852, when Alphonse Loubat developed the familiar grooved rail set flush with the pavement: (Jackson, 1985).

5   283 miles of urban cable track carrying 373 million passengers annually: (Jackson, 1985).

7   inflation cut revenues in half and the company's expenses doubled: (Jackson, 1985).

7   more than thirty thousand miles of track on twelve hundred different urban transit systems and interurban railways: (Lind, 2012).

7   Twenty-three other utilities defaulted on interest payments: (Lind, 2012).

8   declined from 216 in 1938 (when the Act went into effect) to 18 by 1950: (St. Clair, 1986).

11   "not to exceed 6 ounces in weight or to pass a two-inch ring": (FHA, 2011).

11   "This is a road made for ever": (Cobbett, 1822).

12   America's largest special-interest group: (Stilgoe, 2001).

12   to pull the same amount of freight that had earlier required six horses: (Stilgoe, 2001).

13   Rand-McNally's first road atlases: (Norton, 2008).

13   "and upon either side of . . . public roads and streets": (Longhurst, 2013).

14   Vanderbilt, a racing fanatic, built the parkway: (Patton, 2008).

16   The entry for 1996 was the Interstate Highway System: (Weingroff, 2000).

16   "of prime importance in the event of war": (Weingroff, 2000).

16   "the needs of growing peacetime traffic of longer range": (Weingroff, 2000).

17   and seventy everywhere else: (Weingroff, 2000).

19   "probably the greatest single tool": (Weingroff, 2000).

20   "in every house right alongside the wife—the motor car": (Weingroff, 2000).

21   a "ferry suburb" in the early nineteenth century: (Jackson, 1985).

22   "to accelerate the transition to lower class occupancy": (Jackson, 1985).

CHAPTER 2: FOR EVERY ACTION . . .

28   "as well as a *through motor route*": (Federal Writers Project, 1995).

29   "will include . . . a change in its character": (North Side Board of Trade, 1897).

30   and the 1964 New York World's Fair: (Caro, 1974).

30   out of the reach of pedestrians: (Dim, 2012).

31   "an express crosstown facility . . . would be $17,000,000": (NYCRoads, 2014).

32   "took the stuff out with a teaspoon": (Gray, 1989).

32   "one measured in inches and tenths of inches": (Gray, 1989).

32 "It was out of character for Moses": (Caro, 1974).

35 "a crime that cannot be prettied up": (Weingroff, 2006) and (Mohl, 2004).

35 de facto veto over any freeway construction within the city: (Mohl, 2004).

35 "relocation of individuals, families, and business enterprises": (Weingroff, 2006).

36 "They exulted in them": (Moynihan, 1960).

36 "no more white highways through black bedrooms": (Mohl, 2004).

38 "too important to leave to the highway engineers": (Moynihan, 1960).

39 generally worth less, than driver time: (Mokhtarian, 2001).

40 a peak average speed of fourteen miles per hour: Traffic speed from Inrix, Inc., http://scorecard.inrix.com/scorecard/worstcorridors.asp.

40 the "dead-anyway" effect: (Anderson, 2011).

41 spaced twenty-seven or more car lengths apart: (Transportation Research Board, 2000).

46 "pending engineering studies": (Perlmutter, 1973).

46 *Law of Peak-Hour Expressway Congestion*: (Downs, 1962) and (Downs, 1992).

46 *induced demand*: (Duranton, 2009).

46 "The number of automobiles increases to fill all the space provided": (Moynihan, 1960).

47 20 percent of the boulevard's traffic will just disappear: (Cairns, 2002).

59 a "horse-and-buggy remnant": (*New York Times*, 1948).

60 *"if past trends were to continue"*: (Vuchic, 1999).

60 "there is no consistent, statistically significant relationship between lane width and safety": (Potts, 2007).

61 no room for anything other than parking lots in downtown Philly: (Vuchic, 1999).

61 In 1960, when the United States had 64.6 million full-time workers: (McGuickan and Srinivasan, 2003).

CHAPTER 3: THE MILLENNIALS

65 in a predictable and regular pattern: (Straus, 1990).

66 the "most civic-minded since the generation of the 1930s and 1940s": (Winograd, 2008).

67 only 56 percent of Millennials did: (Twenge, 2012).

67 or the opportunity to exercise: (APTA, 2014).

68 2,400 miles a year, or 46 fewer miles a week: (Davis, 2012).

68 117 more miles annually biking, walking, or taking public transit: (Davis, 2012).

68   85 percent more than in 1970: (Dutzik, 2013).

68   driving 6 percent *fewer* miles than in 2004: (Davis, 2012).

69   "VMT may double in the next twenty years": (Peters, 2004).

69   "This is denial": (Walker, 2014).

69   the number of cars being "retired": (Davis, 2012).

70   "22 million unwanted large-lot suburban homes": (Doherty, 2010).

71   from $1,100 to $2,300 (in 2011 dollars): (Dutzik, 2013).

72   2,100 fewer miles than their employed same-age predecessors: (Davis, 2012).

72   "I want to protect the environment, so I drive less": (Davis, 2012).

73   "those who wanted to get a driver's license did so by age 20": (Davis, 2012).

73   within a year of becoming eligible for one: (Ross, 2014).

73   In 1998, the number was 64.4 percent: (Chozick, 2012).

74   an average of more than $1,700 annually: (Reuter, 2012).

74   and 21.1 percent of the trips per household: (Cao, 2009), citing the 2004 NHTS Survey.

74   substitutes for one entire shopping trip: (Ferrell, 2004).

74   Only 18 percent of Baby Boomers answered "yes": (KRCResearch, 2011).

75   "socializing while traveling": (APTA, 2014).

78   Volunteer chauffeuring costs suburban families: (Litman, "Evaluating Household Chauffeuring Burdens," 2014).

79   no more economic output than it did in 1946: (Schmitt, "The Importance of Driving," 2014).

81   nearly 20 percent higher salaries for doing exactly the same job: (Stutzer, 2004).

81   essentially no increase in gratification: (Frank, 1999) and (Haidt, 2005).

81   the more years it goes on, the worse its effects: (Koslowsky, 1995).

82   declined by nearly 30 percent from 2007 to 2011: (Ross, 2014).

82   "techno pink" and "denim": (Chozick, 2012).

82   equals thirty-two cars *not* purchased by civilians: (Rogowsky, 2014).

84   "full of economic, social, and recreational activities": (Doherty, 2010).

84   with a mix of single-family houses: (Beldon, Russonello, & Stewart LLC, 2011).

84   an additional 14 percent said it was "essential": (Lachman, 2011).

84   "suburban neighborhood with a mix of houses, shops, and businesses": (TransitCenter, 2014).

85   only 6 percent of them currently do so: (Goldberg, 2014).

85   larger than at any time since the 1970s: (Ross, 2013).

85   Those in walkable neighborhoods, half that: (Doherty, 2010).

86   "The foundation of orthodox transportation planning is our certainty": (Walker, "How Good Are We at Prediction," 2014).
87   "a gradual accommodation": (Pauly, 1995).

CHAPTER 4: HEALTHIER, WEALTHIER, AND WISER

90   98 percent of the energy produced by the rider: (Wilson, 2004).
94   more lower back pain: (Koslowsky, 1995).
94   less stressful to commute long distance by train than by car: (Novaco, 2009).
94   "I have two doctors: My left leg and my right": (Trevelyan, 1928).
95   and can cut the risk of stroke by a third: (Tanasescu, 2002).
95   Walk thirty minutes a day: (Williams, 2013).
95   a 12 percent reduction in hypertension: (Hayashi, 1999).
95   more than obesity or even smoking: (Blair, 1995).
95   walking thirty minutes a day cut mortality by nearly a quarter: (Lee, 1995).
95   Walking worked *at least* as well: (Ratey, 2008).
96   "people feel better when they have a longer walk to work": (Martin, 2014).
96   every animal from humans to rodents: (Erickson, 2011).
97   when it comes to the hippocampus, size matters: (Vaynman, 2004). A lot of the down-and-dirty research on BDNF has been done on rodents; exercisers perform significantly better in mazes than sluggards.
97   intelligence itself was a side-effect of bipedalism: (Akkerman, 2008). Akkerman makes a good case that an upright gait didn't just help to free human hands to fabricate tools, but that human eyesight, situated at the highest available spot, made it possible to navigate via the fixed northern star, and to measure distance by number of steps taken.
98   the viewpoint of a pedestrian, a cyclist, or a bus rider: (Gatersleben, 2013).
98   the amount of visual information that they receive at fifteen miles per hour: (Dover, 2014).
99   "Oxytocin surges when people are shown a sign of trust": (Zak, 2012).
99   more trust, empathy, and compassion in an entire community: (Mikolajczak, 2010).
99   reduce threats, increase happiness: (Montgomery, 2014).
99   On Appleyard's "Heavy Street": (Appleyard, 1981).
100   as far afield as Bristol, England: (Hart, 2008).
101   "because I can play there when ever I want": (Appleyard, 2005).

104 a little more than 55 cents per passenger mile: (NTSB Bureau of Traffic Statistics, 2014).

104 the more mobility is constrained by tolls or congestion, the higher the GDP: (Litman, "The Mobility-Productivity Paradox," 2014).

105 places with a lot of congestion are economically vibrant: (Dumbaugh, 2014).

105 a group of anthropologists and systems scientists: (Ortman, 2015).

106 "average journey time is at a minimum": (Wardrop, 1952).

110 proximity is ten times more important than speed: (LeVine, 2012). In the unlikely event you're interested in the math behind this, the researchers who came to this conclusion used a technique known as path analysis to show that the weight of the "proximity" path equaled .423, while the "speed" path weighed only .033.

110 transportation costs in San Antonio: (Jaffe, 2014).

112 college degrees were found in only about 35 percent: (Cortright, 2014).

CHAPTER 5: WALK ON BY

117 arrive at their favorite stores on foot: (Forkes, 2010).

117 walkable shopping areas in Los Angeles produced up to four times the sales: (Boarnet, 2011).

117 "Americans would like to live in places that don't really exist": (Vanderbilt, 2010).

118 a bump of more than $30,000: (Cortright, 2009).

119 despite a 144 percent increase in bicycle riding on the street: (Reisman, 2012).

123 as much as 70 percent: (Bunn, 2003).

123 associated with a 20 percent increase in walking: (Morrison, 2004).

124 in order, Orlando, Tampa–St. Petersburg, Jacksonville: (SmartGrowthAmerica, 2014).

124 47 percent more likely to meet the recommended exercise guideline: (Sollis, 2009).

125 planning to narrow portions of Colorado Boulevard: (Branson-Potts, 2014).

130 especially hospitable to that kind of streetscape: (Hawthorne, 2014).

131 "big enough to have scale, and small enough to do something with it": (Tierney, 2014).

132 higher levels of dangerous obesity than the US average: (Green, 2011).

133 afterward the number jumped to 64 percent: (Green, 2011).

135 "infrastructure like safe indoor and outdoor bicycle parking": (NYC, 2010).

136 "required to reach stairs from the building's main entrance": (NYC, 2010).

136 "in the horizontal plane opposite to the direction of travel": (Eves, 2009).

136 an average relative increase in stair use of nearly 50 percent: (Soler, 2010).

138 Cars traveling northbound through West Midtown: (NYC DOT, 2010).

139 a whopping 80 percent fewer pedestrians were now walking in the Times Square roadway: (NYC DOT, 2010).

139 nitrogen dioxide by 41 percent: (NYC Department of Health and Mental Hygiene, 2012).

139 "eighty percent of whom support the Broadway plazas": (Bernstein, 2013).

139 put his entire city . . . on a diet: (Ruiz, 2007).

140 one of the most important factors in walkability was connectivity: (Pratt, 2012).

141 "you *can't* walk anywhere!": (Snyder, 2013).

141 "We're creating a city": (Snyder, 2013).

143 the way people will start a stationary conversation: (Whyte, 1988).

143 "The faster people walk, the narrower their field of peripheral vision becomes": (Underhill, 1999).

146 a crowd of individuals is transformed into a solid mass: (Fruin, 1971).

146 commuters, for example, walk at different speeds than tourists: (Timmermans, 2009)

146 People walk faster when they're wearing headphones: (NYC DOT, 2006).

146 societies where no one minds bumping into another: (Chattaraja, 2013).

147 According to the HCM, the proper shy distance: (NYC DOT, 2006).

147 people will start to swerve as much as seventeen feet: (Pushkarev, 1975).

150 a lot easier to cross the 1,732 points: (ICC, 2002).

150 A 2002 study: (ICC, 2002).

151 the average Japanese adult: (Bassett, 2010). As a baseline, in order to eliminate the confounding element of technological progress, the researchers also persuaded a group of old-order Amish to wear the pedometers. Their daily number of steps exceeded 18,000.

CHAPTER 6: UNLOCKING THE GRID

155 calls "continuous queues of vehicles block[ing] an entire network": (Soanes, 2008).

158　"buying, selling and improving real estate on streets, avenues, and public squares": (Jackson, 1985) and (McNeur, 2014).

158　"a town for the motor age": (Marshall, 2010).

158　The pattern was given the seal of approval in 1934: (Marshall, 2010).

160　the "almost perfect grid": (Walker, 2010).

164　a stronger attraction even at a greater distance: (Rodrigue, 2006). The "law" calculates distance the same way a crow flies—that is, without confounding elements like bodies of water, available roads, limited-access highways, and the like. Well, I said it was simple.

171　by far the largest city in the country with no rail transit at all: (Houston TranStar, 2014).

171　fifty-eight hours a year stuck in traffic: (TTI, 2012). In case you were wondering, Chicago, Washington, DC, and Los Angeles were numbers 1–3.

172　nearly three-quarters of Houston's transit users: (Grabar, 2014).

172　the old system offered far more coverage than patronage: (Walker, 2008).

172　a lot of transit riders in places with no stops at all: (Walker, 2014). The designers of the system included Traffic Engineers, Inc., METRO itself, and Jarrett Walker.

173　"Rail used to be a negative word around this town. It's not anymore": (Grabar, 2014).

176　far more than in a typical American system: (Garrick, 2011).

177　"than all other public purposes combined": (Shoup, 1997). Shoup would later collect his research in a 2005 book with the same title.

178　in Brooklyn, researchers found a whopping 45 percent: (Shoup, 2011).

178　0.5 spaces for every 1,000 square feet: (Garrick N. &., 2011).

179　the system's algorithm uses traffic signals: (Eckerson, 2014).

CHAPTER 7: WHAT MAKES A SMART CITY?

184　the system, which had cost somewhere between $10 and $12 billion: (Sturdevant, 2007).

184　In 2010 alone, just under 110 million were sold: (Pham, 2011).

188　from the services they choose, rather than the products they own: (Botsman, 2010).

190　more than thirty just for the trains and buses of the MBTA: (Barry, 2011).

190　online ticketing, GPS location information, and Wi-Fi service on the region's buses: (Transportation for America, 2010).

191 Automated announcements from CARTA: (Transportation for America, 2010).

191 A lot of people who tended to avoid transit: (Tang, 2011).

191 decreased their *perceived* wait time by an additional 13 percent: (Watkins, 2011).

194 "light rail on rubber tires": (Transportation for America, 2010).

194 As far back as the 2002 Olympics: (Iteris, 2003).

195 One team of researchers from the University of Torino and Yahoo Labs: (Quercia, 2014).

199 the base fee was $8 plus $5 a mile and a $15 minimum: (Jackson, 2010).

200 the price of an exclusive taxi medallion fell 17 percent: (Barro, 2014).

201 less than $17 an hour before gas and tolls: (Hall, 2015).

204 to provide seating space on Manhattan streets at $25 per hour: (Schwartz, 1982).

205 anything that results in better public services: (Null, 2014).

207 The largest single component of that number: (ASCE, 2014).

209 the likelihood of getting a seat, and on which car: (ARUP, 2014).

209 The private software-and-data company INRIX: (ARUP, 2014).

CHAPTER 8: TUXEDOS ON THE SUBWAY: TRANSPORTATION ANYWHERE, ANYTIME, AND FOR EVERYBODY

212 "At the subway station, you wait fifteen minutes for a train": (McInerney, 1984).

213 even 41 percent of riders in the largest transit systems: (Federal Transit Administration, 2002).

214 guaranteed that each state get back between 90 and 92 percent of its residents' contribution: (Altshuler, 2010).

216 The nation's poorest families spend more than 40 percent: (Bullard, 2003).

216 most of that 40 percent in subway turnstiles and bus fare boxes: (Bullard, 2003).

217 a parking lot that is always half empty: (Faheem, 2008).

218 On December 14, she was hit and killed: (Collison, 1996).

221 one of the most dangerous large cities in the world: (Guevara, 2013).

222 no published schedules at all: (Hutchinson, 2011).

223 the entire city, rich and poor, goes car-free: (Guevara-Stone, 2014).

224 "one in which even the rich": (Peñalosa, 2011).

225 a Democratic lever two-thirds of the time: (Troy, 2012).

225 expected to grow by *590,000* square miles: (Seto, 2011). The actual estimate is in a range from 166,000 square miles to 4.8 million square miles. The latter is about the size of the United States and Mexico, combined.

226   overwhelmingly approved by the state's voters: (Schmitt, "The Koch Brothers' War on Transit," 2014).

226   "the houses are smaller and closer to each other": (Pew Research, 2014).

229   *functionally obsolete*: (ASCE, 2014).

231   "and without endangering himself or others": (Bel Geddes, 1940).

232   an initial capital cost that would exceed $200 *billion*: (Kornhauser, 2013).

234   systems that can drive a car into a multistory parking structure: (Khaw, 2014).

235   "*up to* one hundred miles an hour": (IEEE, 2012).

235   Navigant Research predicts that by 2035: (Navigant, 2014).

235   Columbia University's Earth Institute calculated: (Burns, 2013).

235   The consulting and accounting firm PwC goes even further: (Price-waterhousecoopers, 2013).

236   a net addition to the American economy of more than a trillion dollars a year: (Jonas, 2014).

236   anywhere a car can already travel: (Gomes, 2014).

237   temporary portable traffic lights are moved: (Gomes, 2014).

237   after five years of taking transit: (Hoback, 2012). The study of transit use in Michigan projected a drop in obesity from 26.4 percent to 12.4 percent.

238   93 percent of the six million automobile crashes: (Silberg, 2012).

239   anywhere from 36 percent to more than 2,000 percent: (LeVine, 2014).

EPILOGUE: FLATBUSH AND ATLANTIC

248   the highest-grossing venue in the United States: (Li, 2013).

BIBLIOGRAPHY

Adams, Henry. *The Letters of Henry Adams*. Edited by Worthington Chauncey Ford. Boston, MA: Houghton Mifflin, 1938.

Akkerman, Abraham. "The City as Humanity's Evolutionary Link: Walking and Thinking in Urban Design." *The Structurist* 47/48 (2008): 28–33.

Altshuler, Alan. "Equity as a Factor in Surface Transportation Politics." *Urban Affairs Review* (SAGE) 46, no. 2 (November 2010): 155–179.

Anderson, Henrik, and Nicolas Treich. "The Value of a Statistical Life." In *The Handbook of Transport Economics*, Andre de Palma et al. (eds.), 396–424. Northampton, MA: Edward Elgar Publishing, 2011.

Appleyard, Bruce. "Livable Streets for Schoolchildren: How Safe Routes to School Programs Can Improve Street and Community Livability for Children." *NCBW Forum*, March 7, 2005.

Appleyard, Donald, M. Sue Gerson, and Mark Lintell. *Livable Streets*. Berkeley, CA: University of California Press, 1981.

APTA. *Millennials & Mobility: Understanding the Millennial Mindset*. Washington, DC: American Public Transportation Association, 2014.

ARUP. *Urban Mobility in the Smart City Age*. London: ARUP, 2014.

ASCE. *2013 Report Card on America's Infrastructure: Roads: Conditions and Capacity*. Washington, DC: American Society of Civil Engineers, 2014.

Barro, Josh. "Under Pressure from Uber, Taxi Medallion Prices Are Plummeting." *New York Times*, November 28, 2014: A1.

Barry, Keith. "How Smartphones Can Improve Public Transit." *Wired*, April 8, 2011.

Bassett, David R., Jr., et al. "Pedometer-Measured Physical Activity and Health Behaviors in U.S. Adults." *Medicine & Science in Sports & Exercise* 42, no. 10 (2010): 1819–1825.

Bel Geddes, Norman. *Magic Motorways*. New York, NY: Random House, 1940.

Beldon, Russonello & Stewart LLC. *The 2011 Community Preference Survey: What Americans Are Looking for When Deciding Where to Live*. Washington, DC: National Association of Realtors, 2011.

Bernstein, Andrea. *On Times Square Pedestrian Plaza, It's Back to the Future for de Blasio*. Transportation Nation/WNYC.org, October 23, 2013.

Blair, S. N., et al. "Physical Fitness and All-Cause Mortality: A Prospective Study of Healthy Men and Women." *Journal of the American Medical Association* 262, no. 17 (November 1995): 2395–2401.

Boarnet, M.G., et al. "Retrofitting the Suburbs to Increase Walking." *Urban Studies* 48, no. 1 (2011): 129–159.

Botsman, Rachel, and Roo Rogers. *What's Mine Is Yours: The Rise of Collaborative Consumption*. New York, NY: HarperCollins, 2010.

Branson-Potts, Hailey. "Making Pasadena's Colorado Boulevard a Haven for Pedestrians." *Los Angeles Times*, January 20, 2014.

Bullard, Robert D. "Addressing Urban Transportation Equity in the United States." *Fordham Urban Law Journal* 31, no. 5 (2003): 1183–1209.

Bunn, F., T. Collier, C. Frost, et al. "Area-Wide Traffic-Calming for Preventing Traffic Related Injuries." *Cochrane Database of Systematic Reviews*, January 2003.

Burns, Lawrence D., et al. *Transforming Personal Mobility: Program on Sustainable Mobility*. New York, NY: Columbia University, The Earth Institute, 2013.

Burns, Rebecca. "The Day We Lost Atlanta." *Politico*, January 29, 2014.

Cairns, S., et al. "Disappearing Traffic? The Story So Far." *Municipal Engineer* 5, no. 1 (March 2002): 13–22.

Cao, Xinyu. *E-Shopping, Spatial Attributes, and Personal Travel: A Review of Empirical Studies*. Minneapolis, MN: Humphrey Institute of Public Affairs, University of Minnesota, 2009.

Caro, Robert. *The Power Broker: Robert Moses and the Fall of New York*. New York, NY: Alfred Knopf, 1974.

Chattaraja, Ujjal, et al. "Modelling Single File Pedestrian Motion Across Cultures." *Procedia: Social and Behavioral Sciences* (Elsevier) 104 (December 2013): 698–707.

Chozick, Amy. "As Young Lose Interest in Cars, GM Turns to MTV for Help." *New York Times*, March 23, 2012: A1.

Cobbett, William. *A Year's Residence in the United States of America.* London: J. M. Cobbett, 1822.

Collison, Kevin. "Mall Bus Policy Called Anti-City: Death Raises Bias Questions." *Buffalo News*, October 16, 1996: 1A.

Cortright, Joe. "The Young and Restless and the Nation's Cities." *CityObservatory/CityReport*, October 19, 2014.

———. *Walking the Walk: How Walkability Raises Home Values in U.S. Cities.* CEOs for Cities, August 1, 2009.

Davis, B., T. Dutzik, and P. Baxandall. *Transportation and the New Generation: Why Young People Are Driving Less and What It Means for Transportation Policy.* Santa Barbara, CA: Frontier Group/U.S. PIRG Education Fund, April 5, 2012.

Dill, J. "Bicycling for Transportation and Health: The Role of Infrastructure." *Journal of Public Health Policy* 30 (March 2009): S95–S110.

Dim, Joan Maran. "Did Robert Moses Ruin New York City?" *Barrons*, March 17, 2012.

Doherty, Patrick C., and Christopher B. Leinberger., "The Next Real Estate Boom: How Housing (Yes, Housing) Can Turn the Economy Around." *Washington Monthly*, November/December 2010: 22–25.

Dover, Victor, and John Massengale. *Street Design: The Secret to Great Cities and Towns.* Hoboken, NJ: John Wiley & Sons, 2014.

Downs, Anthony. *Stuck in Traffic: Coping with Peak-Hour Traffic Congestion.* Washington, DC: Brookings Institution Press, 1992.

———. "The Law of Peak-Hour Traffic Congestion." *Traffic Quarterly* 16, no. 3 (July 1962): 393–409.

Dumbaugh, Eric, Jeffrey Tumlin, and Wesley E. Marshall. "Decisions, Values, and Data: Understanding Bias in Transportation Performance Measures." *ITE Journal* (August 2014): 20–25.

Duranton, Gilles, and Matthew A. Turner. *The Fundamental Law of Road Congestion: Evidence from US Cities.* Working Paper 15376. Cambridge, MA: National Bureau of Economic Research (NBER), 2009.

Dutzik, T., et al. *A New Direction: Our Changing Relationship with Driving and the Implications for America's Future.* U.S. PIRG Education Fund/Frontier Group, 2013.

Eckerson, Clarence, Jr. "Zurich: Where People Are Welcome and Cars Are Not." *Streetfilms*, October 15, 2014.

Erickson, K. I., et al. "Exercise Training Increases Size of Hippocampus and Improves Memory." *Proceedings of the National Academy of Sciences* 108, no. 7 (February 2011): 3017–3022.

Eves, Frank F., et al. "Increasing Stair Climbing in a Train Station: The Effects of Contextual Variables and Visibility." *Journal of Environmental Psychology* 29, no. 2 (June 2009): 300–303.

Faheem, Karim. "Brooklyn Neighbors Admit a Big Box Isn't All Bad." *New York Times*, August 11, 2008: A1.

Federal Transit Administration. *FY 2002 Statistical Summary*. December 2002. http://www.fta.dot.gov/about_FTA_1094.html (accessed December 27, 2014).

Federal Writers Project. *The WPA Guide to New York City: The Federal Writers Project Guide to 1930s New York*. New York, NY: The New Press, 1995.

Ferrell, C. E. "Home-Based Teleshoppers and Shopping Travel: Do Teleshoppers Travel Less?" *Transportation Research Record* (Transportation Research Board) 1894 (2004): 241–248.

FHA. *The Paintings of Carl Rakeman*. US Department of Transportation, Federal Highway Administration. September 11, 2011. http://www.fhwa.dot.gov/rakeman/1823.htm (accessed June 6, 2014).

Flaherty, C. A. *Highways*, Fourth Edition. Oxford, UK: Elsevier, Ltd., 2002.

Forkes, Jennifer, and Thea Dickinson. *Bike Lanes, On-Street Parking and Business: Year 2 Report: A Study of Bloor Street in Toronto's Bloor West Village*. Toronto, ON: Clean Air Partnership, 2010.

Frank, Richard W. *Luxury Fever: Money and Happiness in an Age of Excess*. New York, NY: The Free Press, 1999.

Fruin, John J. *Designing for Pedestrians*. Washington, DC: Transportation Research Board, 1971.

Garrick, Norman "Zurich, the World's Best Transit City." *Planetizen*, December 12, 2011.

Garrick, Norman, and Christopher McCahill. "Lessons from Zurich's Parking Revolution." *The Atlantic/CityLab*, August 12, 2011.

Gatersleben, Birgitta, Niamh Murtagh, and Emma White. "Hoody, Goody or Buddy? How Travel Mode Affects Social Perceptions in Urban Neighbourhoods." *Transportation Research Part F: Traffic Psychology and Behaviour* 21 (November 2013): 219–230.

Goldberg, David. "Survey: To Recruit and Keep Millennials, Give Them Walkable Places with Good Transit and Other Options." *T4America Blog*, April 22, 2014.

Golenbock, Peter. *Bums: An Oral History of the Brooklyn Dodgers*. New York, NY: G. P. Putnam's Sons, 1984.

Gomes, Lee. "Driving in Circles: The Autonomous Google Car May Never Actually Happen." *Slate*, October 14, 2014.

Grabar, Henry. "Mass-Transit Magic: How America's Fourth-Largest City Can Abandon Its Addiction to Cars." *Salon*, May 25, 2014.

Gray, Edward. *American Experience: The World That Moses Built*. Directed by Edward Gray. 1989.

Green, Christine Godward, and Elizabeth G. Klein. "Promoting Active Transportation as a Partnership Between Urban Planning and Public Health: The Columbus Healthy Places Program." *Public Health Reports* (Association of Schools of Public Health) 126, no. Supp 1 (2011): 41–49.

Guevara, Carlos. "Bajar tasa de homicidios en Bogotá a un dígito es viable: expertos." *El Tiempo*, January 8, 2013.

Guevara-Stone, Laurie. "How Bogota Creates Social Equality Through Sustainable Transit." *GreenBiz.com*, July 21, 2014.

Haidt, Jonathan. *The Happiness Hypothesis*. New York, NY: Basic Books, 2005.

Hall, Jonathan, and Alan Krueger. *An Analysis of the Labor Market for Uber's Driver-Partners in the United States*. Princeton, NJ: Industrial Research Center, Princeton University, 2015.

Hart, Joshua. *Driven to Excess: A Study of Motor Vehicle Impacts on Three Streets in Bristol UK*. Driven to Excess, 2008. http://driventoexcess.org (accessed September 13, 2014).

Hawthorne, Christopher. "'Latino Urbanism' Influences a Los Angeles in Flux." *Los Angeles Times*, December 6, 2014.

Hayashi, T., et al. "Walking to Work and the Risk for Hypertension in Men: The Osaka Health Survey." *Annals of Internal Medicine* 131, no. 1 (July 1999): 21–26.

Hoback, Alan, et al. "Health Effects of Walking to Transit." *Proceedings of the 53rd Transportation Research Forum*. Tampa, FL: Transportation Research Board, 2012.

Houston TranStar. *About Houston TranStar*. 2014. http://www.houston transtar.org/about_transtar/ (accessed November 7, 2014).

Hutchinson, Alex. "TransMilenio: The Good, the Bus and the Ugly." *CityFix*, July 14, 2011.

ICC. *Motorist Delay at Public Highway: Rail Grade Crossings in Northeastern Illinois*. Springfield, IL: Research and Analysis Section, Transportation Division, Illinois Commerce Commission, 2002.

IEEE. "Look Ma, No Hands!" *IEEE News*, September 2, 2012.

Iteris. *Intelligent Transportation Systems at the 2002 Salt Lake City Olympic Games: Traffic Management and Traveler Information Case Study*. Washington, DC: Intelligent Transportation Systems, US Department of Transportation, 2003.

Jackson, Kenneth T. *Crabgrass Frontier: The Suburbanization of the United States*. New York, NY: Oxford University Press, 1985.

Jackson, Nicholas. "Hailing a Cab with Your Phone." *The Atlantic*, November 16, 2010.

Jaffe, Eric. "7 Charts That Show How Good Mass Transit Can Make a City More Affordable." *The Atlantic/CityLab*, August 25, 2014.

Jeon, Cy, et al. "Physical Activity of Moderate Intensity and Risk of Type 2 Diabetes: A Systematic Review." *Diabetes Care* 30 (2007): 744–752.

Jonas A., S. C. Byrd, and R. Shanker. *Nikola's Revenge: TSLA's New Path of Disruption*. New York, NY: Tesla Motors Inc., Morgan Stanley, 2014.

Kahneman, Daniel. *Thinking Fast and Slow*. New York, NY: Farrar, Straus & Giroux, 2011.

Kay, Jane Holtz. *Asphalt Nation: How the Automobile Took Over America, and How We Can Take It Back*. New York, NY: Crown, 1997.

Khaw, Cassandra. "BMW Is Working on Cars Your Smartwatch Can Park." *The Verge*, December 16, 2014.

Kornhauser, Alain. "PRT Statewide Application: The Conceptual Design of a Transit System Capable of Serving Essentially All Daily Trips." In *Urban Public Transportation Systems, 2013*, Steven L. Jones (ed.), 357–368. Reston, VA: American Society of Civil Engineers, 2013.

Koslowsky, M., et al. *Commuting Stress: Causes, Effects, and Methods of Coping*. New York, NY: Plenum Press, 1995.

KRCResearch. *Millennials and Driving: A Survey Commissioned by Zipcar*. Cambridge, MA: Zipcar, Inc., November 2011.

Lachman, M. L., and D. L. Brett. *Generation Y: America's New Housing Wave*. Washington, DC: Urban Land Institute, 2011.

Lee, I. M., C. C. Hsieh, and R. S. Paffenbarger Jr. "Exercise Intensity and Longevity in Men: The Harvard Alumni Health Study." *Journal of the American Medical Association* 273, no. 15 (April 1995): 1179–1184.

Levine, J., et al. "Does Accessibility Require Density or Speed?" *Journal of the American Planning Association* (Routledge) 78, no. 2 (May 2012): 157–172.

LeVine, Scott, Alireza Zolfaghari, and John Polak. "Autonomous Cars: The Tension Between Occupant Experience and Intersection Capacity." *Transportation Research Part 3: Emerging Technologies* 52 (March 2014): 1–14.

Li, David. "Garden Wilting at No. 2 as Barclays Center Named Highest-Grossing Venue in US." *New York Post*, July 24, 2013.

Lind, William S., and Glen D. Bottoms. *Expanding Public-Private Partnerships in Electric Railways: A Zero-Cost Conservative Proposal*. Washington, DC: The American Conservative Center for Public Transportation, American Public Transportation Association, 2012, 1–31.

Litman, Todd. "A New Transit Safety Narrative." *Journal of Public Transportation* 17, no. 4 (December 2014): 114–135.

———. *Evaluating Household Chauffeuring Burdens: Understanding Direct and Indirect Costs of Transporting Non-Drivers*. 2015 TRB Annual Meeting. Washington, DC: Transportation Research Board, 2014.

———. *The Mobility-Productivity Paradox*. I-TED/International Transportation Economic Development Conference. Victoria, BC: Victoria Transport Policy Institute, 2014, 1–18.

Longhurst, James. "The Sidepath Not Taken: Bicycles, Taxes, and the Rhetoric of the Public Good in the 1890s." *Journal of Policy History* 25, no. 4 (October 2013): 557–586.

Marshall, W. E., and N. W. Garrick. "Street Network Types and Road Safety: A Study of 24 California Cities." *Urban Design International* 15 (April 2010): 133–147.

Martin, Adam, Yevgeniy Goryakin, and Marc Suhrcke. "Does Active Commuting Improve Psychological Wellbeing? Longitudinal Evidence from Eighteen Waves of the British Household Panel Survey." *Preventive Medicine* 69 (September 2014): 296–303.

McGuickan N., and N. Srinivasan. *Journey to Work Trends in the Major Metropolitan Areas*. Washington, DC: US Department of Transportation, FHA Office of Planning, 2003.

McInerney, Jay. *Bright Lights, Big City*. New York, NY: Vintage Contemporaries, 1984.

McNeur, Catherine. *Taming Manhattan: Environmental Battles in the Antebellum City*. Cambridge, MA: Harvard University Press, 2014.

Mikolajczak, M., et al. "Oxytocin Makes People Trusting, Not Gullible." *Psychological Sciences* 21, no. 8 (January 2010): 1072–1074.

Mohl, Raymond. "Stop the Road: Freeway Revolts in American Cities." *Journal of Urban History* 30, no. 5 (July 2004): 674–706.

Mokhtarian, P., and I. Salomon. "How Derived Is the Demand for Travel? Some Conceptual Measurement Considerations." *Transportation Research A* 35, no. 8 (September 2001): 695–719.

Montgomery, Charles. *Happy City: Transforming Our Lives Through Urban Design*. New York, NY: Farrar, Straus & Giroux, 2014.

Morrison, D., et al. "Evaluation of the Health Effects of a Neighbourhood Traffic Calming Scheme." *Journal of Epidemiology and Community Health* 58, no. 10 (October 2004): 837–840.

Moynihan, Daniel P. "New Roads and Urban Chaos." *The Reporter*, April 14, 1960: 13–20.

Navigant. *Autonomous Vehicles, Self-Driving Vehicles, Advanced Driver Assistance Systems, and Autonomous Driving Features: Global Market Analysis and Forecasts*. Boulder, CO: Navigant Consulting, Inc., 2014.

New Scientist. "The Day the Sweet Track Was Built." *New Scientist* 1721 (June 16, 1990).

New York Times. "New Ebbets Field to Have Hot Dogs and Hot Seats." *New York Times*, March 6, 1952: 34.

———. "Brooklyn Bridge to Be Modernized as Highway for 6,000 Cars an Hour." *New York Times*, September 4, 1948: 17.

North Side Board of Trade. *The Great North Side: Or, Borough of the Bronx*. New York, NY: North Side Board of Trade, 1897.

Norton, Peter D. *Fighting Traffic: The Dawn of the Motor Age in the American City*. Cambridge, MA: MIT Press, 2008.

Novaco, Raymond W., and Oscar I. Gonzalez. "Commuting and Well-Being." In *Technology and Psychological Well-Being*, Yair Amichai-Hamburger (ed.), 174–205. Cambridge, UK: Cambridge University Press, 2009.

NTSB Bureau of Traffic Statistics. *Table 3-17: Average Cost of Owning and Operating an Automobile(a) (Assuming 15,000 Vehicle-Miles per Year)*. September 17, 2014. http://www.rita.dot.gov/bts/sites/rita.dot.gov.bts /files/publications/national_transportation_statistics/html/table_03_17 .html (accessed December 4, 2014).

Null, Schuyler, et al. *Dawn of the Smart City: Perspective from New York, Ahmedabad, Sâo Paulo, and Beijing*. Washington, DC: Woodrow Wilson International Center for Scholars, 2014.

NYC. *Active Design Guidelines: Promoting Physical Activity and Health in Design*. New York, NY: NYC Departments of Design and Construction, Health and Mental Hygiene, and Transportation, 2010.

NYC Department of Health and Mental Hygiene. "The New York City Community Air Survey: Results From Years One and Two: December 2008–December 2010." New York, 2012.

NYC DOT. *Green Light for Midtown Evaluation Report*. New York, NY: New York City Department of Transportation, January 2010. http://www.nyc .gov/html/dot/html/pedestrians/broadway.shtml (accessed January 6, 2015).

———. *New York City Pedestrian Level of Service Study*. New York, NY: New York City Department of City Planning, 2006. http://www.nyc.gov/html /dcp/pdf/transportation/td_fullpedlosb.pdf (accessed January 6, 2015).

NYCRoads. *Cross Bronx Expressway: Historic Overview*. 2014. http://www .nycroads.com/roads/cross-bronx/ (accessed July 7, 2014).

Ortman, Scott, et al. "Settlement Scaling and Increasing Returns in an Ancient Society." *Science Advances* (AAAS) 1, no. 1 (February 2015).

Patton, Phil. "A 100-Year-Old Dream: A Road Just for Cars." *New York Times*, October 9, 2008.

Pauly, Daniel. "Anecdotes and Shifting Baseline Syndrome of Fisheries." *Trends in Ecology and Evolution* 10, no. 10 (October 1995): 430.

Peñalosa. Enrique. "Latin America Must Look to Amsterdam More Than Miami." *Semana*, January 13, 2011.

Perlmutter, Emanuel. "Indefinite Closing Is Set for West Side Highway." *New York Times*, December 17, 1973: 41.

Peters, Mary. *The Perfect Storm*. Remarks as prepared for delivery, National Stone and Gravel Association, Washington, DC. Federal Highway Administration, January 24, 2004. http://www.fhwa.dot.gov/pressroom /re040124.cfm (accessed November 12, 2014)

Pew Research. *Political Polarization in the American Public*. Pew Research Center for the People & the Press, Washington, DC: Pew Research, 2014.

Pham, Nan D. *The Economic Benefits of Commercial GPS Use in the U.S. and the Costs of Potential Disruption*. Washington, DC: NDP Consulting, 2011.

Potts, I., D. Harwood, and K. Richard. *Relationship of Lane Width to Safety for Urban and Suburban Arterials*. Washington, DC: Transportation Research Board, 2007.

Pratt, Richard. "Chapter 16: Pedestrian and Bicycle Facilities." In *Traveler Response to Transportation System Changes*. Transit Cooperative Research Program (TCRP) Report 95, 16–29. Washington, DC: National Research Council, 2012.

Pricewaterhousecoopers. *Look Mom, No Hands!* New York, NY: Pricewaterhousecoopers, 2013.

Pushkarev, B. and J. Zupan. "Capacity of Walkways." *Transportation Research Record* 538 (January 1976): 1–15.

———. *Urban Space for Pedestrians*. Cambridge, MA: MIT Press, 1975.

Quercia, Daniele, et al. "The Shortest Path to Happiness: Recommending Beautiful, Quiet, and Happy Routes in the City." *Proceedings of the 25th ACM Conference on Hypertext and Social Media*. New York, NY: Association for Computing Machinery, 2014, 116–125.

Ratey, John J., MD. *Spark: The Revolutionary New Science of Exercise and the Brain*. Boston, MA: Little, Brown and Company, 2008.

Reisman, Will. "Road Diets Used as Tool for Reclaiming Neighborhoods in San Francisco." *San Francisco Examiner*, August 24, 2012.

Reuter, Thad. "E-retail Spending to Increase 62% by 2016." *Internet Retailer*, February 27, 2012.

Rodrigue, Jean-Paul, Claude Comtois, and Brian Slack. *The Geography of Transport Systems*. New York, NY: Routledge, 2006.

Rogowsky, Mark. "Zipcar, Uber, and the Beginnings of Trouble for the Auto Industry." *Forbes*, February 8, 2014.

Ross, Casey. "Boston Humming as Appeal of Life in City Booms." *Boston Globe*, March 3, 2013.

Ross, Darren. "Millennials Don't Care About Owning Cars, and Car Makers Can't Figure Out Why." *Fast Company*, March 26, 2014.

Roth, Matthew. "Enrique Peñalosa Urges SF to Embrace Pedestrians and Public Space." *StreetsBlog SF*, July 8, 2009.

Ruiz, Rebecca. "America's Most Obese Cities." *Forbes*, November 7, 2007.

Schmitt, Angie. "The Importance of Driving to the U.S. Economy Started Waning in the 70s." *StreetsBlog USA*, December 18, 2014. "

———. The Koch Brothers' War on Transit." *StreetsBlog USA*, September 2014.

Schwartz, Samuel I., and Shauna Tarshis Colasuonno. "VIM: Not Just Another Acronym." *ITE Journal* (September 1982): 23–27.

Seto, Karen C., et al. "A Meta-Analysis of Global Urban Land Expansion." *PLoS One* 6, no. 8 (August 2011): e23777.

Shoup, Donald C. "Free Parking or Free Markets." *Access: The Magazine of the University of California Transportation Center* 38 (Spring 2011).

———. "The High Cost of Free Parking." *Journal of Planning Education and Research* 17, no. 1 (Fall 1997): 201–216.

Silberg, Gary, and Richard Wallace. *Self-Driving Cars: The Next Revolution.* KPMG and the Center for Automotive Research, 2012.

SmartGrowthAmerica. *Dangerous by Design 2014.* Smart Growth America/National Complete Streets Coalition, 2014.

Snyder, Tany. "Oklahoma City Mayor Mick Cornett: We Have to Build This City for People." *StreetsBlog USA*, January 24, 2013.

Soanes, Catherine, and Angus Stevenson. *Concise Oxford English Dictionary.* Oxford, UK: Oxford University Press, 2008.

Soler, R. E., et al. "Point-of-Decision Prompts to Increase Stair Use: A Systematic Review Update." *American Journal of Preventive Medicine* 38, no. 2S (2010): 290–291.

Sollis, J., et al. "Neighborhood Environments and Physical Activity Among Adults in 11 Countries." *American Journal of Preventive Medicine* 36, no. 6 (June 2009): 484–490.

Span, Guy. *Paving the Way for Buses: The Great GM Streetcar Conspiracy,* 2003. http://www.baycrossings.com/Archives/2003/04_May/paving _the_way_for_buses_the_great_gm_streetcar_conspiracy.htm (accessed June 20, 2014).

St. Clair, David J. *The Motorization of American Cities.* New York, NY: Praeger, 1986.

Stilgoe, John. "Roads, Highways, and Ecosystems." The Use of the Land: Perspectives on Stewardship. Research Triangle Center, NC: National Humanities Center, July 2001. http://nationalhumanitiescenter.org/tserve /nattrans/ntuseland/essays/roads.htm (accessed June 15, 2014).

Straus, William, and Neil Howe. *Generations: The History of America's Future, 1584–2069.* New York, NY: William Morrow, 1990.

Sturdevant, Rick W. "NAVSTAR, the Global Positioning System: A Sampling of Its Military, Civil, and Commercial Impact." In *Societal Impact of Spaceflight.* NASA et al., 331–351. Washington, DC: NASA/Government Printing Office, 2007.

Stutzer, Alois, and Bruno Frey. *Stress That Doesn't Pay: The Commuting Paradox*. Discussion Paper No. 1278. Zurich: University of Zurich, Institute for Empirical Research in Economics, 2004.

Tanasescu, M., et al. "Exercise Type and Intensity in Relation to Coronary Heart Disease in Men." *Journal of the American Medical Association* 288 (2002): 1994–2000.

Tang, L., and P. Thakuriah. "Will the Psychological Effects of Real-Time Transit Information Systems Lead to Ridership Gain?" *Transportation Research Record* 2216 (February 2011): 67–74.

Tierney, John. "Remaking Columbus's Most Downtrodden Neighborhood." *The Atlantic*, October 1, 2014.

Timmermans, H.J.P. *Pedestrian Behavior: Models, Data Collections, and Applications*. Bingley, UK: Emerald, 2009.

TransitCenter. *Who's on Board? Mobility Attitudes Survey*. New York, NY: Transit Center, 2014.

Transportation for America. *Smart Mobility for a 21st Century America: Strategies for Maximizing Technology to Minimize Congestion, Reduce Emissions and Increase Efficiency*. Washington, DC: Transportation for America, 2010.

Transportation Research Board. *Highway Capacity Manual*. Washington, DC: National Research Council, 2000.

Trevelyan, G. M. *Walking*. London: E. V. Mitchell, 1928.

Troy, Dave. *The Real Republican Adversary: Population Density*. November 19, 2012. http://davetroy.com/posts/the-real-republican-adversary -population-density (accessed December 26, 2014).

TTI. *Urban Mobility Information*. December 2012. http://mobility.tamu .edu/ums/report/ (accessed November 7, 2014).

Twenge, J. M., E. C. Freeman, and W. K. Campbell. "Generational Differences in Young Adults' Life Goals, Concern for Others, and Civic Orientation, 1966–2009." *Journal of Personality and Social Psychology* (March 2012): 1045–1062.

Underhill, Paco. *Why We Buy: The Science of Shopping*. New York, NY: Simon & Schuster, 1999.

US Navy. "US Ship Force Levels, 1886–Present." History and Heritage Command, July 31, 2014. http://www.history.navy.mil/research/histories /ship-histories/us-ship-force-levels.html (accessed March 22, 2015).

Vanderbilt, Tom. "What's Your Walk Score?" *Slate*, April 12, 2010.

Vaynman, Shoshanna, Zhe Ying, and Fernando Gomez-Pinilla. "Hippocampal BDNF Mediates the Efficacy of Exercise on Synaptic Plasticity and Cognition." *European Journal of Neuroscience* 20 (September 2004): 2580–2590.

Vuchic, Vukan R. *Transportation for Livable Cities*. New Brunswick, NJ: The Center for Urban Policy Research, 1999.

Walker, Jarrett. *Houston: Transit Reimagined*, May 2014. http://www .humantransit.org/2014/05/houston-a-transit-network-reimagined.html (accessed November 7, 2014).

———. *How Good Are We at Prediction?* Human Transit, July 14, 2014. http://www.humantransit.org/2014/07/how-good-are-we-at-prediction .html (accessed Aug 4, 2014).

———. "Purpose-Driven Public Transport: Creating a Clear Conversation about Transport Goals." *Journal of Transport Geography* 16, no. 6 (November 2008): 436–442.

———. *Vancouver: The Almost Perfect Grid*. Human Transit, February 24, 2010.   http://www.humantransit.org/2010/02/vancouver-the-almost -perfect-grid.html (accessed November 5, 2014).

Wardrop, J. G., and J. I. Whitehead. "Some Theoretical Aspects of Road Traffic Engineering." *ICE Proceedings: Engineering Division* 1, no. 5 (October 1952): 767–768.

Watkins, K. E., et al. "Where Is My Bus? Impact of Mobile Real-Time Information on the Perceived and Actual Wait Time of Transit Riders." *Transportation Research Part A: Policy and Practice* 45, no. 8 (October 2011): 839–848.

Weingroff, Richard F. "Essential to the National Interest." *Public Roads* 69, no. 5 (March–April 2006).

———. "The Genie in the Bottle: The Interstate Highway System and Urban Problems, 1939–1957." *Public Roads* 60, no. 2 (September–October 2000).

Whyte, William H. *City: Rediscovering the Center*. New York, NY: Doubleday, 1988.

Williams, Paul T. "Effects of Running and Walking on Osteoarthritis and Hip Replacement Risk." *Medicine and Science in Sports and Exercise* 45, no. 7 (2013): 1292–1297.

Wilson, David Gordon, and Jim Papadopoulos. *Bicycling Science*, Third edition. Cambridge, MA: MIT Press, 2004.

Winograd, Morley, and Michael Hais. *Millennial Makeover: MySpace, YouTube, and the Future of American Politics*. New Brunswick, NJ: Rutgers University Press, 2008.

Zak, Paul. *The Moral Molecule: The Source of Love and Prosperity*. New York, NY: Dutton, 2012.

INDEX

SAMUEL I. SCHWARTZ, aka "Gridlock" Sam, is one of the leading transportation experts in the US. He served as New York City's traffic commissioner and the New York City Department of Transportation's chief engineer. He currently runs Sam Schwartz Engineering, which operates out of Chicago, Los Angeles, New York, Newark, Tampa, and Washington, DC. Schwartz has been profiled by the *New Yorker* and the *New York Times*. He has been a columnist at the *New York Daily News* and is regularly interviewed in dozens of professional publications.